高等学校应用型特色规划教材

实用英语口译教程
(第 2 版)

PRACTICAL ENGLISH INTERPRETATION COURSE BOOK
(Second Edition)

主　编　冯伟年
副主编　乃瑞华　任蓓蓓　查新舟
　　　　秦晓梅　富娅琳

清华大学出版社
北　京

内 容 简 介

本书共分四个部分。第一部分介绍口译基础知识、无笔记口译训练、数字口译、交替传译中的笔记技术和演讲的技巧。第二部分是口译实践，内容包括迎来送往、礼仪性口译、旅游观光、商贸洽谈、环境保护、经济与贸易、外交与政治等双语口译实践。第三部分是全国翻译专业资格考试简介，重点介绍三级口译考试题真题。第四部分是时文语林，介绍包括政治、经济、金融、法律、汉语习语等十四个方面的实用口译必备词汇。

本书适用于高等院校英语、翻译、商务英语、旅游英语、英语教育、应用英语等专业学生的口译课教学，也可供从事口译、外事、外贸、旅游等行业的涉外人员和具有一定英语基础的口译自学者学习使用。

本书封面贴有清华大学出版社防伪标签，无标签者不得销售。
版权所有，侵权必究。举报：010-62782989，beiqinquan@tup.tsinghua.edu.cn。

图书在版编目(CIP)数据

实用英语口译教程/冯伟年主编. —2版. —北京：清华大学出版社，2016（2022.7重印）
（高等学校应用型特色规划教材）
ISBN 978-7-302-42333-1

Ⅰ. ①实… Ⅱ. ①冯… Ⅲ. ①英语—口译—高等学校—教材 Ⅳ. ①H315.9

中国版本图书馆 CIP 数据核字(2015)第 286936 号

责任编辑：桑任松
封面设计：杨玉兰
责任校对：周剑云
责任印制：宋 林

出版发行：清华大学出版社
网　　址：http://www.tup.com.cn, http://www.wqbook.com
地　　址：北京清华大学学研大厦A座　　邮　编：100084
社 总 机：010-83470000　　邮　购：010-62786544
投稿与读者服务：010-62776969, c-service@tup.tsinghua.edu.cn
质量反馈：010-62772015, zhiliang@tup.tsinghua.edu.cn
课件下载：http://www.tup.com.cn, 010-62791865

印 刷 者：北京富博印刷有限公司
装 订 者：北京市密云县京文制本装订厂
经　　销：全国新华书店
开　　本：185mm×260mm　　印　张：15.5　　字　数：375千字
版　　次：2009年7月第1版 2016年1月第2版　　印　次：2022年7月第8次印刷
定　　价：45.00元

产品编号：066771-03

前　言

口译是一项艰巨而紧张的脑力劳动。译员要面对各种意想不到的挑战，承受很大的思想压力。首先是无法完全预测交际双方的谈话内容，必须对随时出现的意外状况有思想准备。其次，口译过程中译员随时可能遇到语言、知识、文化等方面的困难和障碍。另外，译员可能在各种气氛紧张的现场进行口译。因此，译员工作时必须精力充沛，思想高度集中，做到耳、眼、手、脑、口同时并用，既要迅速高效，又要准确无误；既要忠于原意，又要灵活应变。因此，口译是一项极富挑战性的工作。

为了迎接新世纪的挑战，进一步扩大我国的对外交流与合作，21世纪的中国比过去任何时候都更加需要口译人才。为国家培养合格的口译人才是高等院校的当务之急。而培养高素质的口译人才，一本具有时效性、针对性、实用性的口译教材至关重要。本书是编者根据长期从事口译实践、教学和科研中所积累的丰富经验和资料，同时结合国内外形势的发展，不断收集、更新和补充新材料，在反复实践和总结提高的基础上编写而成的。为适应新的发展形势和需要，又在第一版基础上进行了修订。

本书的特点如下。

一、理论联系实际，题材广泛，内容新颖

本书集口译理论、技巧和实践为一体，内容主要包括口译的基本理论、方法和技巧以及口译工作所涉及的各种话题的英汉互译。本书收集的大部分材料都是近几年来我国对外交流活动的各种最新口译资料，其中包括李克强总理2015年在瑞士冬季达沃斯的致辞、国家主席习近平发表的2015羊年新年贺词、2014年李克强总理在天津第八届夏季达沃斯论坛上的致辞、2015年政府工作报告、2015年习近平主席在博鳌亚洲论坛年会上的演讲等。选材的目的是通过大量形式多样的英汉互译实例，使学生掌握口译的基本理论和技巧，熟悉涉外工作的礼仪和程序，获得最新的政治、外交、经济、社会、文化等背景知识，培养他们在各种场合灵活运用不同的口译技巧进行英汉互译的实践能力，尽快缩短他们与实践运用之间的距离，使得学生走上工作岗位就能很快胜任口译工作。

二、英译汉、汉译英并重，双向训练同步进行

口译通常是在两种语言连续交替转换的模式中进行。因此，口译教学也应采取英汉互译、双向训练同步进行的模式。口译实践是本书的核心。这一部分的每一章都选用了英译汉和汉译英两种训练材料。同时，除第五章外，每一章在口译实践材料之前还选用了两篇与该章专题相关的英语阅读材料作为口译训练前的热身材料，这些材料都附有重点词汇的中文注释。

三、形式多样、实用性强、可操作性强

本书分为四大部分，第一部分是口译理论与技巧，包括口译基础知识、无笔记训练、数字口译和口译笔记法。第二部分是口译实践，包括七个章节，涉及口译常见的主题，选

用了大量时效性、针对性和实用性强的材料。在设计上，并不是把口译材料堆砌在一起，而是出于方便教学和学生学习的角度，难点呈阶梯式分布。除了第五章"迎来送往"主题外，其他六个章节包含从"热身阅读"、"句子口译"、"对话口译"、"段落口译"再到"篇章口译"几大版块，内容由简到难，使学生避免产生畏惧心理，从而逐渐建立自信。在第三部分，对全国翻译专业资格考试英语三级证书的口译综合能力真题和口译实务真题做了详解，以帮助学生了解翻译专业资格考试的内容并顺利获得翻译资格证书。第四部分的时文语林，列举了涉及学位名称、教育机构名称、职业名称、企业和商店名称、政治、经济、金融、贸易、法律用语的英译和常用汉语成语、谚语、典故、歇后语和《四书》语录的英译等14个方面的实用口译必备词汇。以上内容是区别于全国同类教材的特色之处。另外，教材配有MP3，帮助学生学习，请在清华大学出版社网站搜索下载。

本书适用于高等院校英语、翻译、商务英语、旅游英语、英语教育、应用英语等专业学生的口译课教学，也可供从事口译、外事、外贸、旅游等行业的涉外人员及有较好英语基础的口译自学者学习、使用。书中不少篇章已在编者所在高校的口译课和同声传译课上使用多年，效果很好，深受学生欢迎。

本书是陕西省教育厅批准的省级精品资源共享课程——口译课程的主打教材。主编冯伟年教授(我国资深翻译家、陕西省普通高校教学名师、英语语言文学专业翻译方向和MTI硕士研究生导师)提出本书的编写理念和原则，设计了各章编写体例，完成了对全书的修改、统稿和定稿工作。

本书具体章节编写的分工如下：冯伟年和乃瑞华负责第一、二、三、四、五章的编写；任蓓蓓负责第六、七章及第三部分的编写；查新舟负责第八、九章的编写；秦晓梅负责第十、十一章的编写、富娅琳负责第四部分——时文语林以及部分音频的录制和合成工作。

在编著过程中，编者引入了一些网站的多媒体资源，并参考了一些已出版的口译音像资料，本书所选题材来源均在"参考文献"中列出，在此谨向原作者、原编译者和相关网站表示诚挚的谢意，同时感谢杨振刚老师、张立电老师提出的许多宝贵意见和技术上的支持。

由于编者水平有限，疏漏和错误在所难免，恳请专家和读者们批评指正，我们将不胜感激。

编 者
2015年8月

目 录

第一部分　口译基础理论和技巧 Basic Theories and Skills of Interpretation

第一章　口译基础知识 Basic Knowledge of Interpretation 1
　一、口译与笔译 1
　二、口译的分类 3
　三、口译的过程和主要环节 4
　四、译员的基本素质要求 8

第二章　无笔记口译训练 Interpretation Training Without Taking Notes 10
　一、信息的接收与分析 10
　二、信息的视觉化和形象化 14
　三、对信息进行逻辑分析 17
　四、口译记忆力训练 25
　五、影子训练 27
　六、对信息做出积极反应 28
　七、演讲的技巧 29

第三章　数字口译 Numeral Interpretation 32
　一、数字反应训练 32
　二、数字的记录 35
　三、数字的口译 36

第四章　交替传译中的笔记技术 Skills of Note-taking in Consecutive Interpretation 40
　一、笔记的功能和本质 40
　二、笔记的过程 41
　三、笔记原则和方法 42
　四、口译笔记的格式和结构安排 45
　五、习语的口译 50
　六、译前准备 54

第二部分　口译实践 Interpretation Practice

第五章　迎来送往口译 Reception of Foreign Guests 59
　一、机场迎送 59

	对话口译/Dialogue Interpretation	60
二、	住宿接待	60
三、	宴会饮食	61
	篇章口译/Passage Interpretation	63
参考译文/Reference Version		65
	对话口译/Dialogue Interpretation	65
	篇章口译/Passage Interpretation	67

第六章　礼仪讲话口译 Ceremonial Speech 69

一、热身阅读材料/Warming-up Reading Material 69

二、口译实践/Interpretation Practice 72

  句子口译/Sentence Interpretation 72

  对话口译/Dialogue Interpretation 73

  段落口译/Short Passage Interpretation 73

  篇章口译/Passage Interpretation 75

参考译文/Reference Version 78

  句子口译/Sentence Interpretation 78

  对话口译/Dialogue Interpretation 79

  段落口译/Short Passage Interpretation 80

  篇章口译/Passage Interpretation 81

第七章　旅游观光口译 Tour and Sightseeing 87

一、热身阅读材料/Warming-up Reading Material 87

二、口译实践/Interpretation Practice 95

  句子口译/Sentence Interpretation 95

  对话口译/Dialogue Interpretation 96

  段落口译/Short Passage Interpretation 97

  篇章口译/Passage Interpretation 98

参考译文/Reference Version 100

  句子口译/Sentence Interpretation 100

  对话口译/Dialogue Interpretation 101

  段落口译/Short Passage Interpretation 102

  篇章口译/Passage Interpretation 103

第八章　商贸洽谈口译 Business Negotiation Interpretation 106

一、热身阅读材料/Warming-up Reading Material 106

二、口译实践/Interpretation Practice 109

  句子口译/Sentence Interpretation 109

　　　　对话口译/Dialogue Interpretation 110

　　　　段落口译/Short Passage Interpretation 111

　　　　篇章口译/Passage Interpretation 112

　　参考译文/Reference Version 114

　　　　句子口译/Sentence Interpretation 114

　　　　对话口译/Dialogue Interpretation 114

　　　　段落口译/Short Passage Interpretation 115

　　　　篇章口译/Passage Interpretation 116

第九章　环境保护口译 Environmental Protection Interpretation 118

　一、热身阅读材料/Warming-up Reading Material 118

　二、口译实践/Interpretation Practice 121

　　　　句子口译/Sentence Interpretation 121

　　　　对话口译/Dialogue Interpretation 122

　　　　段落口译/Short Passage Interpretation 123

　　　　篇章口译/Passage Interpretation 124

　　参考译文/Reference Version 127

　　　　句子口译/Sentence Interpretation 127

　　　　对话口译/Dialogue Interpretation 127

　　　　段落口译/Short Passage Interpretation 128

　　　　篇章口译/Passage Interpretation 129

第十章　政治和外事口译 Interpretation of Politics and Diplomacy 131

　一、热身阅读材料/Warming-up Reading Material 131

　二、口译实践/Interpretation Practice 142

　　　　句子口译/Sentence Interpretation 142

　　　　对话口译/Dialogue Interpretation 143

　　　　段落口译/Short Passage Interpretation 143

　　　　篇章口译/Passage Interpretation 144

　　参考译文/Reference Version 149

　　　　句子口译/Sentence Interpretation 149

　　　　对话口译/Dialogue Interpretation 150

　　　　段落口译/Short Passage Interpretation 151

　　　　篇章口译/Passage Interpretation 151

第十一章　经济和贸易口译 Interpretation of Trade and Economy 156

　一、热身阅读材料/Warming-up Reading Material 156

　二、口译实践/Interpretation Practice 159

句子口译/Sentence Interpretation 159
　　对话口译/Dialogue Interpretation 160
　　段落口译/Short Passage Interpretation 161
　　篇章口译/Passage Interpretation 161
参考译文/Reference Version 166
　　句子口译/Sentence Interpretation 166
　　对话口译/Dialogue Interpretation 167
　　段落口译/Short Passage Interpretation 168
　　篇章口译/Passage Interpretation 168

第三部分　全国翻译专业资格(水平)考试 China Accreditation Test for Translators and Interpreters (CATTI)

一、三级口译考试简介 175
二、"口译综合能力"备考 176
三、"口译实务"备考 199

第四部分　时文语林——实用口译必备词汇 Practical Phrases of C-E Translation in Current Politics, Economy, Law, Education and Culture

一、学位名称/Academic Degrees 207
二、教育、教学机构名称/Educational Institutions 208
三、职业名称/Various Positions 210
四、常见企业和商店名称/Names of Common Enterprises and Stores ... 214
五、二十四节气/Twenty-four Solar Terms of China 216
六、经济用语/Economic Terms 217
七、金融、贸易用语/Terms in Finance and Trade 219
八、政治用语/Political Terms 221
九、法律用语/Legal Terms 223
十、常用汉语成语/Common Chinese Idioms 224
十一、常用汉语谚语/Common Chinese Proverbs 227
十二、常用汉语典故/Common Chinese Allusions 231
十三、歇后语/Two-part Allegorical Sayings 233
十四、《四书》语录/Quotations of Four Books 234

参考文献/Reference Books 239

第一部分　口译基础理论和技巧
Basic Theories and Skills of Interpretation

第一章　口译基础知识
Basic Knowledge of Interpretation

一、口译与笔译

　　口译(interpretation)与笔译(translation)作为翻译活动的两种实践形式，从本质上来讲都是在寻求原语(source language)与目标语(target language)之间的意义对等。翻译行为旨在"理解话语篇章"，然后用另一种语言"重新表达"这一"话语篇章"。"话语篇章"从根本上来讲是语言知识同语言外知识结合的产物，是翻译的对象。"理解"离不开语言外知识，"重新表达"的质量也和译者所掌握的知识息息相关。口译和笔译的最终目的在于保证使用不同语言的人们之间顺利交际，因此，翻译的重点应当着眼于原语与目标语之间的意义上对等，而并非是其语言形式上的机械对应。

　　口译和笔译都有很长的历史。口译活动是随着人类各民族相互交流的需要而产生和发展起来的，可以上溯到人类各种语言逐渐形成后的时期。从这个意义上讲，口译的历史比笔译的历史久远得多。

　　口译活动在历史上的记载甚少。哥伦布发现新大陆后曾将大量印第安人运到西班牙学习西班牙语，并将他们培养成口译译员。明清时期中国的一些小说中对口译译员有了正式的称呼——通事。直到20世纪初，口译活动的开展仍以粗放式为主。第一次世界大战之后，各个国家之间的交往日益频繁，对口译译员的需求急剧增加。1919年，"巴黎和会"首次借助英法两种语言的翻译进行谈判，当时的口译方式主要是发言人讲一段，译员翻译一段，即交替传译，也可称连续口译或接续口译。这是口译历史上的一个重要转折点，标志着第一次正式出现了现代意义的口译技术，即口译的记忆、笔记、复述等基本技术。此后，美国发明了一种让译员使用耳机听辨原语，同时使用话筒传送译语的"共时翻译"设备，这种设备在当时并没有获得口译界的认同。在第二次世界大战之后的纽伦堡战犯审判中，人们正式启用了同声传译，以保证在大量繁杂的听证、辩护、审判工作中能在原语话语结束时"同时"结束译语，从而节省宝贵的时间。"同声传译"因此大出风头，很快在大多数国家普及，并且代表着口译工作的一种发展方向。一批专门为国际会议培养高级译员的翻译学院在德国、瑞士、法国和美国应运而生。1953年"国际会议译员协会"的成立，标志着口译人员社会地位的确立。口译作为一门语言艺术开始兴旺起来，并成为一个令人羡慕和追求的高尚职业。

口译与笔译在质量标准上基本相同，都要强调"信"(faithfulness)、"达"(expressiveness)、"切"(closeness)。

"信"就是忠实于原语的内容，口译译员要听懂讲话人的意旨，捕捉讲话人的意思。准确是口译的最基本标准，准确就是"信"。在口译中，"信"就是忠实地传达说话人的原意，即口译的信度。具体地说，在内容上，译员要全面完整、准确无误地传达谈话的议题、观点，对涉及的事实、细节、数字、时间、地点等不能有任何疏漏和差错。准确是口译的生命线，是译员工作责任心和业务能力的集中表现。口译内容的范围很广，有涉及立场、观点的政治会谈，有包括各种数字的经贸谈判。即使是日常生活翻译，也常常涉及具体的时间、地点或细节。口译内容上的任何差错或失真，都可能造成政治上的原则性错误、经济上的重大损失或工作上的严重失误。因此，口译中，译员不可只顾速度而忽视口译的准确性。任何粗心大意、马虎从事的作风都可能造成难以挽回的影响。

口译的准确性也表现在语言表达方面。在语言表达上译员要做到语音、语调正确，准确掌握词义、词性、词的变化与搭配，正确运用句型、时态、语气和衔接，做到语音、语调、词法、语法准确无误。译员语言表达上的任何错误都可能造成交际双方谈话内容上的含糊其词、似是而非，甚至引起严重误解。这样的口译不可能真实地传达说话人的意愿，也不符合口译的准确原则。

"达"是指用符合目标语言表达习惯的语言形式"重新表达"原语内容。在口译中，"达"是指语言通达、通顺、流畅。口译要做到流利，一要"快"，二要"畅"。译员必须迅速、及时地把一方的话语信息传达给另一方，做到语速流畅、节奏适当、反应敏捷、出口利落，不能吞吞吐吐、慢条斯理。

"切"是指尽可能地贴近原语的风格，正确运用语态、语气、情态等，再现说话人的情感、情绪和口气，真正做到传情达意，再现说话人"原汁原味"的谈话风格。口译时，译语的表述时长最好不超过原语的表述时长。译员必须集中精力抓住说话人的中心意思，把话语所含信息完整、准确、及时地表达出来。译员不可能也不必把原话的每个词语和句子逐一不漏地译出，那样做反而会影响下一步的听译。因此，口译最重要的是传情达意，把说话人的意思和话语的效果表达出来。

译语要口语化，简短明了、通俗易懂、准确、及时、通顺。笔译的成果是永久性的作品，有广泛的读者。笔译要求忠于原文、语言规范、行文流畅、再现原文的风格和艺术魅力。为此，笔译工作者必须遵循书面语言规范和句法规则，选择确切的词语和表达方法，忠实、流畅、艺术地再现原作的内容、信息和风格。

口译是一种特殊的语言交际过程，首先是速度快。口译的全过程，从语言信息的接收、解码、记忆、编码到输出只在短短的时间内进行。译员一旦进入工作状态，就像一台自动运转的机器，必须全神贯注、连续不断地进行语言信息的处理和转换工作。即使译员对前面口译的效果不够满意，也难以返工或更改。

口译是一项艰巨而紧张的脑力劳动。译员要面对各种意想不到的挑战，承受很大的思想压力。首先是无法完全预测交际双方的谈话内容，因而无从事先对谈话细节内容做充分的准备。其次，口译过程中译员随时可能遇到语言、知识、文化等方面的困难和障碍。另外，他们可能在各种气氛紧张的现场进行口译。因此，译员工作时必须精力充沛，思想高度集中，做到耳、眼、手、脑、口同时并用，既要迅速高效，又要准确无误；既要忠于原意，又要灵活应变。口译的确是一项极富挑战性的工作。

口译的这些特点和规律决定了口译与笔译有很大的区别，二者的差异主要有以下两方面。

1. 工作方式不同

口译是从口头语言到口头语言的翻译。口头语言转瞬即逝，从听入信息到译出信息，译员只有短短几秒钟的时间。特别是同声传译，口译和讲话几乎是同时进行的，真可谓"一言既出，驷马难追"，一旦出错，很难补救。口译中译员要在瞬息之间把获得的语言信息输入大脑，经过判断、处理，迅速转换成另一种语言，再准确、流畅地表达出来，使交谈双方达到沟通、交流之目的。译员必须独立地完成这一切，不可能参考任何文件、资料，也不可能求教于任何专家、学者。

然而，笔译则不同，笔译人员面对的是书面语言。他可以不受时间的限制，反复阅读，从容思考，充分理解原文，必要时还可借助各种工具书，反复推敲，仔细琢磨。同时，笔译人员可以使用各种修辞手段，对译文进行修改、润色；还可以请教别人或与同行切磋，或请专家审校。总之，笔译工作者有较充分的时间对译文进行加工，使其精益求精，达到最佳境界。

2. 工作环境不同

口译人员直接面对各类听众。他们可能是国家元首，政府要员，各方面的专家、学者，或者是从事各种职业的各行各业的人。译员要在各种各样的场合工作，如礼节性的接见或宴请、气氛比较宽松的观光旅游、严肃正规的政治会晤、针锋相对的外交谈判，甚至无法预料讲话人要说什么的即兴发言、辩论、记者招待会，或者是有数百听众的大会演说。口译是异常复杂而紧张的脑力劳动，口译人员特别是同声译员工作时承受着巨大的精神压力和心理负担。难怪有的联合国会议译员把其翻译时所在的玻璃小间叫作"恐怖的密室"。因此，口译人员需要有良好的心理素质和身体素质。

相比之下，笔译人员却是在另一种环境中工作。他们的工作对象是看不见的广大读者，可以任意选择一个舒适、安静的环境，专心致志、从容不迫地工作。

二、口译的分类

口译按其翻译形式可分为以下四类。

1. 交替翻译

交替翻译(consecutive interpretation)是指译员在说话人每讲完几句或一段话后自然停顿

时，当即译给听众的翻译方式。这种方式可以用于交际一方单向连续讲话的情况，也可以用于交际双方连续交替式的谈话，因此也叫连续翻译或即席翻译。交替翻译是最常用的一种口译形式，口译人员的业务训练一般都是从交替翻译开始的。交替翻译主要用于交谈和演讲时的双语交际场合，如日常接见、宴请、会晤、谈判、讲座、演讲、记者招待会、旅游观光等活动。

2. 同声传译

同声传译(simultaneous interpretation)是指译员在说话人讲话的同时边听边译的口译方式。使用这种方式，翻译和讲话几乎是同时进行的。同声传译是一种高效率、高难度的口译形式，是在熟练掌握交替翻译技巧的基础上经过特殊强化训练后才能达到的境界。同声传译主要用于各种国际会议和重要国际学术会议的翻译，因此也叫会议翻译(conference interpretation)。目前，世界上80%～90%的国际会议都使用同声传译。这种翻译需要一定的设备。通常是发言人对着一个与传译室相连接的话筒讲话，译员在传译室里对着第二个话筒把听到的讲话内容译成另一种语言，与会者通过耳机接收到译入语。如果听众是讲多种语言的，为使大家都跟上会议的进程，需要为每种语言各配备1～2名译员，增加传译室的传送线路，并在每个听众座位上都安上相应的可以选择不同语言的接收装置。

3. 耳语传译

耳语传译(whispering interpretation)简称耳译，是指译员把听到的讲话内容连续不断地小声传译给身边听众的翻译方式。耳译也属于同声传译，不同的是同声传译用于国际会议和国际学术会议的大会发言，而耳译则多用于小组讨论、观看文艺演出等场合。耳译往往只针对一两名听众。

4. 视阅传译

视阅传译(sight interpretation)简称视译，是指译员看着事先准备好的原文讲稿或文件，用另一种语言直接连续不断地把讲稿译给听众的翻译方式。视译也属同声传译，是一种边看边译的特殊口译形式。

口译按其内容和文体也可分为以下几种：
(1) 交谈式口译，包括一般性交谈、访谈、谈判等口译；
(2) 礼仪式口译，包括礼宾迎送、欢迎词、告别词、宴会祝酒词、开幕词等口译；
(3) 介绍式口译，包括观光、导游、演讲等口译；
(4) 会议口译，包括各种国际会议、学术交流会等口译。

三、口译的过程和主要环节

从表面上来讲，口、笔译都包括理解和表达两个主要环节。那么理解和表达这两个程序是如何关联并顺利进行的呢？或者说译员的智力机制内部是如何进行信息代码的转换的呢？确切地说，在翻译中从原语理解到译语理解的过程中，人的智力因素是非常重要的。

基于这种考虑，巴黎释意派翻译理论指出，翻译(包括口译和笔译)存在三大主要环节：原语理解、脱离原语词语外壳和译语表达。这三大主要环节都涉及译员的心智活动过程。"原语理解"涉及译员对原语的感知、辨析和综合理解，包括词义检查、意义单位的构建与组织、语篇层次意义的建立等。"脱离原语词语外壳"涉及从原语信息储存到译语表达过渡的某种中间状态，包括依据内部言语等信息载体实施"不完全脱离"，依据抽象符号和概念、意象、情感等信息载体实施"完全脱离"等。"译语表达"涉及译员的译语言语准备、译语内部言语组织和译语产出，包括对要点信息的加工、对隐性关键信息等重要信息的加工、句法组织和语音发布等。各个主要环节内部所包含的分程序有机地连接在一起，形成了口译中连续不断的工作链。

巴黎释意派翻译理论的创始人 D. 塞莱科斯维奇曾使用口译"三角模式"，简单、明确地阐释了口译工作过程，该三角模式如图 1.1.1 所示。

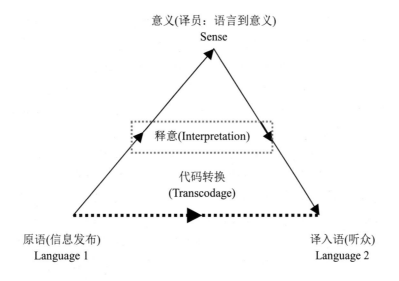

图 1.1.1　口译工作过程的"三角模式"

如图 1.1.1 所示，原语至译入语的转换过程可以有直接的代码转换形式(例如术语、数字、专有名词等语言信息的代码转换现象)，也可以有从原语直达三角模式顶端的"意义"以传至译入语的"释意"形式；而意义是从三角模式的顶端开始发送的，因为原语一旦还原成原始信息，原语的词语外壳就被"脱离"，那么线性的语言外在形式对译员来说便不应再有影响。D. 塞莱科斯维奇讲道："假设口译过程为一个三角模式。从三角形的顶端开始传送自发表达的思想，因为变成意思的原语形式已不再有约束力。底部表示未经语境或情景更改的概念从语言到语言的直接翻译，这些概念只是知识的目标而不是理解的目标。"这就是说，口译的过程不仅是简单的双语互换，三角顶端的"意义"起到了相当大的作用。"意义"反映着口译实践的本质，是脱离语言形式并解释出其中的含义。这一"释意"过程就是口译工作的根本所在。简而言之，口译工作的关键在于"得意忘言"或"得意忘形"，这样的口译才能出"神"入"化"。

具体实践过程中，口译过程可以分为四个环节：听清、理解、记忆和表达，且这四个环节紧密衔接，有时几乎是同步进行的。对中国译员来说，英译汉和汉译英时，各个环节的难度和侧重会有所不同。

1. 听清

口译的运作过程是从语言信息的输入开始的。除视译是通过视觉接收信息外，绝大多数情况下，译员通过听觉从说话人那里接收语言信息。因此，译员的听觉和对听入信息的理解是口译的第一道关口。对中国译员来说，英译汉时尤其如此，因为我们对英语的掌握远不如母语那样熟练。英译汉时听力理解始终是我们的薄弱环节。不难想象，如果译员没有听清或听懂说话人讲的英语，那么译成汉语将无从谈起；如果没有完全听懂或听错了，也不可能准确、完整地传达说话人的原意，甚至会造成误解，导致双方交际的失败或更严重的后果。因此，译员必须有敏锐的听觉、很好的语感和善于区分不同语音、语调、词汇和句法的能力。

一个称职的译员不仅能听懂英美国家人士讲的标准英语，而且能听懂以英语为母语国家的人士所讲的各种不同的英语变体，如爱尔兰英语、苏格兰英语、加拿大英语、澳大利亚英语、新西兰英语、南非英语等。他们还必须能听懂把英语作为第二语言或官方语言使用的人所讲的英语，如印度英语、新加坡英语、菲律宾英语、西非国家的人士讲的英语等，还必须能听懂把英语作为外语使用的非英语国家人士讲的英语。与标准英语相比，以上国家的人士讲的英语可能发音不准，用词不当，甚至还有语法错误。但对中国译员来说，能够听懂不同国家和地区的英语十分重要，尤其是现在，我国实行的是全方位的对外开放，我们不仅要同英语国家打交道，而且要同全世界各国人民发展交流与合作。英语是全世界使用最广泛的语言之一，但以英语为母语的国家并不多。大多数国家是把英语作为第二语言、官方语言或者外语来使用的。不同国家的人讲的英语各有特点，与标准英语在发音、词汇、语法上都有一定的区别。因此，译员平时要有意识地训练和培养自己适应各种不同英语变体的语音、语调、词汇、句法的能力，努力提高自己的英语听力理解能力，这是提高口译质量的重要环节。

汉译英时情况有所不同，除了浓重的地方口音、方言、习语、俚语或专业术语外，对中国译员来说，听懂汉语一般不成问题，其中重要的环节是理解，从而进行语言转换和英语表达。

2. 理解

理解是译员对接收的语言信息进行分析、解意、综合等加工处理而后做出正确判断和理解的过程。说话人传递的信息是由多种因素组成的，有语言的和非语言的。译员对接收信息的理解包括下述几个层面的内容。

(1) **语言性的理解**。语言是信息的主要载体。口译是一种语言交际活动，信息的传递主要靠译员对原语的理解，包括对说话人的语音、语调、语法、词汇、词义及语篇等语言因素的理解。因此，译员必须有扎实的语言知识、丰富的词汇，不但要熟练掌握两种交际语的常用语、成语、谚语、俗语等，而且要善于捕捉"言外之音"、"话外之意"，从说话人的语气、语调、隐语和语境中体会其话语的真正含义。由此可见，语言层面的理解根本在于译员对参与交际的两种语言掌握的娴熟程度。译员应该精通两种语言，尤其是外语水平应接近母语水平。

另外，语言性的理解与文化背景知识密切相关。由于交际双方使用的两种语言各有其社会意识和文化内涵，如果不了解一种语言的社会文化背景，就很难理解和掌握这种语言，当然也就无从翻译。因此，译员要有良好的双语文化修养，既了解原语文化，又熟悉本民族的文化，只有这样，口译时才能从两种文化的对比中找出相互"对等"的概念和词语进行语义转换。译员对两种文化了解得越透彻，就越能深刻理解说话人的原意。

(2) **知识性的理解**。口译涉及的内容极为广泛。当今世界，各种国际交流活动非常频繁。除了经常性的政治外交、经济贸易、文化体育等交流外，各种专业性、学术性的会议和交流活动也越来越频繁。双方谈话的内容可能涉及许多方面。译员如果掌握了足够的相关方面的专业知识，就能从专业的角度去分析和理解谈话内容。反之，如果译员缺乏有关谈话主题的专业知识，即使外语水平再高，也不可能充分理解谈话的内容。由此可见，知识与理解密切相关。译员的知识越丰富，对谈话的理解就越深刻，口译也就越顺利。

成功的译员应是多面手，具有丰厚扎实的知识底蕴。当然，这不是要求译员事事通、样样懂，但译员必须掌握起码的国际常识，具有政治、经济、商贸、法律、人文、科技等方面的基本知识，了解原语国的政治、经济、史地、社会等基本概况，熟悉我国的国情，尤其是我国的对内对外政策及在重大国际问题上的立场、观点和态度。在条件允许的情况下，译员要事先有所准备，尽量熟悉交际双方将要讨论的主题及可能涉及的知识范围。

译员的知识获取主要靠平时坚持不懈的努力。译员应善于抓住每次实践机会，不断积累和扩充知识，提高口译水平。

(3) **逻辑性的理解**。译员除靠说话人发出的语言信息和对谈话主题的了解来理解说话人的意思外，还可以借助对谈话内容的分析和逻辑推理加深理解。交际中双方各以不同的身份、地位参与谈话，双方谈话时都有各自的思路、方式和目的，谈话内容有内在的逻辑和联系。译员要了解说话人的身份、地位、职业等情况，尽快理解其谈话的意图，抓住其谈话的内在联系，通过对其谈话的分析和逻辑推理，确切理解说话人的真正含义，这样就不会因为偶尔没有完全听清说话人的谈话而中断思维和理解。译员可通过逻辑推理，跟上说话人的思路，理解其本意。即使在说话人发生口误或谈话前后颠倒的情况下，译员也能正确推导出他的意思，并将其正确地口译出来。

3. 记忆

译员在对接收的语言信息进行处理的过程中，需要把获取的信息暂时留存在记忆里，以防在转换和表达时信息流失或漏译、误译。因此，译员要有较强的记忆力，特别是交替翻译时记忆力尤其重要，因为交替翻译时说话人常常是讲2～3分钟甚至4～5分钟才停下来。译员对说话人的谈话内容不能随意增减，更不能违背其原意进行编造，必须把说话人的原意忠实、完整、及时地表达出来。

因此，译员必须在理解的瞬间最大限度地调动自己的记忆力，把谈话的意思记下来，再选择恰当的措辞和句子表达出来。可见，记忆和理解紧密相连，相辅相成，几乎是同时进行的。理解了的东西最易记忆，记忆又能影响理解和表达。实际上，口译过程中译员是边听、边记、边理解。

记忆有两种形式：心记和笔记。同声传译时讲话和翻译几乎同时进行，来不及做笔记，因为笔记会分散精力，影响下一句的听和译。一般情况下，译员全凭心记。交替翻译则不同，译员要等说话人讲完一段停下来再翻译；译员需要借助笔记来帮助记忆，但是不要过度依赖笔记，否则容易本末倒置，影响翻译的效果。不管是同声传译还是交替翻译，都要求译员有出众的记忆力。因此，译员要通过实践锻炼强化自己的记忆力。记笔记是一项专门的口译技巧，将在本书第四章专门讨论。

4. 表达

表达是译员在充分理解原语的基础上，用译入语表达说话人原意的过程。听清、理解、记忆的最终目的是为了表达。表达的过程中，译员要对理解的信息和概念进行语码转换，重新编码，综合概括，选择适当的词语，最后将其及时准确地译出。表达时译员要做到发音清晰、语调准确、措辞得当、语句通顺、自然流畅。这些是表达的基本要求，也是体现口译质量高低的重要标志。成功的表达既能完整、准确、流利地传达说话人的信息，又能保持说话人的风格和特点。出色的口译能使双方的交谈"水乳交融"，没有任何语言障碍。在一些国际会议上，常常会看到这种现象：与会者在聆听一位代表慷慨激昂的发言时，会发现传译室里的译员以同样的激情，一边口译，一边情不自禁地挥动手臂。译员如此传情达意、完美理想的表达效果取决于其语言功底和演讲才能。译员不仅要有纯正的母语和熟练的外语，而且要有一定的演讲技巧，表达时口齿伶俐、声音洪亮、音色优美、节奏适宜，遣词造句要有一定的功力，这样的口译才能吸引和打动听众。

四、译员的基本素质要求

在全球化的今天，国际交往日益密切，口译越来越受到重视，已经成为一种重要、崇高而令人向往的工作，同时也是一种入门门槛很高、很难进入的职业。口译人员任务艰巨，责任重大，工作艰辛，没有良好的思想素质和过硬的业务能力是很难胜任的。一名合格的译员，应具备以下基本素质。

1. 思想素质和职业道德

一名合格的译员要有良好的政治思想素质和崇高的职业道德，具有较高的政策水平和严格的组织纪律性。在涉外工作中，译员的工作和表现代表国家的形象、民族的精神、国家或集团的利益。译员对工作要有强烈的责任感和高度负责的精神。在对外交往中要忠于祖国，正确执行党和国家的方针、政策，严守国家机密，严格遵守外事纪律和涉外人员守则，忠于职守，洁身自爱，不谋私利，不自行其是，不做任何有损国格和人格的事。

2. 语言能力

一名合格的译员必须有过硬的语言能力，其中包括扎实的母语和外语功底，不仅要对两种语言有扎实的语音、语调、词法、句法、语法等基本知识，而且要有熟练的语言运用能力和跨文化交际能力，要有敏锐的听力和丰富的词汇，翻译时口齿清晰、语调自然、措辞得当，表达准确、流畅。同时，译员要熟练掌握一定数量的习语、谚语、缩略语、委婉语、诙谐语、专业术语、诗句、名言、警句的译法，灵活运用各种口译的方法和技巧，只有这样，才能在各种口译场合从容不迫，将两种语言运用自如，闯过一道道难关，达到传情达意的效果。

3. 知识储备

译员的业务素质还包括知识的储备。口译过程中，译员会遇到各类题材的谈话，其内容几乎包罗万象，无所不及。因此，一个称职的译员必须具备丰富的知识，能够迅速适应不同专业的翻译任务，同时还必须比较深入地掌握相关专业知识，例如国际事务、经贸、金融、电信、化工、机械、计算机、生物等方面的知识，这样可以更好、更稳定地为某些机构提供服务。

4. 综合能力

译员还必须有敏锐的头脑，快速的反应，出众的记忆力，高度的判断能力，较强的综合分析能力，逻辑思维能力和随机应变能力，只有这样，才能在各种场合的口译中立于不败之地。

5. 个人修养

译员还必须有良好的个人修养，在涉外活动中要做到仪表端庄、举止大方、彬彬有礼、态度谦和、风度文雅，既要热情友好，又要不卑不亢，在工作实践中，译员要注意不断提高自己的政治、业务素质和个人修养。

第二章　无笔记口译训练
Interpretation Training Without Taking Notes

谈到口译，很多人往往认为首要的是记口译笔记。无可否认，记口译笔记能够极大地促进口译的准确性和条理性，但是作为口译学习者，在入门阶段最重要的一点是听懂讲话，全面把握讲话者的讲话信息以及信息的逻辑层次和关系，从语言中提取出意思，并且通过刻苦的训练增强短期记忆能力。在这个阶段，学习者应当不记书面笔记，而是用大脑记忆来存储信息内容。

一、信息的接收与分析

口译中信息接收的最主要途径就是听，在口译中听的不是语言，而是语言表达的内容。在英语学习中，有一定英语水平的人已经掌握了如何记住一段话的几个要点，判断一段话会产生的结果，在听到对方讲话后形成自己的赞同或反对意见，或是捕捉到对方讲话中使用到的字词，考虑字词在用法上的特点，或是从语法、修辞、逻辑上挑对方的毛病等，但这些都不是口译员需要做的。口译员是个很特别的听众，他用不着以自己的想法进行干预，而只需要注意讲话人要表达的意思，领会意思中的细节。口译员需要对信息进行分析，但是讲话人在不停地讲，那么他就必须在很短的时间内捕捉到必要的信息。所谓"把注意力集中在讲话人的话语上"，是指避免注意不适当的东西。比如，当你听到一位发言人的讲话时，你在心中暗自抱怨"怎么老是嗯啊呀？"或是心里想"他的美音真是到了炉火纯青的地步，我要是能说得一样好就好了"，等等，这都表明你的注意力没有集中到讲话人的意旨上。

口译过程中，不仅要听懂原话，还要对讲话内容的整体和细节有全面的把握。口译初学者要想达到上述要求，需要以正确的方法进行训练。语言同意义的分离练习或者说口头概述大意练习是常用的方法。原语复述训练，也就是说听到的是中文就用中文复述，听到的是英语就用英语复述。这种练习看似简单，实践时可能会有意想不到的困难，比如要点遗漏，表述混乱，缺乏逻辑性，表达不流畅，等等，练习时要努力克服。要学会听意义，而不是语言，这是口译训练成功的关键。听完一段讲话后，不要停留在语言上，要把注意力集中在信息意义上，下意识地忘记语言，做到"得意而忘言"。听意义也可以减轻记忆的负担，因为记意义比记词汇容易。

复述练习 I

请看下文，然后用原语将其主要内容概述出来，注意文中的逻辑关系，不要试图背诵原文。

2-1.mp3

　　努尔哈赤的一生啊,应当说是成功的一生。作为一个男人来说,作为一个政治家来说,作为一个军事家来说,应当说是成功的。由边远山区的那么一个少年,逐渐逐渐成长,成为大清国的奠基者,大清国的开创人,应当说是成功的。那他成功的基本的经验是什么?我说啊,努尔哈赤人生喜剧、人生成功的经验很多。我认识一个国际级的裁判。有一次开会,我们俩住一屋,他跟我说,他说他们总结了,拿一个世界级的金牌要有156个因素,当然有主有次了。你平常锻炼非常好,那天感冒了,你金牌就没了。156个因素综合在一起,发挥最好,你才可以得到金牌。清太祖努尔哈赤44年,建立一个清帝国,我想比拿一个世界冠军总体来说应当更难,所以努尔哈赤的喜剧,他成功的因素应当是很多的。今天不可能都讲,我就讲两个字"四合"——一二三四的"四",谐合的"合",就是"天合","地合","人合","己合",努尔哈赤事业成功的基本经验"四合"。

——节选自阎崇年中央电视台"百家讲坛"《清十二帝疑案》之努尔哈赤(下)

2-2.mp3

　　老子和我们现代生活有关吗?老子他在哪儿呢?这个问题呀我曾经做了一个测试。我到苏州玄妙观,碰到三个天真活泼的孩子,一看太可爱了,我就测试一下。我说:"你们知道老子吗?"他们说:"爷爷,知道!"他们中一个男孩说了,他说:"老子就是我爸!"还有一个男孩,他说了:"老子不就是玄妙观当中的那个塑像吗,那个道士的塑像吗?"我会心一笑。一个小女孩嫣然一笑,她说:"不,不,不,《老子》是一本书,我爸爸的书桌上就有这本书!"我笑了,老子不就是和我们三个现代孩子生活在一起吗,而且这三个孩子心目当中有三个不同的老子:一、老子是我爸;二、老子是那个道士的塑像;三、《老子》是一本书。

——节选自姚淦铭中央电视台"百家讲坛"《老子其人其书》

2-3.mp3

　　Since my last message of Christmas greetings to you all, the world has witnessed many great events and sweeping changes. But they are already part of the long record of history. Now, as ever, the important time for mankind is the future. The coming years are full of hope and promise, and their course can still be shaped by our will and action. The Christmas message of peace on earth, goodwill toward men, remains the same. But we can only achieve this if we are all truly ambitious for what is good and honorable. Humanity can only make progress by determination and concerted effort. One such concerted effort has been the campaign to free the world from hunger. I am very happy to know that the people of the Commonwealth have responded so generously to this campaign. Much has been achieved but there is still much to do and on this day of reunions and festivities in the glow of Christmas. Let us remember the many undernourished people, young and old, scattered throughout the world. All my family joins me in sending every one of you best wishes for Christmas and may God's blessing be with you in the coming year!

2-4.mp3

Memory is our most important possession. Without memory, you wouldn't know who you are. You couldn't think about the past or plan for the future. Memory is essential for everything we do as human beings. It's amazing that we have this magical time machine in our heads that enables us to record experiences and then use that information at a later time. Discovering how the brain makes and preserves memories has to be one of the most important of all scientific pursuits.

People who feel they must apologize for having a bad memory should stop using a poor memory as an excuse for forgetting things. The only people who have a poor memory are those whose memory function has been compromised by disease or damage. All the rest of us must accept the responsibility to make an effort to remember things. You must associate it with something. You must exercise it or risk losing its effectiveness. Students and faculty should understand that a good education involves an emphasis on understanding rather than sheer memorization. Second, cramming for finals is a very bad way to learn bad way to learn something that will last. Information from cramming will come in and go out. If you want retain what you learn, you must spread out the learning process.

相信通过上述复述练习，大家已能够从讲话中大致区分出哪些是语言，哪些是信息。从讲话中找出信息以后，我们还应当对这些信息进行逻辑分析，以便能够透彻、全面地把握这些信息，以加深记忆。在逻辑分析中，我们要构建起话语的逻辑框架，框架中首先要分清层次，概括出中心内容，以及从几个方面来说明这个中心意思。然后要分析每个方面有哪些信息，信息之间又是什么关系，比如是因果关系、对比关系、分类关系、时间先后关系、空间上的顺序关系、重要性的序列关系，或是列举关系等。

在上述练习中我们来看看2-1，这是一篇关于清太祖努尔哈赤成功人生的讲座，中心内容是努尔哈赤的一生是成功的一生，然后讲了他成功的因素——"四合"。这样便掌握了逻辑层次。在讲到他的一生是成功的一生时，提到他作为男人、政治家和军事家这三个方面都是成功的，可简单概括为：他从边远山区少年成长为大清国的奠基者和开创人，是成功的。在讲到其成功的因素时，举了一位国际级的裁判总结拿国际级金牌所需因素的例子来说明努尔哈赤的成功因素很多，然后突出主题：如此多因素最主要的只有两个字"四合"，即"天合"、"地合"、"人合"和"己合"。有了这样的分析，我们就可以从整体到局部很好地把握讲话的内容，有条不紊地记忆讲话的信息，缓解"听"过程中的压力，为流畅表达打下良好的基础。

复述练习Ⅱ

请听下面的讲话，然后用原语将其中心内容概述出来，分析讲话中的逻辑关系，形成一个逻辑框架，然后将讲话内容按照逻辑关系展开并复述出来。

 2-5.mp3

同学们好！今天很有运气，跟大家一起来讨论一个相关于人类健康的问题。那我们现在首先要考虑一个问题。我们最怕听到三种声音,你们说是哪三种?大概一下子想不起来,我想第一种是属于我们所见到的一种,"哎呀,老啰!"什么意思呢?就是这个人到了一定年龄以后,这一个生理的器官逐渐衰老,这个衰老的器官该怎么办呢?换掉。我们现在人类已经进入很大程度上的老龄化阶段,美国 2010 年,大约 50 岁以上的就超过了 32%。我们国家也有一个统计,在 2010 年,大约 60 岁以上的超过 24%。你可以算一算,我们人口基数是 13 亿,这样算下来,是多大的一个数目。第二个声音呢,最怕听到的是"砰","哎呀,糟了!车子给撞上了"。战场上也是"砰"一枪打过去,不是打断了人的腿,就是穿过人的胸。那么这些组织损伤创伤,目前已经逐年上升,在我们国家的统计数字上看,已经达到了临床住院数目的第二位。第三个声音就是你们可能经常听到的声音"咔嚓"。什么意思呢?人生病了,到医院去了,组织器官坏了,医生拿一个剪刀就给你剪掉了,手术化疗。

——节选自王远亮中央电视台"百家讲坛"《人体零件制造》

2-6.mp3

我觉得《易经》给我们最宝贵的东西,四个字,也是中华文化里面最可贵的四个字,叫做"持经达变"。

什么叫经?经,就是不能变的东西,它叫经。你一个人有了经以后,你还不会变,那就是你不会用嘛,不会用。原则是不能变的,但是方法是一定要变的。可是我们现在受美国影响很严重,我们说:"什么都在变。"我是不接受这句话的。各位,你如果相信一切一切都在变,什么都在变的话,请你今天晚上回去,看看你自己的爸爸变了没有?还是老一个!哪里有变!可见还是有人不变嘛?如果你今天回去发现全家人都变了,你爸爸也变了,那真的变了。没有那回事。其实《易经》告诉我们,世界上如果没有不变,你就不可能有变;如果没有变,你就不可能有不变,它根本就是相对的。其实《易经》是全世界最高明的辩证法。

你从这个角度来看我们中国人,你会发现,中国人说要就变成不要,说不要他就是要。你送礼给外国人,外国人会当场拿来,告诉你,我最喜欢这个东西。中国人会吗?中国人你送礼给他,他说:"不要,千万不要!好了,搁那儿好了。"最后还是要了。我小时候也是很讨厌这个的,根本虚伪,假的嘛!后来我才懂,我读了《易经》才懂,学理很简单,叫做"站在不要不要的立场来要,才不会乱要,这样就对了。站在没有没有意见的立场来发表意见,才不会乱讲。这样就对了。站在退让的立场来不让,最后当仁不让嘛!当仁就不应该让嘛!这就是最好的逻辑。"《易经》告诉我们:当不当就是应该不应该的意思。只有一句话,尤其是对年轻人,特别特别要小心"少问喜欢不喜欢,多问应该不应该"。现在不是,我喜欢。你喜欢就糟糕了。你喜欢?!对不对?我经常讲,外国人因为他脑筋是一半的,我们脑筋是全的,因为我们有阴有阳,同时要兼顾。所以外国人讲话经常讲一半的话。你看,他们最流行的一句话叫什么:"不自由,毋宁死。"现在年轻人都上当,说"对,对对对。"你就糟糕了。他只讲了一半"不自由,毋宁死"。还有一半他没讲,从来没讲,只有中国人才懂:"一自由就堕落。"不自由当然不好,但太自由更不好。你说有钱多好,这句话也不对啊！钱是怎么样？钱是不够，很紧张；太多了，很烦恼；刚刚好，最愉快。那就好了嘛！

——节选自曾仕强中央电视台"百家讲坛"《易经与人生》

2-7.mp3

Mastery of interpretation techniques seems to be as essential to an interpreter as mastery of boxing technique is to a boxer. True, normally every boxer has got to have two fists to fight with. Yet not all who have two fists are good boxers. It usually takes an arduous process of training and coaching integrated with a great number of "bouts" to master adequately the techniques of boxing, thereby eventually making a first-rate boxer. Similarly, not all those who have a good command of the languages involved and have acquired a wide range and scope of general knowledge are necessarily good interpreters. An arduous process of training and coaching integrated with an enormous amount of practice is called for, in order to master the basic techniques of interpretation, including dexterity in note-taking, and to be able to cope with various difficult situations.

——Extracted from *A Practical Handbook of Interpretation (Enlarged and Revised Edition)* by Zhong Shukong

2-8.mp3

The South African author Andre Brink who was a prominent critic of apartheid has died aged 79. Andre Brink was a white South African who wrote in Afrikaans and English. Some of his novels were burned for challenging the apartheid system. In his later work he was deeply critical of the African National Congress after South Africa became a democracy. His most famous books include *A Dry White Season and Looking on Darkness*.

——From BBC News

二、信息的视觉化和形象化

在口译中当我们听到一段讲话时，我们可以快速对其逻辑关系进行分析，加强记忆效果。实际上，我们还可以使用其他办法来增强记忆效果，对信息进行视觉化和形象化处理就是常用的策略。日常生活经验和常识告诉我们，我们的大脑在识记言语材料时，如果该材料内容生动、形象、丰富，则可以给我们留下较深刻的印象，而内容空洞的材料则容易被人遗忘。不少心理学实验也证明"意象"因素在人脑的记忆中有重要作用。脑对意象材料的记忆效果普遍好于对词语材料的记忆效果，同理，视觉记忆的效果一般来说也普遍好于听觉记忆的效果。这就是说，虽然口译工作者无权对原语内容进行挑选，但是可以充分利用原语的意象载体增强对原语信息的记忆效果。信息的视觉化和形象化策略常常可以运用在口译活动涉及叙述某一事件，描述过程，介绍产品、人物、景点、团体、企业时，等等。

译员可以边听边将听到的内容形象化，用视觉跟踪事态的发展，借助形象综合记忆听到的内容，这样做既可以避免只听字词，还可在表达时做到通畅和清晰。

复述练习Ⅲ

请看下文，将讲话中的内容进行信息的视觉化和形象化处理，然后复述讲话内容。

2-9.mp3

春天来了！春天来了！

我们几个孩子，脱掉棉袄，冲出家门，奔向田野，去寻找春天。

春天像个害羞的小姑娘，遮遮掩掩，躲躲藏藏。我们仔细地找啊，找啊。

小草从地下探出头来，那是春天的眉毛吧？

早开的野花一朵两朵，那是春天的眼睛吧？

树木吐出点点嫩芽，那是春天的音符吧？

解冻的小溪叮叮咚咚，那是春天的琴声吧？

春天来了！我们看到了她，我们听到了她，我们闻到了她，我们触到了她。她在柳枝上荡秋千，在风筝尾巴上摇啊摇；她在喜鹊、杜鹃嘴里叫，在桃花、杏花枝头笑……

——选自《找春天》

2-10.mp3

那么，诸位不管是来自城市，还是来自农村，不论是年长，还是年少，那么，都会接触到不少的昆虫。确实，在我们的周围，在自然界当中，有着各种各样的昆虫。那么，有的呢，长得像棍子，像枝条；有的呢，长得像叶片。那么，有的长，有的短，有的头尖；有的呢，头是圆的，头圆；那么，有的是腰比较粗，有的呢，腰非常细，像杆一样。那么，有的昆虫能够发音歌唱，那么，有的呢能够发光。那么，为什么昆虫会大小不同，形状各异？为什么它们会发光？为什么它们会歌唱？那么，我们的民族啊，各个民族各个国家，都有不同的传说。比如，这个蝉，就是我们北方常见的黑蚱蝉。它是怎么来的？它为什么会唱歌呢？据传说，在大概是远古的时代，有一家有三口人，其中呢，老两口和一个女儿。那么，女儿从外表上长得是非常的漂亮，那么，并且针线活儿也做得非常好，人也非常善良。那么，好多人来提亲，但是老两口就是不松口，就是不答应。直到有一天，有个要饭的小伙子，长得又黑又瘦，来了。老两口就悄悄地跟他说："你愿不愿意做我们的女婿？"那个小伙子当然说愿意了。但是呢，老两口告诉他一个秘密，就说这个女孩，这个女孩呢，长了个尾巴。这个，自然界是有这种现象的。结果，小伙子说："行，有尾巴也不要紧。"但是，老两口告诉他："你不能告诉任何人。如果告诉任何人，那么女儿可能就会死去。"刚开始的时候还挺好。过了一段时间，小伙子有一次喝醉了，人们就说他，说："你长得这么丑，那么，又穷，为什么娶个貌若天仙的女子？是不是有问题啊？"他就告诉大家说："哎呀！我媳妇长了个尾巴。"结果，很快消息在周围传开了。那么，他的媳妇呢，就投河自尽了。投河自尽以后就变成了就是在湖北那边的凤尾鱼。小伙子呢，一看媳妇死了，他也非常难受，他也投河自尽，就变成了这个黑蚱蝉，整天叫着"妻啊，妻啊"，所以，那么这个蝉就会发音了，"妻、妻、妻。"

——节选自彩万志中央电视台"百家讲坛"《中国昆虫文化》

2-11.mp3

The last hidden world — China

For centuries, travelers to China have told tales of magical landscapes and surprising creatures. Chinese civilization is the world's oldest and today is largest with well over a billion people. It's home to more than 50 distinct ethnic groups and a wide range of traditional life styles often in close partnership with nature. We know that China faces immense social and environmental problems, but there is great beauty here too. China is home to the world's highest mountains, vast deserts ranging from searing hot to mind numbing cold, steaming forests, harboring rare creatures, grassy plains beneath vast horizons and rich tropical seas. Now, for the first time ever we can explore the whole of this great country, meet some of the surprising and exotic creatures that live here and consider the relationship of the people and wildlife of China to the remarkable landscaping which they live. This is wild China.

——节选自 BBC 纪录片 *Wild China* 片头语

 2-12.mp3

A Stormy Night

Reina de Los Angeles is a Spanish village in southern California. In the village there is a military presidio with Spanish soldiers and their horses. There is also a Spanish church called a mission. The Spanish friars live here. All around the village there are big homes with patios.

Tonight there is a terrible storm and it is raining. Inside the village tavern there are soldiers and other men. They are eating and drinking. Sergeant Pedro Gonzales is at the tavern. He is a big, strong man.

"What a horrible night! It always rains in February. Where is Zorro on this stormy night?" asks one soldier.

"Zorro! Don't say that name! He is a bandit and a criminal," says Sergeant Gonzales.

"He is the terror of southern California," says another soldier.

"People say that he takes from the rich and gives to the poor. He is a friend of the natives and the friars. He punishes dishonest people," says an old man.

"Ha! Zorro is a big mystery. Who is he? Where is he from? He wears a black mask and no one can see his face. He travels on the El Camino Real on his fast horse. He is very good with his sword," says the Sergeant.

"Yes, and he leaves his mark—the Z—everywhere," says the old man.

"No one can stop him. The Governor of California offers a big reward for the capture of Zorro," says one soldier.

At that moment a man enters the tavern. He is young and handsome. He has black hair and dark eyes. He has fine clothes.

"Don Diego Vega, my friend!" says Sergeant Gonzales. "Your clothes are wet. Why are you out on this rainy night?"

Don Diego smiles and says, "I am going home, but I am cold and wet. I want something to drink."

"Come and stand near the fire," says the Sergeant. "Here is a glass of wine."

"Thank you, my friend," says Don Diego.

"We are talking about Zorro. Everyone is scared of him, but I am not! I am ready to fight Zorro and win! I am a champion with the sword. What do you think, Don Diego?" asks the Sergeant.

"Everyone talks about this mysterious man with a mask. Many people say good things about him," says Don Diego.

"I want to fight him and capture him! I want the big reward," says Sergeant Gonzales.

"No, no! Don't talk about fighting. I hate fighting and I hate violence. I think Zorro is sincere. He punishes only bad people. He protects the poor, the natives and the friars. Let Zorro do his work," says Don Diego.

"You are a kind man. You like music and poetry. You don't understand, my friend. You are rich and noble," says the Sergeant.

Don Diego smiles and says, "It's 6 p.m. I must return to my hacienda. Good night everyone." He opens the tavern door and goes out into the rain.

——From *Black Cat*

三、对信息进行逻辑分析

口译过程中接受和分析的主要是口语，但是不完全等同于我们在一般生活中所使用的口语。生活中的口语风格是很随意的，不太讲究语词的修饰，歇后语、俚语、俗语、俏皮话等较多，语级较低，所谓语级就是一定的言语社会层次可以有高雅、低俗等区别，使用的场合也不同，与语体类似；语体大致可分为庄严体(frozen)、正式体(formal)、普通体(general)、非正式体(informal)以及随意体(causual)等。生活中的口语很少涉及正式体和庄严体，也不存在正式体、庄严体所涉及的某些修辞方式和正式场合特有的一些正式的"套话"结构，题材也非常有限，交流过程中逻辑不严密，结构松散，伴随着大量的副语言信息和一些超出语言的信息，有时甚至是一个眼神或一个表情，双方就可以心领神会。

口译工作现场所使用的口语自然也包括"生活口语"，但是典型的口译工作却包罗万象，仅能说两句生活中常用的口语、俚语是难以胜任口译工作的。口译中的口语通常语级较高，多为正式或庄严语体，交际现场常为正式或半正式场合，多用"套话"，涉及的题材也常为政治、经济、科学技术、文化交流、学术探讨等方面。这种口语逻辑性较强，有一定的结构完整性，信息量较大，较注意用词，有时候在用词、结构等层次上可能还会很"专业化"。其信息量大且较为浓缩、不易记忆，在有些场合必须依赖笔记等某些特定的口译技术。这就是说"生活口语"并非是口译的语言难点，仅仅靠与以英语为母语的人士进行对话等方法来提高"生活口语",或者是生搬硬套死记大量俗语俚语,是无法有效地提高口译水平的。

口译学习应当重点分析研究口译中实际需要的口语言语,即口译"工作言语"。这种"工作言语"是口译工作人员的基础,主要是像庄严体、正式体、普通体等拥有较高语级的语体和特定题材类别的话语语篇结构,如会议发言、谈判、技术研讨、产品介绍、景点描述、商务沟通、法律纠纷等特定的语篇结构。掌握了这些内容后,可以很好地帮助口译人员把握口译工作语言的特点,更好地理解、分析、记忆信息,高水平地完成口译工作。鲍刚教授在《口译理论概述》一书中指出口译工作言语主要可分为四种话语结构类别:叙述语类、介绍语类、论证语类和联想语类。

1. 叙述语类

叙述语类主要是原语中的典故、故事、笑话等所使用的话语结构。这种语类有两个方面需要口译学习者注意:叙述的"时序性"和"空间线索"。所谓叙述的"时序性",是指话语的结构与叙述的时间顺序紧密相关。口译中遇到的叙述语类话语一般都遵循着一条时间线索,不同于书面语中数条线索同时展开或者日常生活中想到哪儿说到哪儿的"跳跃"式叙述。这条叙述线索主要表现为时间上的线性推移,同时串联着一定的空间、景物、人物等描述、造成时间推移过程中的"停"下来进行观察的现象。这是一条时而描述、时而叙说的话语语篇发展线索,描述与叙说既相互交织,又分别有所侧重,显示着言语者的言语特点。在起始阶段有一个"引子",使用一些言语交流双方所习惯接受的"套话"结构给言语受话者以一种"故事开始了"的感觉,如"我听说过有这么一件事儿……","我们国家有一个关于……的传说"等。在"引子"阶段,言语者一般会交代故事发生的时间、地点和主要人物,亦可引出某种悬念。"引子"后面是结合了描绘、悬念、铺垫等手法的故事情节的发展,然后往往还有一个高潮,最后还必定有一个结尾,除非原语话语被打断。译员可以利用这种结构对原语内容进行某种"标定",从而便于对话语内容进行存储。一般来讲,极少有违反这一叙述规律的话语现象出现。其结构图如图1.2.1所示。

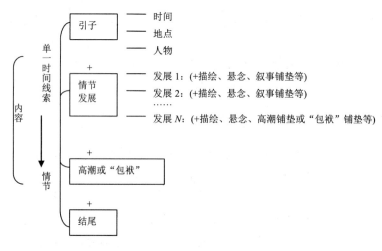

图1.2.1　叙述语类的时间结构

结构分析练习 1

请用前面所学的叙述语类的时间结构知识分析下面这段话，然后用汉语复述出来。

2-13.mp3

我想讲一个例子，是吧！这个也是发生在离我们不远的地方了。有一个小女孩上初二，长得很漂亮，学习委员。老师跟她交代，就是说啊："你是学习委员，要把咱们班的学习搞上去。"她特别当一回事儿，高度重视，每天给同学补课。考试之前最忙的就是她，结果这学习成绩还上不去，他们班。最后这孩子怎么办呢？她就急了，她形成一种焦虑，心理有毛病。她就在日记本上写，她说："如果下一次考试成绩再上不去，我就要采取最后一条措施了。"她要自杀。老师也不知道，同学也不知道，她形成焦虑了。但是呢，她跟她妈妈很亲，她就跟她妈妈说。结果，吃饭的时候，她跟她妈妈说什么呢？她说："妈妈，我告诉你啊，我不想活了。"这孩子把心里话说了，结果，她妈妈不懂这个，不懂得孩子有心理问题。妈妈说什么呢，她说："你胡说八道什么呀？！咱们家条件这么好，这两个还是知识分子，有三居室，你是学习委员。你胡说什么啊？！"就把她给堵了，她就没言语。转天吃饭的时候，她又说。她说："妈妈，我真的不想活了！"她妈妈说："你怎么又来了？胡说八道！"又给堵了。第三次，她又说，她说："妈妈，我前两次说的都是真的，我不想活了。"她妈就很生气，她一拍桌子："你这孩子真不像话，竟胡说八道！"这孩子把碗筷撂下，爬到八楼上跳下来，粉身碎骨。这么好的一个孩子就这样没了。在埋葬的时候，她的姥姥在她的坟前说了一句话，说："孙女啊，你的死就是我们教育的失误！"如果这个家长明白，孩子可能有心理问题，大人都可能有心理问题呀！是不是？这时候问一问孩子："你为什么呀？"孩子就会说："我们班学习上不去，我作为学习委员有责任。"孩子她这时候年龄啊，她偏激呀，她全归她自己身上，妈妈这样说就行了："你敢于负责任太好了。你想过没想过，你们班有多少老师，有责任没有？有班主任，有科任老师，每个孩子还有家长，他们有责任没有？你们班，还有别的班干部有责任没有？"一下子她就会缓解了，这件事就不会出来了。那当然，我举的是这么一个极端的例子。一般的情况下，孩子可能轻微的焦虑，交往障碍，是吧！本来这个平常比较活跃的孩子忽然就比较闷了，等等，就出现一种反常的现象，所以我想，这个要把关注孩子心理健康提上日程，这也是现在这个时代特别需要提醒的。

——节选自王宝祥中央电视台"百家讲坛"《可怜天下父母心》

叙述语类的另一个特点是叙述过程中所插入的描绘总是遵循着一定的空间线索，以构成特定的画面，同时这一空间线索又必须能够为多数人所接受，因此原语描述线路大同小异。多数人在言语描绘时共同遵循的描绘线路基本上都是先上后下、由外及内、先左后右、从前到后等。译员掌握了这些特点就可以对描述主线做出某种预测，进而可能利用某种鲜明的立体坐标图为原语的意象信息勾勒出一幅清晰的画面，而无须借助语言记忆。

2. 介绍语类

介绍语类常常用于对科技成果或产品、商品的介绍，对人物的介绍，对旅游景点的介绍，对企业、团体的介绍等。这一语类的线索主要是按照人类对一般事物的认知规律发展的：正式介绍前存在某种"引言"语段，有时介绍者在这一语段内启用一些修辞手段，以吸引受话者注意；介绍时一般是由表及里、由浅入深，基本上符合多数人的思维线路，介绍"主线"有时可循着一定的空间或时间线索；介绍多具有层次感，表现出一定的逻辑顺序；语篇结尾时一般有一处小结。其层次结构如图1.2.2所示。

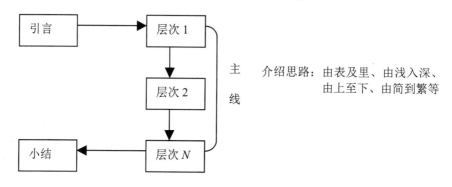

图1.2.2　介绍语类的层次结构

结构分析练习2

请用前面所学的介绍语类的层次结构知识分析下面这段话，然后用汉语复述出来。

2-14.mp3

华为公司此次推出的三款小灵通手机充分借鉴 GSM、CDMA 手机的设计理念，并考虑了国内消费者的文化背景、使用习惯以及个人偏好的因素，全部为折叠机型，总计六种颜色。具有造型时尚美观、色彩新潮、功能丰富等诸多特点，并在功能和款式上已完全可以与现在 GSM、CDMA 手机相媲美，可以满足不同消费者的差异化需求。由于华为小灵通手机完全根据用户需求设计，我们预计此次推出的三款手机一上市将会受到消费者的青睐。

3. 论证语类

这一语类在口译中很常见，是口译工作言语的典型话语结构之一。这种话语结构逻辑性非常强，以"论点+论证"为基本层次结构，逻辑关联词出现的频率很高。一般来讲，这种语类结构清晰，转折明确，逻辑严谨。然而，话语者也可能出现"离题"的情况，尤其是在没有充分准备发言的情况下，这时译员要特别注意话语者何时离题，在话语结构的何处离题，并要做好话语者回到话语主题的精神准备。论证语类的层次结构如图1.2.3所示。

论证语类总的来说是有一定难度的，比较接近书面语，语体多采用正式体，往往有自己独特的、较正式的"套话"结构，多数情况下由较长的复合句组成，信息量很大，语句比较精炼，给口译工作带来相当大的困难。这种语类多数直接采用"念稿发言"的形式，专业性很强，如果译员无法事先得到稿子，在口译时将会陷入被动的局面，因此口译学习者一定要心中有数。对于事先拿到稿子而进行的口译，通常称为"视译"，这也是口译技术训练之一，在以后的章节中另作讨论，这里暂不讨论。

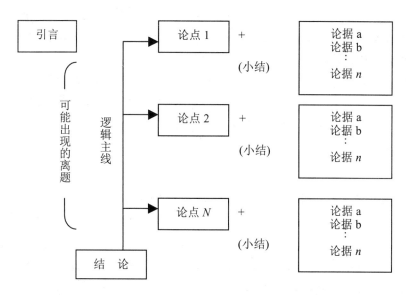

图 1.2.3　论证语类的层次结构

结构分析练习 3

请用前面所学的论证语类的层次结构知识分析下面这段话，然后用原语复述出来。

2-15.mp3

很高兴来到塔什干出席上海合作组织成员国总理第十二次会议。感谢乌兹别克斯坦政府为本次会议所做的周到安排。

当今世界，政治经济形势发生复杂深刻变化。我们在变化中要保持传统，坚持原则，也要拓展合作方式，共同迎接挑战。我们要落实好今年9月比什凯克元首峰会达成的共识，积极作为，打造安全、便利、互惠和绿色的发展环境，推动本地区加快发展，造福各国人民。为此，我提几点建议：

第一，深化安全合作。任何一个国家和地区，没有安全，就没有发展。打击恐怖活动是各国的共同利益，也是共同责任。各方应把打击恐怖活动和禁毒作为当前安全合作的重点，同时尽快赋予上合组织反恐怖机构禁毒职能。我们需要提高综合安全能力，提供更好的安全保障。

第二，加快道路互联互通。各成员国都在"丝绸之路经济带"上。各方深化务实合作，互联互通是基础。希望各方积极参与新亚欧大陆桥和渝新欧国际铁路联运通道建设，进一步畅通从东到西的大通道，促进物畅其流。中方愿在技术、装备以及融资等方面给予支持。

第三，促进贸易和投资便利化。各成员国应在通关、检验检疫等方面简化手续，降低关税，消除贸易壁垒，创造条件实现上海合作组织框架内的自由贸易。中国愿在新亚欧大陆桥东端的连云港，为成员国提供物流、仓储服务。

第四，加强金融合作。为满足成员国互联互通与产业合作的融资需求，支持重大项目建设，应进一步发挥好上合组织银行联合体的作用。要推进建立上合组织开发银行。加快实现成员国之间的本币结算。中方愿设立面向本组织成员国、观察员国、对话伙伴国等欧亚国家的中国欧亚经济合作基金，欢迎各方参加。

第五，推进生态和能源合作。各方应共同制定上合组织环境保护合作战略，依托中国-上合组织环境保护中心，建立信息共享平台。完善能源合作机制，做好组建上合组织能源俱乐部的研究和推进工作。

第六，扩大人文交流。要在尊重文化多样性的基础上，加强人文交流，使各国关系发展达到更高境界，夯实民意基础。中国愿增加面向成员国青年学生的政府奖学金留学生名额，未来5年将为成员国2000名中小学生举办夏令营。

——节选自李克强总理2013年在上海合作组织成员国总理第十二次会议上的讲话

4. 联想语类

这是一种"想到哪儿说到哪儿"的话语形式，确切地讲是一种跨语类的话语结构。最主要的特点是逻辑性非常差，结构相对松散，语级语体较低级，非常接近于"生活口语"，多见于寒暄、问候、会谈或者宴会中主宾较随便的对话，甚至是相当长的自顾自地"独白"，这种话语在整理其思维路线时比较困难。这种话语在中国的口译活动中比较常见，在西方文化背景下比较少见。我国译员在口译工作中应该对此类话语特别留意，中国原语话语者很可能以"意会"作为出发点，在交际话语中产生"跳跃"式的联想，译员作为中介者应为交际的最终受者提供力所能及的帮助。其实，不管言语的变化如何，其内部总是有一定的规律可循。表面上"逻辑混乱"的话语只不过是把某种"联想"的线索隐藏在言语之中。联想线索可以呈现三种规律：相似型联想规律、相反型联想规律和接近型联想规律。相似型联想规律反映着两个联想客体之间"类似"性质的关联，相反型联想规律反映着联想客体之间"对立"性质的关联，接近型联想规律反映着二者之间"依存"性质的关联，其中相似型联想规律是最常见的"基础型"联想方式。从思维角度来看，关于联想规律的分析可用图1.2.4所示。

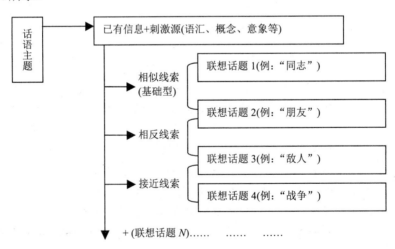

图1.2.4 话语中的联想规律

由图1.2.4可以看出，这种话语反映了一种"离题"的话语思维方式，呈现出某种思维的"跳跃"，讲话者很可能直接从"联想话题1"一跃而至"联想话题4"或"联想话题N"，隐去中间环节。这种"跳跃式言语思维"往往给译员带来很大困难。译员在遇到这种类型的话语时，要特别留意讲话者进行言语联想时话语"主线"上的思维刺激源，随时注意讲话者思路何时转化、"跳跃"，以及其中的联想线索沿着何种规律发展等。如果可能，最好能够了解讲话者的言语习惯等"背景信息"，看讲话者是惯于相似联想还是相反联想，是善于逻辑表达还是跳跃式"意会"思维。对此，应对措施是对讲话者用过的发言稿进行一定的分析，最好是对讲话者本人有所了解。

结构分析练习 4

请用前面所学的联想语类的知识分析下面这段话，然后用汉语复述出来。

2-16.mp3

很多人以为，武侠小说就是武打小说。我们很多中学老师没收学生的书就说："不许看武打小说。"所谓武打小说，在他们理解起来就是暴力文学，教孩子怎么打架的教科书，就是粗制滥造的低俗文学。而这些朋友不了解，武侠小说也好，通俗小说也好，其实只是我们给文学分的类，只是文学中的某一个类别。这些类别只是说它们有不同的特点，而不是说它们在艺术价值上有高有低，通俗小说不见得它不高雅，不见得不严肃，而那些所谓的非通俗小说，我们想想发表在所谓严肃刊物上的那些小说，它们都是精品吗？它们都高雅吗？不是说你写某一种类别的东西，就决定了你的高下，就好像我们大家从事的工作。当教授就一定高雅吗？在木樨地卖馒头就一定低俗吗？这可不见得。所以类别只是一种特点上的划分，而不能决定它的高下。看文学作品跟看人一样，不能看表面上的名目。比如大家看我今天穿这衣服，不能代表我就会武功。其实我不会打架，我连我的夫人都打不过，我可能只能打过我家那只猫。所以不能只看这个表面现象，武侠小说里面它就不能写出非常精彩的爱情吗？我想读过武侠小说的人，会对这个问题呢，有非常清楚的认识，特别是金庸的武侠小说。金庸的武侠小说当然是一流的武侠小说，这个是毫无疑问的，没有人会对这个提出疑问。但是，我们不去讲他的武侠，就看金庸小说里边的爱情，从这个角度看，也可以说金庸的小说是一流的爱情小说。今天我们可以说，金庸写爱情之广，写爱情之深，写爱情之奇，可以跟世间任何言情大师一决高下。

——节选自孔庆东中央电视台"百家讲坛"《金庸小说的情爱世界》

结构分析练习 5

请用前面所学的联想语类的知识分析下面这段话，理清其中的联想规律。

2-17.mp3

Oh! Thank you very much! Earth Wind & Fire in the Black Eyed Peas, everybody! As I'd like to call them "Earth Wind in Fiber". It's an ice-breaker, don't judge me yet.

Welcome to the 57th Annual Primetime Emmy Awards. That's right, 57, which means 57 years ago today, people who worked in television could only suspect that they were inadequate.

You've noticed some of us are wearing a magnolia for support of the victims of Hurricane Katrina. New Orleans is my hometown, and I have family in Mississippi. Our thoughts and our prayers go out to everyone affected. I guess I don't have to point out that this is the second time

I've hosted the Emmy's after a national tragedy, and I just want to say that I'm honored, because it's times like this, we really, really need laughter.

But today, we're here to celebrate television. Personally, I love TV. Some people call it "the idiot box". Really, well, if we didn't have television then how could we be watching a show honoring the people who make television on television if there was no television? Idiot!

I think the reason that we love award shows so much is because they're exciting. We don't know who is gonna win or lose, well we know that HBO is gonna get a butt load of awards, but, you know, people say that HBO wins because they can show cursing and naked people. Let's be honest, we like to watch naked people cursing in real life, not in real life. It's actually not that pleasant. Grandma, put your clothes on, it's Thanksgiving. We're trying to watch the parade. Ah? Where did you learn that word? Which reminds me if Ian McShane from that Deadwood wins tonight, uh, get the children out of the room, and the pets. They don't need that.

You know what, I keep hearing myself saying words like wining and losing and awards as if that's what tonight is about. Like somehow, wining an award will validate you. Come on, if you don't win tonight, it doesn't mean you're not a good person, it just means you are not a good actor.

I'm kidding. I'm kidding. It just means that you're not as good as the other people in that category. Kidding again. Winning is not important, what is important is how you feel about yourself, and of course you're gonna feel a lot better about yourself if you win. But let's be realistic. Most of you tonight will not win, so, let's look at the bright side of not winning. Give me a minute, there's gonna be something.

Well, you don't have to get up, you can stay comfortably seated, and you don't have to make an acceptance speech, which is, that's not easy, that's a lot of pressure, because no matter how hard you try to thank everybody, somebody is gonna feel left out, somebody is gonna have their feelings hurt. You know, well, I guess those eyebrows've just waxed themselves. She'd look like a monkey if it weren't for me.

Here is a tip the best acceptance speech you can give is, I'd like to thank everyone who helped me get this, and you know who you are, followed by a ... It's the best thing. But please don't say you didn't expect it. You're nominated; you had a one-in-five chance. Except for Blythe Danner. Blythe Danner is nominated for 3 categories this year. Blythe, your speech? Yours should be the shortest. Just walk up and say, "I knew it."

Let's face it. Everybody wants to win, this is show business. But tonight, let's try something; let's just try to put aside our ego, our envy, our jealousy, our judgment. What am I saying? That's what we've got this year.

But seriously, I think overall in the scheme of things, winning an Emmy is not important. Let's get our priority straight. I think we all know what's really important in life, winning an

Oscar. They're for movies. Man, I'd love to host that show.

All right, everybody! Have fun, relax. Everybody win a drunk tonight. I'll see you in a minute.

——第57届艾美奖(Emmy Awards)主持人开场白

上述四种主要的语类构成了口译主要"工作言语"的整体，了解这些话语类别，可以深化对各种话语的结构认识，有利于促进发展口译的各种工作。

四、口译记忆力训练

1. 口译记忆的难点

人的记忆有长时记忆(long-term memory)和短时记忆(short-term memory)之分。长时记忆力储存的是平时积累的生活常识、专业知识、各种经历，等等，其容量是无限的，信息在此储存的时间相对较长，有的甚至终身不忘。而短时记忆只是暂时储存刚刚接收到的信息，随后有些信息可能进入长时记忆得以保存，有的则很快被忘记。

口译中译员刚刚接收到的信息暂时储存在短时记忆中，同时激活长时记忆的部分，使其参与译员的在线记忆运作。口译中这种处于活跃状态的记忆被称为工作记忆，它是短时记忆和长时记忆的一种结合，以短时记忆为主，加上长时记忆中被激活的部分。

口译记忆的困难一般可以归为三个方面的原因：一是短时记忆的局限性，二是长时记忆中储存的信息处于不活跃状态，三是心理压力大。

有关记忆的研究表明，短时记忆具有很大的局限性，不仅容量有限，一般仅为七个左右的信息单位(chunk)，而且信息在此保留的时间非常短暂，不超过一分钟。如果接收的信息较多，而且没有经过深度加工，信息便很容易被遗忘。

译员在口译时并不是机械地接收语音信息，而是从长期记忆中提取相关的语言和知识，如果所听到的是译员平时反复使用、非常熟悉的话题，说明这些内容处于活跃状态，更容易被理解记忆。

因此平时要注意扩大知识面，熟悉各种话题，扩大长期记忆的容量，记忆熟悉的话题比不熟悉的要容易得多。

2. 提高口译记忆的效率

提高口译的记忆效率，需要从长时记忆和短时记忆两个方面入手。口译课的记忆训练主要是针对短时记忆，目的是克服短时记忆容量的有限和信息储存时间短的局限，以提高有限空间的使用效率，延长信息储存的时间。对信息进行视觉化训练和逻辑化训练是提高记忆效率的两种有效方法。

人的记忆中 70%~80%的信息是视觉的，视觉化要求我们在大脑中形成对信息的整体图像。不仅用耳朵听到信息，而且仿佛同时"看"到信息，即语言所描述的内容。这种训练是针对大脑对意象语料的敏感性而设计的，旨在训练译员通过将信息内容现实化、视觉化来记忆信息的能力。视觉化也是缩小信息占用记忆空间的有效办法,它将信息细节完整地结合起来,把对零散文字的记忆变成对一个生动画面的记忆,记忆负担得到很大的缓解,记忆也更加深刻。对于描述性、叙述性的语篇,视觉化非常有效。

信息逻辑化要求对信息进行逻辑分析。逻辑分析是为了更透彻地理解信息,加深对信息的印象。通过加工整理,将散乱的信息点有机结合起来,形成大的整体信息单位,这样就可以使用较小的记忆空间。就好比一个凌乱的抽屉,如果将其中的东西放整齐,就可以腾出更多的空间,存放更多的东西。信息逻辑化训练要求我们不仅要记住逻辑线索,还要找出关键词,这样对一整段话的记忆就变成了对几个关键词和逻辑线索的记忆。关键词可以是原语讲话中的重要信息词汇,也可以是译员自己归纳的词语,只要记住这些关键词和逻辑线索,便能激活译员对整段话的回忆。

训练方法:原语复述和目的语复述。

原语复述是在认真听完一段语篇之后,用同一种语言将讲话的中心内容复述出来。练习的过程要循序渐进,语篇的长度可以依照个人实际情况逐渐增加。刚开始的时候,由于表达能力有限、技巧缺乏等原因,复述可能会近似于背诵。但熟悉之后,这一现象就会大为改观,学生会逐渐学会如何抓住"主要信息",放掉"次要信息"。此外,由于汉语是母语,对汉语做原语复述就容易很多,因此篇章可以稍微长一些。训练还是要以英文的原语复述为主。

例文 1　It's a great pleasure to be here today to talk about one of the key challenges of the future — the challenge of sustainability. Because sustainable development is something on which we all need to work together — not just governments and businesses, but also communities and individuals — to ensure the future of our peoples and even our planet.

这段话就可以概括为:Sustainable development is of great importance to our future and needs our joint efforts.

目的语复述比原语复述又前进了一步。即在听完一段语篇之后,用目的语复述中心内容。原语复述练习和目的语复述练习在提高短时记忆能力的同时,也让学生逐渐适应口译过程,向口译过渡。

2-18.mp3

The Olympic Games are believed to have begun more than 3,000 years ago, although written records only exist from 776 BC.

The records show that these Games consisted of activities that were the skills of soldiers, like boxing, javelin throwing and marathon running. At just over 26 miles (or 42 kilometres) long, the marathon is the longest race run in the Games. It is named after the site of a battle in ancient Greece. According to legend, a Greek messenger ran from Marathon to Athens to bring news of the Greek victory and died of exhaustion just after giving his message.

The ancient Olympic Games continued for nearly 1,200 years until the Roman Emperor, Theodosius I, abolished the Games because of their pagan influences.

About 1,500 years later, in 1894, the Frenchman, Baron Pierre de Coubertin, helped to re-establish the Games. He also created the structure of the modern Olympic Movement.

Nowadays the aim of the Olympic Movement is to promote peace, friendship and understanding between different nations through sport.

The first modern Olympic Games were held in Greece in 1896. Just over 200 men, representing 14 countries, competed in a total of 43 events. Winners received a silver medal, a certificate and a crown of olive leaves. Runners-up were given bronze medals and a crown of laurel, while those who finished third went home empty-handed.

The Olympic Games are held every four years with one country being responsible for the organization of the event. There is often fierce competition to be the host city. In 2008, Beijing hosted the Games and in 2012 they were held in London.

五、影子训练

影子练习(shadow-exercise)，即跟读训练。这种方法就是用同一种语言几乎同步地跟读原语发言人的讲话，它可以训练听说同步技巧和注意力的分配，培养口译员"一心多用"的能力，从而为后期的同声传译学习打好基础。刚开始训练时可以比原语推迟3～5秒钟，待练习了一段时间后，可以迟于原语片刻至一句话的时间跟读。跟读时耳朵、嘴巴和大脑要一起派上用场，耳朵听、嘴巴说、脑子记。这是需要精神非常集中的一种练习，也是提高语速、提高理解速度、修改语音语调的最好方法。在高语速条件下，边跟读边完全理解语义是有相当难度的，但这种训练能为口译打下扎实的基础。各种新闻、谈话节目、研讨会、音乐体育节目、演讲等都是练习的上好材料。

另外还可增加一些"干扰性"练习，譬如一边听、一边写些不相关的内容，如数字、人名等，分散使用注意力，那样效果会更好。

以下是三种训练方法：

(1) 单纯做跟读训练，看看能不能完全跟下来；

(2) 在做跟读训练的同时，要求学生手上写数字，比如要求他们从100写起，99、98、97这样倒退着写，培养对多项任务同时处理的能力；

(3) 在完成跟读和干扰性训练之后，马上要求学生用原语概述所听到的原声录音的内容。

2-19.mp3

This is the VOA Special English Economics Report.

In recent years, the government has taken steps to deal with those concerns.

Andrew Batson is with the China research company Gavekal Dragonomics. He says it is unclear whether the SAIC's accusations against Alibaba are related to intellectual property rights.

Chinese officials are also closely watching consumer safety, seeking to stop the sale of fake products after many problems with product safety. A new consumer protection law enacted last

March increases possible payments to those who buy damaged or fake goods. The State Administration for Industry and Commerce says $610 million worth of poor-quality goods were sold in China from 2010 to 2012.

However, some experts question if the accusations against Alibaba are connected to China's campaign against fake products. Shaun Rein wrote the book, "The End of Copy Cat China." He says protecting consumers may be one of the reasons for the regulators' actions.

"I think part of it is consumer protectionism, part of it though might be to sort of pull Alibaba down. I think over the last year Jack Ma might have become too powerful according to some areas. He is taking on vested interests in the financial sector, and retail sales, and entertainment, and some might feel he is getting too powerful."

The SAIC said it waited to release its report on Alibaba until this year so it would not damage the company's IPO. However, last week, a U.S. law firm announced it was taking action against Alibaba. The lawyers said the company did not tell the public about its communications with the Chinese regulator before the stock offering.

This week, Jack Ma spoke in Hong Kong. He said that the company will be open in its dealings with the legal action. He said the situation should give western observers a better understanding of Alibaba and China.

And that's the Economics Report from VOA Learning English. I'm Mario Ritter.

六、对信息做出积极反应

前面提到，口译中重要的是讲话中的信息，并非语言形式，也讲到了如何更好地理解、分析、记忆话语篇章等，作为口译学习者，仅仅知道上述知识是远远不够的，还需要付出艰辛的努力，进行刻苦的口译训练，要有耐心，更重要的是要对练习的每篇材料感兴趣，哪怕只是在做练习期间保持短暂的兴趣，因为只有能够触动心弦的事，才会使人深刻地记住。一般来讲，与自己个人利益无关的事很少能够引起人们的联想和反应。电视机前的观众面对政治家的演说常常表现得无动于衷，但如果是感兴趣的话题，如物价上涨、贪污腐败等就会激发他们的情感，让他们很容易记住。

为了记住讲话人说的话，口译学习者必须根据接收的信息进行积极的联想，不断获得新知识，把新的信息纳入更加广泛的知识中去。这就要求每听到一句话都应当积极地去联想，运用已有的知识去理解，理清话语的层次结构，理解迅速而深刻。复述或是口译表达时要做到话语清晰，意义明了，逻辑清楚，前后一致，整个过程都要关注信息的传达，即"得意忘言"。

请听下面的讲话，注意分析其层次结构，抓住中心思想，然后复述出来。

2-20.mp3

A hundred and fifty years ago, no American girls and few boys went to college, but those young men hoping to become doctors, lawyers, or teachers began studying at seven or eight years of age to develop skills in five general subjects: English, foreign languages, mathematics, history and science. The study of English often required six years. During these six years, the pupils studied spelling, punctuation, parts of speech and grammar. A thorough knowledge of Latin grammar was also required, and to gain proficiency to pass their college entrance examinations. Most boys studied the language for five or six years. In addition, they took three or four years of French and another two or three years of German or Greek. Like English, mathematics often required six years of study, but history usually took only four. Science was generally a three-year course, two years devoted to general science and one year to physics. With no time wasted in such classes as art, typing, band, or crafts, young men were usually fully prepared to begin their serious college programs at the age of thirteen or fourteen.

七、演讲的技巧

演讲这门艺术可以有效地运用在口译表达中，因为演讲是一门语言艺术，它的主要形式是"讲"，即运用有声语言并追求言辞的表现力和声音的感染力；同时还要辅之以"演"，即运用面部表情、手势动作、身体姿势乃至一切可以理解的态势语言，使讲话艺术化起来，从而产生一种特殊的艺术魅力。

一名优秀的译员必须是一位杰出的演讲者。译员作为次级讲话人(secondary speaker)，与发言人同时出现在听众面前，必须要将发言人的发言效果(impact)体现出来。这不仅指语言内容要准确，也指译员要合理地运用声音、姿势、动作、眼神等。出色的译员能通过良好的演讲表现增加听众对其翻译能力和译作质量的信任度。

但是译员对于发言的题目、内容和目的没有决定权，也不能随意更改发言内容。

译员可以通过有声(口头表达)和无声(肢体语言)的手段表达发言人要传达的效果。

请听下面的讲话，注意有声和无声手段的运用，然后复述出来。

2-21.mp3

Remarks of President Barack Obama Weekly Address, the White House
March 7, 2015

Hi, everybody. Sunday is International Women's Day — a day to celebrate remarkable women and girls worldwide, and to re-dedicate ourselves to defending the fundamental rights and dignity of all people.

That's why, this week, Michelle and I launched a new initiative on a topic that's close to both our hearts: girls' education.

It's called "Let Girls Learn." And its goal is to help more girls around the world go to school and stay in school. Right now, 62 million girls who should be in school are not. And that's not an accident. It's the direct result of barriers, large and small, that stand in the way of girls who want to learn.

Maybe their families can't afford the school fees. Maybe the risk of being hurt or kidnapped or even killed by men who will do anything to stop girls from learning is just too great. Or maybe they aren't in school because they're expected to get married and become mothers while they're still teenagers — or even earlier. In too many parts of the world, girls are still valued more for their bodies than for their minds. That's just plain wrong. And we all have to do more to stop it.

That's the idea behind "Let Girls Learn." We're making it clear to any country that's our partner — or that wants to be our partner — that they need to get serious about increasing the number of girls in school. Our diplomats and development experts are already hard at work. Our Peace Corps volunteers will play a big role, too. And we're putting our partnerships with NGOs, businesses and foundations to work on behalf of girls everywhere.

I come to this issue as the leader of the world's largest economy, and Commander-in-Chief of the world's most powerful military, and I'm convinced that a world in which girls are educated is a safer, more stable, more prosperous place. When girls are educated, their future children are healthier and better nourished. Their future wages increase, which in turn strengthens their families' security. National growth gets a boost, too. And places where women and girls are treated as full and equal citizens tend to be more stable and more democratic.

But I also come to this issue as the father of two wonderful young women. And I know that there are lots of girls just like Malia and Sasha out there — girls who are funny and caring and inquisitive and strong, and have so much to offer the world.

It's a privilege to be the parent of girls. And we want to make sure that no girl out there is denied her chance to learn — that no girl is prevented from making her unique contributions to the world. Because every girl — every girl — deserves our respect. And every girl deserves an education.

Thanks, and have a great weekend.

——选自普特英语网

 2-22.mp3

中国发展虽然取得了巨大成就，但中国仍然是一个拥有13亿多人口的发展中大国，仍然处于并将长期处于社会主义初级阶段。中国人民正在努力实现现代化，这是人类历史上前无古人的伟大事业，需要付出十分艰苦的努力。

"艰难困苦，玉汝于成。"在过去30多年间，有6亿多中国人摆脱了贫困，对全球减贫事业贡献率达70%。中国经济占世界经济总量的比重从1%提高到12%，目前中国经济增长对全球经济增长贡献率将近30%。中国取得如此巨大的发展成就，最重要的一条经验就是我们坚持立足本国国情，坚持改革开放，走出了一条中国特色社会主义道路。

——节选自习近平主席接受拉美四国媒体联合采访

本章"结构分析练习(华为公司)"参考译文

2-14 参考译文：The three types of Hua Wei Personal Hand-phone System (PHS) cellphones launched this time have been designed based on the designing concept of GSM and CDMA cellphones. Domestic customers' cultural backgrounds, and individual habits and preferences of using cellphones have been taken into consideration in designing. These folding-type fashion-styled cellphones have six new trend colour options and feature such new functions that they can match GSM and CDMA cellphones, satisfying of consumers diverse needs. Hua Wei PHS cellphones are so customized that we predict these types of PHS cellphones will be welcomed by the customers.

第三章 数字口译
Numeral Interpretation

一、数字反应训练

数字是口译中遇到的比较棘手的问题之一。一般来讲，我们经常听到的讲话中的推理、形象、思想等，一听就能听懂。数字与上述内容不同，往往在大脑中是以无意义的形式存在的，难以与已有的知识相关联，因此很难记忆。数字在口译内容中极其重要，如果翻译错了，有可能造成灾难性的后果，所以一般都需要用笔记下数字，但是有不少场合无法记录，比如在参观途中，在光线不充足的条件下，或在工地、车间等比较严酷的口译环境中，这时就需要译员有较好的短时记忆能力。即便是有条件记录数字，也需要译员对数字有快速的反应能力，因此数字反应训练在口译训练中是很有必要的。

对于口译初学者来讲，数字的反应练习主要分为"数字广度"和"数级转换"练习。"数字广度"练习主要用来训练不相关数字的短时记忆，分为顺背练习和倒背练习。顺背练习时将数字分成3位一组，4位一组……，9位一组，一组一组或者两组两组地视读或听辨，然后口头复述出来，练习时不要做任何笔头记录，学生记忆时可以采取任何自己认为有效的方法记住尽可能多的数字，比如可以采取形象化、谐音法、视觉化等方法。倒背练习和顺背练习方法基本相同，可以从两位一组开始，学生在听到或看到数字后"倒"着把这些数字复述出来，这样可以加强学生以阿拉伯数字的视觉形式储存数字的能力，能够在需要的时候随时"看到"要看的数字，从而提高对数字的反应和记忆能力，但是这不能替代其他的数字练习。

数字练习 1
请看下面的数字，看完一行，复述一行。

985	652
1,687	9,573
19,674	36,795
689,547	257,964
3,579,546	1,648,537
68,745,924	13,579,864
358,964,234	356,874,628

数字练习 2
请看下面的数字，看完一行，从最后一个数字开始倒着复述。

62	84
519	732

4,835	8,376
46,752	64,795
549,327	468,537
3,572,496	4,978,615
38,957,642	85,893,412
138,412,863	637,954,281

"数级"转换是我们在口头翻译中的一大难题。英汉两种语言中对数字的表达分级不同：英语是以"个、十、百"三位一组的进位组合单位，"数级"由低到高依次用"thousand"（千）、"million"（百万）、"billion"（十亿）、"trillion"（万亿）等；汉语是以"个、十、百、千"四位一组的进位组合单位，"数级"由低到高依次用"万"、"亿"、"万亿"等，尤其要注意"万"以上又分成了十万、百万、千万、亿、十亿、百亿、千亿、万亿等。汉语中的数的读法和英语中数的读法的这种差异性给双语之间的数字转译工作带来了额外的负担，一不小心就会失误，解决的重要途径是扎实的数级互换练习加上必要的记录和标记。在无笔记的数级互换练习中，可以列出一个英汉数字表达对照表，如表1.3.1所示。

表1.3.1　英汉数字表达对照表

数　　字	英　　语	汉　　语
10	ten	十
100	one hundred	百
1,000	one thousand	千
10,000	ten thousand	万
100,000	one hundred thousand	十万
1,000,000	one million	百万
10,000,000	ten million	千万
100,000,000	one hundred million	亿
1,000,000,000	one billion	十亿
10,000,000,000	ten billion	百亿
100,000,000,000	one hundred billion	千亿
1,000,000,000,000	one trillion	万亿

在口译练习中必须牢记上述对照表，多做互译练习，熟练掌握数的表达，才能够取得好的效果。

数字练习3

3-1.mp3

请听下列数字，然后用英语复述出来。

32,000	205,600	37,480,000	5,140,500	113,303
1,321,290,000	69,016	368,545	18,830	45,552,900

86-10-65961114	001-613-7893434		001-202-3282500
0044-20-72994049	13,846,795,241		15,967,853,480
1315849270	029-85874628		0711-3546875

请听以下用英语报出的数字,请不要做笔头记录,用汉语口头译出。

637	930	58,000	65,080
64,558	2,987	1,863	62 thousand
159.9 billion	970 million	2.25 billion	280 million
56.97 million	131.87 million	1.5282 billion	37,871
13.4 percent	12.1381 trillion	16.2 percent	101,480

请听以下用汉语报出的数字,请不要做笔头记录,用英语口头译出。

360,058	23,150	17万	82,000
1540	302,000	2100.8亿	17.52亿
20万	60.72亿	两千亿	508.5亿
10,222	1.12亿	6.98万	48.49万

数字练习 4

请听下面的汉语讲话,不要做任何笔记,讲话结束后,用英文口头译出。

3-2.mp3

上海东方明珠广播电视塔是上海旅游新地标。塔高468米,享有亚洲第一、世界第三的殊荣。它集广播电视发射、娱乐、游览于一体。263米高的上体观光层和350米处太空舱是游人360°鸟瞰全市景色的最佳处所。267米处是亚洲最高的旋转餐厅。底层的上海城市历史发展陈列馆再现了老上海的生活场景,浓缩了上海自开埠以来的历史。

3-3.mp3

中国和外国的教育合作和交流日益活跃。国际交换学生是其中的重要组成部分,中国在海外学习的留学生人数比其他国家都多。自1979年以来,有超过100万中国人在世界100多个国家和地区学习,其中将近30万人学成归来。来中国的外国留学生人数也在迅速增加。自1979年以来,来自188个国家的102.6万多留学生在中国的544所大学学习。

数字练习 5

请听下面的英语讲话,不要做任何笔记,讲话结束后用汉语口头译出。

3-4.mp3

The May 2002 merger of Hewlett-Packard and Compaq Computer Corporation forged a dynamic, powerful team of 140,000 employees with capabilities in 160 countries and doing business in 43 currencies and 15 languages. Revenues for the combined companies were $72 billion for the fiscal year that ended October 31, 2002. Chairman and CEO Carly Fiorina leads HP, which has corporate headquarters in Palo Alto, California.

3-5.mp3

Tourism is a major industry in Australia, representing about six percent of the gross domestic product and providing, directly or indirectly, around 440,000 jobs. More than two million tourists visit Australia each year, spending about $4,000 million.

二、数字的记录

数字的记录可谓让人煞费苦心，各国译员也做了种种努力，但到目前为止尚未取得一致的最终方案，在我国很多译员比较推崇的实用做法是直接用阿拉伯数字做笔记。以下是几种常用的数字记录方法。

1. 英语数字记录

比如当听到英文：thirteen billion fifty million five hundred and twenty-nine thousand and one，可以用以下方法记录：

(1) 13b 050 m 529 t 001   b, m, t, tr 分别表示 "billion, million, thousand, trillion" 等段位。但是 billion 最好用大写 B 表示。

(2) 13，050，529，001   可以在听到 "billion, million, thousand" 时迅速在记下数字之后标下逗号，在空出的位置补零。

2. 汉语数字记录

比如听到 25 亿 3 千 5 百 64 万 5 千，可以记录为：25 亿 3564 万 5 千

数字记录练习

3-6.mp3

请听下面的数字，记录数字，然后译成英语或汉语。

1416.6	6340.5	1041.21	3525	1378.86 万
499.22 万	12,001.16 亿	2102.63 亿	190 亿	30.3%
4458.61 亿	53.71 万	342.75 万	2100.8 亿	14,377.29 亿
74.519 billion	37.301 billion	119.572 billion	110,400	266,800
38 trillion	30.54 trillion	3.031553 trillion	11.22 million	2,182
26.152 million	634.62	10.46 million	3,130.54	11.1223 million

数量单位的记录可以采用汉字、自创简化字或是国际通用的缩略符号即可，地名人名比较熟悉的可采用(英语单词或拼音)首字母或前两三个字母加最后一个辅音字母记录。术语的记录根据自己熟悉的程度选择适当的汉字、英文单词或缩略语。

三、数字的口译

1. 单纯数字的口译

口译时要学会"点三杠四"法。"点三"指逗号之间的三位数,"点"的作用如同分节号;而"杠四"则指斜杠之间有四位数,即汉语的数字进位关系。比如听到英语 13,050,529,001。为了进行口译迅速从个位向左每四位用斜杠隔开:13,0/50,52/9,001,这样可以直接读数:一百三十亿五千零五十二万九千零一。汉译英时,忽略"万"和"亿"等单位,把各位数字迅速准确地写下,再按英语数字进位规律从右至左每三个分成一节,比如 25 亿 3564 万 5000。这样,在口译时只需照着英语数字表达习惯点逗号 2,5 亿 35,64 万 5,000,然后读出即可,two billion five hundred thirty five million six hundred and forty five thousand.

2. 模糊数字的口译

模糊数字的口译也很重要,平时注意积累,熟记于心。

几个 — several, a few, some

十几个 — over a dozen; less than twenty; more than ten

几十个 — dozens of

几十年 — decades

二十出头 — a bit over twenty

八十好几了 — well over eighty

好几百 — hundreds of

几百万 — millions of

几十亿 — billions of

3. 分数、小数的口译

(1) 分数

分子用基数词,分母用序数词,分子大于 1,序数词要用复数。

1/2 — a (one) half   1/3 — one third
2/3 — two thirds   3/4 — three quarters

比较复杂的分数:

20/87 — twenty over eighty-seven   33/90 — thirty-three over ninety

4 2/3 — four and two thirds

(2) 小数

小数点后面的数字必须一一读出

0.0035 — zero/naught/point zero zero three five

单纯数字听译练习

3-7.mp3

请听下面的数字，记录数字，然后译成汉语。

Country	Area (km²)	Population
Estonia	45, 277	1, 340, 000
Finland	338, 417	5, 352, 000
France	632, 834	6, 545, 000
Greece	131, 957	11, 310, 000
Hungary	93, 030	10, 010,000
Iceland	103, 000	10, 010, 000
Ireland	70, 282	4, 420, 000
Italy	301, 333	60, 020, 000
Luxembourg	2, 586.3	493, 500
Macedonia	25, 713	2, 048, 000
Malta	316	413, 600
Moldova	33, 800	3, 560, 000
Monaco	2	34, 021

带有数字的英汉数字听译练习

3-8.mp3

请听下面的句子，进行简单的记录，然后译成汉语。

1. In the first three quarters of 2008, the annual fiscal income of the province increased by 350 billion yuan.

2. The four-star tourist garden hotel has 97 deluxe suites, 268 standard rooms, and a convention hall with a seating capacity of over 450 people.

3. In recent years, Shanghai has pumped some 10 percent of its GNP and 40 percent of its total fixed assets investment into the construction of the city's infrastructure.

4. Australia is one of the most urbanized countries in the world, with about 70 percent of the population living in the 10 largest cities.

5. January 26, the date of the first European settlement of the continent in 1788, is Australia's National Day.

带有数字的汉英数字听译练习

3-9.mp3

请听下面的数字，记录数字，然后译成英语。

1. 去年这个公司汽车的销售量增长了1.5倍。

2. 1978年至2007年，中国人均生产总值增长了43.4倍。
3. 中国的钢产量，1949年为15.8万吨，1978年为3,178万吨，1989年为6,124万吨，1997年为2.02亿吨，2007年为4.89亿吨。
4. 中国内地现有二亿七千六百九十万个家庭，平均每户有3.96人。
5. 20世纪70年代，每公顷土地平均供养2.6人。

带有数字的段落口译练习

3-10.mp3

请听下面的英语，进行简单的记录，然后译成汉语。

Since the founding of the People's Republic of China, the State has attached great importance to agricultural development. Especially since the nation's implementation of the policies of Reform and Opening-up in 1978, including the policy of taking agriculture as the foundation of the national economy, China has scored great achievements in agricultural development. To cite a few examples, the total grain output grew from 304 million tons in 1978, to 492.5 million tons in 1997. Cotton output grew from 2.16 million tons in 1978, to 4.2 million tons in 1997. Sugar-cane grew from 21.11 million tons in 1978 to 78.79 million tons in 1997. Aquatic products grew from 4.66 million tons in 1978 to 35.6 million tons in 1997. China is now one of the leading producers in the world of grain, cotton, rapeseeds, sugar-yielding crops, peanuts, soybeans, tea, meat and livestock, and ranks first in total output of grain, cotton and rapeseeds.

本章练习部分参考译文

3-2 Orient Pearl Broadcasting and Television Tower is one of the Shanghai's tourist landmarks. Serving for radio and television broadcasting as well as recreation and sightseeing, the 468-meter-tall tower is the highest TV tower in Asia and the third highest in the world. Tourists can get a bird's eye view of the city at the 263-meter-high observatory room and the 350-meter-high "space cabin". At 267 meters high, it is a rotating restaurant, the highest one of its kind in Asia. The ground floor of the structure is a historical museum featuring the city's history, including the life-like scenes of old Shanghai streets.

3-3 China is seeing active cooperation and exchanges in education with the rest of the world. Exchange students are a major part in this regard, and no other country has more people studying abroad than China. Since 1979, over 1,000,000 Chinese have studied in over 100 countries and regions, of whom nearly 300,000 have returned after finishing their studies. The number of foreign students in China has also increased rapidly. Since 1979, over 1,026,000 students from 188 countries studied at 544 Chinese universities.

3-4 2002年5月，惠普与康柏电脑公司合并，组成了一个充满动力的强大的公司，14万员工在160个国家运作，以43种货币和15种语言经营业务。合并后的营业额在2002年

10 月 31 日结束的财政年度里，达到 720 亿美元。董事长兼首席执行官卡莉·菲奥里纳是惠普的领导人，惠普的总部在加州的帕洛·阿尔托。

3-5 旅游业是澳大利亚的一大主要产业，产值约占其国内生产总值的 6%，旅游业直接或间接地为 44 万澳大利亚人提供了就业机会。每年来此观光的游客超过 200 万人，这些游客在澳大利亚的消费高达 40 亿澳元。

3-8 带有数字的英汉数字听译练习

1. 2008 年前三个季度，全省财政收入增收 3,500 亿元。

2. 这家四星级花园宾馆拥有 97 间豪华套房、268 间标准客房，以及可容纳 450 多人的会议厅。

3. 近年来，上海在基础设施建设中投入了占国民生产总值 10%和固定资产 40%的资金。

4. 澳大利亚是世界上城市化程度最高的国家之一，约 70%的人口居住在十个最大的城市里。

5. 每年 1 月 26 日，即 1788 年首批欧洲大陆定居之日，被指定为澳大利亚的国庆节。

3-9 带有数字的汉英数字听译练习

1. The sales volume of automobiles of this company increased nearly 1.5 times last year.

2. China's per capita GDP went up by 43.4 times between 1978 and 2007.

3. China's output of steel was 0.158 million tons in 1949, 31.78 million tons in 1978, 61.24 million tons in 1989, 202 million tons in 1997, and 489 million tons in 2007.

4. In the Chinese mainland, there are 276,900,000 households, each of which has 3.96 people on average.

5. In the 1970s, each hectare of land could support 2.6 people on the average.

3-10 自从 1949 年中华人民共和国成立以来，国家高度重视发展农业。特别是自从 1978 年我国实行"改革开放"的各项政策以来，其中将农业作为国民经济基础的政策，使我国在发展农业方面取得了巨大成就。例如，粮食总产量从 1978 年的 3.04 亿吨，增加到 1997 年的 4.925 亿吨。棉花总产量从 1978 年的 216 万吨，增加到 1997 年的 420 万吨。甘蔗从 1978 年的 2111 万吨，增加到 1997 年的 7879 万吨。水产品从 1978 年的 466 万吨，增加到 1997 年的 3560 万吨，等等。现在，中国是世界上粮食、棉花、油菜籽、制糖作物、花生、大豆、茶叶、肉类牲畜等产量最多的国家之一，其中粮食、棉花、油菜籽的总产量在世界居第一位。

第四章 交替传译中的笔记技术
Skills of Note-taking in Consecutive Interpretation

第二章讲的是无笔记口译训练，重点在于抓住讲话人的意思，高效率地记忆下来，流利清晰地表述出来。如果能够三五分钟不记笔记精确地口译讲话内容，那自然很好。然而每个人记忆的能力是有限的，俗语有云，"好记性不如烂笔头"，在口译中也适用。一般而言，译员在开始的 20 分钟工作效率是非常高的，但是口译活动往往不止 20 分钟，有时在和一些初次涉及口译活动的客户打交道时，可能一口气讲了 8~10 分钟甚至更长的时间，出现人名、地名、时间等专有名词过多的时候，就不得不依靠笔记来帮助回忆讲话的线索和具体细节，还有当听到非常生疏、难懂的内容时，往往也需要笔记来辅助。总之，口译笔记是口译学习和实践中很重要的内容之一。但是笔记到底应该记多少？是不是有了笔记就不需要记忆力训练了？笔记应该用什么语言来记？本章将通过讲解、示范和练习，引导大家掌握笔记的方法和技巧，平衡听辨记忆和笔记的注意力分配。

一、笔记的功能和本质

你可能已经观摩过一些大型国际会议的场景：在学术研讨会、记者招待会、商务谈判等场合，发言人侃侃而谈，连续讲话十几分钟后，才停下来让译员进行翻译；而优秀的口译员几乎立刻就能把几百甚至几千字包含的信息迅速、准确、流利地用目的语表达出来，他们是如何完成这个看来起是"不可能完成的任务"的呢？

有经验的口译员经过长期的训练和实践，其短期记忆能力确实得到了加强；不过要完全靠记忆力记住发言者讲话中的全部信息，包括根本没有规律的数字、人名、地名等，再准确地传达出来仍然是非常困难的。因此，口译员需要适度的笔记来辅助记忆。

从技术角度上说，笔记可以帮助弥补短期记忆的不足，减轻口译环节记忆的负担，让译员更高效地记住庞杂的信息群落，并且可以有更多的精力兼顾其他环节。从心理方面来说，有了笔记，译员就会感觉心里有底，更加自信。

口译笔记很重要，但是不是替代我们的大脑记忆，也不是把讲话的每个字都记下来，这是口译笔记和上课做课堂笔记或者会议记录的重要差异。课堂笔记是用一种语言记录完整的内容(当然省略了很多次要信息)供课后复习参考之用，很多时候使用比较完整的句子来记录。速记员记录会议内容为了保持真实性，往往要保留一定数量的原话，是采用特定的记音符号、速记符号记录语音的形式，一般需要长时间的培训才能掌握。口译笔记则不同，在口译活动中需要在讲话者发言停顿后数秒就开始用另一种语言翻译出来，这就是说不能等口译开始后才将记录的笔记进行翻译，这样大脑的负担就非常重了。我们需要的是可以"一目十行"，可以迅速帮助我们启动并提示记忆，唤起某种联想，找回"遗忘"的比较重要的细节，如数字、专有名词等。从这个意义上来讲，口译笔记只是记忆的辅助手段，其作用是帮助译员把精神集中在讲话的内容上，在翻译的时候起提醒作用。

口译活动中大脑记忆是占首要地位的，口译笔记是非常重要的辅助手段，如果因为记笔记干扰了大脑的记忆，就得不偿失了。为了不干扰大脑记忆，我们始终要把注意力集中在讲话者表达的意思上，记下的词或符号必须能够提示某个意思，而不是讲话者所说的某个词或某句话。这就要求我们记的笔记是通过一个字符记住相关的意思，这个字符可以是文字、符号、图形等，形式上没有任何的限制，当然字符所表达的意思也是因人而异的，因此，口译笔记是非常个性化的记录形式。

二、笔记的过程

口译初学者切忌为了记笔记而记笔记，忽视了理解分析。如果没有准确理解和把握原语内容，笔记不仅不能起到辅助记忆的作用，反而会干扰译员的注意力，使口译效果大打折扣。实际上，对于有经验的口译员来说，真正花在"记录"上的精力其实比较少，对原文的理解才是他们做笔记的前提和基础。

你可能有过这样的经历，就是什么都听懂了，没有遇到生词，但是还是说不出讲话人想要表达的意思，翻译得不准确，甚至偏离了主题。是你真听懂了吗？还是你只是听到了语言的表层结构和单词罗列的意思却没有理解句子的深层结构？在记笔记时，一边听，还要一边揣摩发言人想表达怎样的信息，语气是怎样的，怎样才能准确传达发言人的意图等。这就是对原语内容进行意义分析，意义分析也就是意义记忆。心理学家的统计结果显示，意义记忆的效果比机械记忆要高25~30倍。

在意义分析的过程中，译员首先要关注原文所包含的意义，而不是某个具体、孤立的词语或某种句法的表现形式，也就是"脱离原语外壳"，"抓住意义"。译员要捕捉关键词句，识别重要信息，把握实质内容。其次，在意义分析过程中，译员要把握原语的框架结构和逻辑关系，原语中可能出现了很多细节，涉及了一些人物、事件，列举了一些例子，这些细节不是凭空加进来的，是有目的的；其排列也不是随机无序的，而是有其内在逻辑关系。知道了这些细节为什么会出现及其出现的逻辑依据，就能从容应对貌似琐碎的内容，提供完整清晰的翻译。最后，意义分析还表现在对发言人讲话意图的深层次把握上。在听的过程中，通过上下文对发言的情境(context)作出判断，从而跳出字面意思，准确地把握发言人的真实意图。

当你完成原语的意义分析并简要记录之后，当发言人结束一个段落的讲话后，就可以通过阅读笔记来协助提取储存在短期记忆里的信息并进行口译表达了。笔记要记得简明扼要，一目了然，尽量写得疏朗一些，不要怕浪费纸(一张纸可以只写几个字，但这几个字是你经过意义分析之后记下的信息"指引牌")。在你记下了一个段落的笔记之后，脑海里应当继续保留你在听辨理解时记下的内容(而不是转而依赖笔记)，然后以笔记为依托，用目的语重新表达意思。笔记的简要和疏朗，恰恰表明记笔记的人在听讲话的时候经过了意义分析。

笔记记得过分详细、密集，往往是由于信息理解不够。口译员出于恐惧加补偿的心理，拼命在纸上记，之后在翻译的时候，把所有希望都寄托在笔记上，极力辨认笔记里的每一个字，希望能从中找到自己没有听懂的内容，其效果也就可想而知。这样的笔记没有起到信息传递的作用，反而变成了障碍。

三、笔记原则和方法

(一) 口译笔记记什么？

通过前面的讲解，相信大家对于口译笔记已经有一定的了解。尽管口译笔记有个性化的差异，但是在记录的内容上差异并不太大。除个别情况之外，口译笔记的内容可以分成三类，一类是包含核心含义的关键词以及能反映逻辑线索的指引词，这类内容需要译者在分析理解的基础上简单记；另一类是不涉及过多分析理解的数字、专有名词、技术术语以及列举的项目等，这些内容不容易存储在短期记忆中，通常听到就要立刻记下来以防遗忘。还有最好记第一句话和最后一句话，内容特别熟悉的根据情况适当减少。

当听到数字时，必须立刻记下来，因为数字表达的意思不依赖于上下文，一旦忘记就再也想不起来了。专有名词主要指人名、地名、机构名称等，人名、地名除发音需要稍加变化外，没有必要进行翻译，但是不容易记忆，应该尽可能按照原语发音记录下来，如果未能准确记录人物的姓名，在翻译时一定不要贸然使用，把名字说错会让人感到愤怒，这个时候不妨用其身份代指，比如说"秘书长先生"、"澳大利亚的代表"等。列举词类也是我们要记录的内容，连续的列举会造成很大的记忆负担，记在纸上则可以提供极大的方便，不至于遗忘，或是在努力回忆其排列顺序时会造成对大脑中短时记忆的其他信息不必要的干扰。技术术语对于译员来讲也是比较难的内容，译员往往是利用术语、主题知识准备临时突击强记技术术语，难免会比较生疏；另一方面，技术术语在讲话中一旦出现，就对整个话语起重要的框架支撑作用，因此技术术语需要记录下来，除非译员有很好的相关行业背景，可适当减少术语的笔记。逻辑关系的记录主要是对于表示逻辑关系的连接词的记录，一般借用数学符号或者自创的缩略词等。另一个非常重要的内容就是必须小心地记下讲话的第一句话，或者某个新的意思的第一句话，这类句子不是在阐述某个意思的过程中所讲的话，在认识上没有上下文作为依托，在笔记中必须记得特别清楚，以便在讲话者结束一段讲话后能够立即开始翻译。最后一句话也要记清楚，这对于译员来说是不容易的，听众往往期望讲话人一停止译员立刻跟上，实际上，记笔记总是要花一些时间的，记录的速度也稍微落后于口头表达的速度。讲话最后的内容也和前面一样重要，花几秒钟记下来，避免出现"狼狈"结束讲话翻译的状况，做到"有始有终"，增加听众的信任感。

(二)口译笔记怎么记？

1. 记录语言的选择

有些口译学者建议口译笔记刚开始阶段尽量用目的语来记笔记，目的在于"强迫"自己摆脱话语的外在形式而把握实质内容，从而培养良好的笔记习惯。他们认为用目的语记核心内容，这本身就是一个思维深度加工的过程；另外，用目的语记录可以使译员在听辨理解阶段就参与到语言转换的过程中，减少之后口译过程的思维压力。

不过，也有口译学者认为，在听辨过程中译员要耗费很多认知精力去理解发言内容，抓住关键信息，把握逻辑结构，如果在此阶段再进行语言转换就会加重译员的负担，分散注意力，造成译员压力过重。

在实际操作中，不同译员的习惯也不同，有的用原语言，有的用目的语，也有的混合起来用。但是不论你选择用何种语言，有一点都是相同的，笔记的内容要有选择性，笔记的数量要简练浓缩。

2. 记录语言的简略书写

简略书写是为了用最少的字符和笔画表达最丰富的含义。这里包括两个步骤：译员首先要进行意义的提炼，把原文的字、词、句经过理解加工后提取意义要点，然后再把浓缩的意义要点用缩略的方式记录下来。

如果选择用英文记录，且单词本身很短，不超过 5 个字母，可以直接写下。如果单词较长，可以选择英文词汇的头 1~4 个字母，例如：

economy — eco   government — gov   education — edu
ignorance — ign   situation — situ   company — com
medical — med   pharmaceutical — pharm
information — info   agriculture — agri

你也可以用省略元音的方法记录单词，例如：

business — bz   bank — bk   development — dvlp
trade — td   possible — psb   limited — ltd
experience — xpr   fundamental — fdmt

和英文相比，汉语的信息浓度更高一些，很多单个汉字本身已经可以表示很明确的意思，所以在口译笔记中可以用一个汉字来传达一个词语的含义，例如：

文化——文   科学——科   基础设施建设——基建
房地产——房   框架——框   旅游观光——旅

当然，你也可以混合使用中英文，例如：经济合作——eco 合，教育改革——edu 改，文化交流——文 exch。

3. 缩略语

译员应当熟悉并记住一些社会经济等领域的常用缩略语，并在口译笔记中使用，例如，

research and development —— R & D
foreign direct investment —— FDI
Hong Kong Special Administrative Region —— HKSAR
state-owned enterprise ——SOE
joint venture —— JV
small and medium-sized enterprise —— SME
merger and acquisition —— M & A
intellectual property right ——IPR
the European Union —— EU
the United Nations — UN
for example —— e.g.

缩略语在使用时如果针对的是印欧语系的语言词汇时，笔记主要省略的是元音，一般仅保留主要音节辅音的第一个字母，也可以视情况保留第一个元音或重要的元音。在涉及缩略词组、短语甚至语句的情况下，口译笔记一般按语言的通用规则去做，不过有时可更简略一些。无论符号、缩略词或缩略语，都尽量符合多数人的应用习惯，这样可以让人脑更快地适应系统，避免不必要的麻烦。

4. 常用口译笔记符号

符号和缩略语从原则上来讲完全是因人而异的，译员在口译实践中要结合自己的语言、知识、经验、喜好，不断地完善自己的符号系统，从而提高笔记效率。然而也没有必要自己别出心裁设计一套完整的系统，可以从其他同行的符号中得到启示，使用多数译员共同使用的某些符号，从中筛选出简洁明了、适合表达、具有普遍性意义且没有歧义的符号，这样可以节省探索合适的记录符号的时间。符号系统是在使用中不断完善的，但是一定不要试图在进行口译的过程中临时发明符号，也不要无休止地"开发"新奇的符号。需要记忆的符号越多，越不便于记忆，表达时就会发生"识别危机"，影响表达质量。下面是一些口译笔记中常使用的符号，供大家参考。

↑　　上升、增加等
↑↑　　越来越强等
↓　　下降、减少等
↓↓　　越来越弱等
→　　导致，见下文，结论，发展，从某地到某地，从某时到某时等
←　　由……导致，原因，见前面……处
<　　少于，更少
>　　多于，更多
=　　等于，相同，相当于，即：意味着
≠　　不等于，不相当，不是，不同于，差异
≈　　大约，粗略，差不多

≡	坚持		
//	与……比较而言		
∵	因为，由于，多亏		
∴	所以，因此，结果		
Σ	总共，合计，总和		
∈	属于		
max	最大，最高，最高级(上标与形容词的缩略形式，如 $^{max}magni$ 表示"最华丽的")		
min	最小，最低	☆	重要的(人或事)，重要性
:	认为，相信，觉得，以为，希望	"	说，表示，陈述，指出
re"	重申	!"	强调
?	问题，疑问，难题	¿	答案，解答
☺	高兴，满意，荣幸	☹	不快，不满，悲伤，忧虑，难过
pt⊥	观点分歧	«	波折
√	正确，对，好	×	错误，否定，不……，没有效果
⌐	之前，直到	⌐	之后，自从
⌐ verb	动词过去时	verb ⌐	动词将来时
<u>verb</u>	进行时	><	冲突，战争
h	主席	□	国家
|·	国内	□.	国外
∠	人民，人类	∧	稳固，巩固

四、口译笔记的格式和结构安排

记录内容的结构安排同样不可小觑。每个译员都有不同的笔记习惯，但大部分专业口译员的笔记格式都符合一些共同原则。

首先，整体的布局要少横多竖，即采取纵向阶梯式缩进结构，这样可以形象地展现上下文的逻辑结构，帮助整理思路。即使是记录列举词也不要横着写在一行，不要吝啬纸张，每个列举的词占一行，纵向排列，不仅可以加快记录速度，也便于翻译时快速判读意群。其次，记录的时候要少写多划，写的字要尽可能少，能够表达清楚含义、能够在几分钟内辨认即可。符号不要太繁杂，有些可以用线条来简化。记录的速度也要相对快一些。遇到重复的内容，可以用线条箭头标指。最后，每次结束一段翻译的同时不要忘了在结束的位置画一条横线，然后再示意讲话人继续。

口译笔记示范如图 1.4.1 所示。

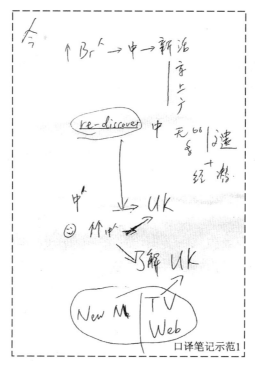

图 1.4.1　口译笔记示范(1)

以下是两篇口译笔记样本仅供参考。

例文 1：Today, more and more British people are visiting China to see for themselves the new dynamism of great cities like Beijing, Shanghai and Guangzhou. We are re-discovering China's incomparably rich cultural heritage, as well as its immense economic potential. The Chinese are re-discovering Britain, too. We are delighted to welcome more Chinese visitors to our country each year. Many more Chinese are finding out about Britain through modern media like television and the Internet.

参考译文：今天，越来越多的英国人来到中国，目睹像北京、上海、广州这样的大城市的新活力。我们正在重新发现中国无与伦比丰富多彩的文化遗产，以及其巨大的经济潜力。中国人也在重新发现英国。我们很高兴每年接待越来越多的中国来访客人。越来越多的中国人通过像电视和互联网这样的现代媒体了解英国。

例文 2：20世纪90年代以来，上海以承办国内外重大体育赛事为契机，不断加快体育设施建设，相继建成了上海体育场、上海国际赛车场、上海虹口足球场、中国残疾人体育和艺术培训基地、旗忠网球中心等一批多功能的体育场馆。

参考译文：Since the 1990s, Shanghai has speeded up construction of sports facilities to meet the need of domestic and international sports events. The multifunctional sports venues completed in the city include Shanghai Stadium, Shanghai International Circuit, Hongkou Soccer Stadium, China Disabled People's Sports and Art Training Center, and Qizhong Tennis Center.

图1.4.1 所示是该例的口译笔记。

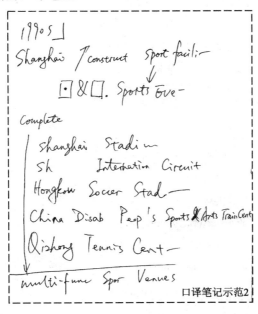

图 1.4.1　口译笔记示范(2)

口译笔记归纳起来有以下四条原则：纵向记录，换行缩进，标明分隔，简约疏朗。

纵向记录，换行缩进的意思是笔记内容要竖向书写，一个意群占一行，并且使用缩进的阶梯式排列，每记录一个新的意群就要另起一行。

标明分隔的意思是当发言人一句话或一个较大意群结束时，需要在结束处做出明显的标记，这样做的好处是可以让口译员在阅读笔记时对信息结构一目了然，可以很快定位信息。

简约疏朗是指笔记不要记得太密集，一行可以只写一两个字，一页纸上空白的地方哪怕占了大多数空间也是正常的。如果字写得太多、太密，反而不容易把握重要信息，增加口译时阅读笔记的难度。

例文 3：我很高兴地宣布我们论坛的第三次会议正式开幕，并在这里欢迎来自我们两国杰出而有影响力的人士。

参考译文: It is a real pleasure to be here to open the third meeting of our forum and to be welcoming such a distinguished and influential group of people from both our countries.

例文4：今晚，我很高兴在南京大学接待我们的老朋友布朗博士。我代表南京大学向布朗博士表示热烈的欢迎。我相信，布朗博士这次对我校的访问，必将为进一步加强两校的友好合作关系做出重要的贡献！明天，您将要赴苏州和上海访问，我预祝您一路旅途愉快！

参考译文：It is with great pleasure that we meet our old friend Dr. Brown at Nanjing University. On behalf of Nanjing University, I wish to extend my warmest welcome to him. I believe that this visit will surely greatly improve the friendly cooperation between the two schools. Tomorrow you will leave for Suzhou and Shanghai. I wish you a pleasant journey.

例文5：Two-way trade has risen sharply in a few short years. The United States is now China's third largest trading partner. Our bilateral trade and economic cooperation show great promise for the future.

参考译文：中美双边贸易在短短几年中大幅度增长。美国已成为中国的第三大贸易伙伴。我们的双边贸易和经济合作前景广阔。

例文6：我代表中国政府和人民向各位来宾表示热烈的欢迎，并预祝大会取得圆满成功！

参考译文：On behalf of Chinese government and Chinese people, I would like to extend our warm welcome to all the guests. I wish the meeting a great success!

笔记练习

请听下面的录音，进行笔记记录，然后译成英语或汉语。

4-1.mp3

1984年，中国派出了350多人组成的代表团，参加在洛杉矶举行的第23届奥林匹克运动会；该团胜利归来，夺得15枚金牌、8枚银牌和9枚铜牌，从而结束了中国未曾在奥运会上得过金牌的那段历史。

4-2.mp3

From VOA Learning English, this is the Economics Report.

Most West Coast ports in the United States have been busy since Friday. That is when negotiators reached a tentative settlement in a nine-month labor dispute and work slowdown. Now that goods again are being unloaded. The dockworkers and employers say they can talk about long-term problems.

Many ships have been docked or have been waiting offshore at 29 West Coast ports. Port officials say it will take months to process all the cargo. Most dockworkers have returned to work. But they still must vote on a tentative five-year contract.

U.S. Secretary of Labor Thomas Perez went to San Francisco to urge both sides to settle their differences quickly. Craig Merrilees is with the International Longshore and Warehouse Union. He said the negotiations have been difficult. "You know, there are a lot of tough issues in this process that lasted over nine months, and some of them are the kinds of issues that are affecting all workers. That includes the outsourcing of good jobs."

Workers say administrative jobs at the port have been moving to other states and other countries. Workers say they also worry about increasing automation of port operations, reducing the need for workers.

Those who move goods in and out of the country include the San Francisco coffee company, Ritual Coffee Roasters. Eileen Rinaldi is the owner. "We are reliant on constant arrivals of coffee in order to have a fresh supply."

Many other businesses depend on goods passing through the ports, such as beer makers that use imported hops, farmers with crops to ship. One California children's clothing company has been waiting for its products trapped in ships near the Port of Oakland.

Tom O'Brien is a transportation expert at California State University, Long Beach. He says long-term problems at the ports must be addressed. Mr. O'Brien also says not only the port but roads, bridges and railways need to be upgraded.

"The fact that we have larger ships coming now, that is creating peak demand for labor and for equipment is putting a lot of pressure on our infrastructure, not only the ports, but the road network, rail capacity, distribution center and warehousing."

The labor dispute began in July when a labor agreement ended. The work stoppage has affected 29 West Coast ports for months and slowed U.S. trade with Asia. Those ports process more than 25 percent of all U.S. maritime trade and more than 70 percent of the nation's imports from Asia.

请听下面的汉语，进行笔记的记录，然后译成英语。

4-3.mp3

一年来，我国经济社会发展总体平稳，稳中有进。"稳"的主要标志是，经济运行处于合理区间。增速稳，国内生产总值达到63.6万亿元，比上年增长7.4%，在世界主要经济体中名列前茅。就业稳，城镇新增就业1322万人，高于上年。价格稳，居民消费价格上涨2%。"进"的总体特征是，发展的协调性和可持续性增强。经济结构有新的优化，粮食产量达到1.21万亿斤，消费对经济增长的贡献率上升3个百分点，达到51.2%，服务业增加值比重由46.9%提高到48.2%，新产业、新业态、新商业模式不断涌现。中西部地区经济增速快于东部地区。发展质量有新的提升，一般公共预算收入增长8.6%，研究与试验发展经费支出与国内生产总值之比超过2%，能耗强度下降4.8%，是近年来最大降幅。人民生活有新的改善，全国居民人均可支配收入实际增长8%，快于经济增长；农村居民人均可支配收入实际增长9.2%，快于城镇居民收入增长；农村贫困人口减少1232万人；6600多万农村人口饮水安全问题得到解决；出境旅游超过1亿人次。改革开放有新的突破，全面深化改革系列重点任务启动实施，本届政府减少三分之一行政审批事项的目标提前实现。

——节选自2015年《政府工作报告》

五、习语的口译

习语是一种以简洁的语言来表达深刻道理的语句。在国际交往中，领导人常常喜欢引用本国或到访国的谚语、成语、格言、俗语、典故、名人名言等，以示亲切友好。

习语是语言中的精华，是人们在日积月累的社会生活中提炼出来的表达思想的方式，是一种文化沉淀。从广义上讲，习语包括成语(idioms)、短语(set phrases)、谚语(proverbs)、格言(sayings)、俗语(colloquialisms)、警句(epigrams)、名言录(quotations)、典故(allusions)、俚语(slangs)、歇后语(two-part sayings)等，是一种在意义和结构上都相对稳定的语言结构。一方面，人类共同的情感及人生阅历使生活在不同社会、不同文化背景下的人们拥有相似的表达思想的习语，如"Facts speak louder than words"(事实胜于雄辩)；"Out of sight, out of mind"(眼不见，心不烦)；"One swallow does not make a summer"(一只燕子不成夏；不可光凭偶然现象就下断语)等。另一方面，文化历史、生活环境、风俗习惯、宗教信仰等的不同，也使各民族产生了自己独特的习惯用语。

例如，1984年11月访华的挪威首相维洛克(Willoch)在欢迎宴会上说道："Although I have tried to follow the development in your country from afar, I am very conscious of the truth of the Chinese proverb 'Seeing is believing.' (中国谚语：眼见为实/百闻不如一见)"

再如美国前总统里根(Reagan)1984年4月访华时热情洋溢地说："Since we arrived the graciousness with which we have been received has been heartwarming. A Chinese proverb best describes my feeling: 'When the visitor arrives, it is as if returning home.' (中国谚语：宾至如归)"

经常为政府首脑、高级官员、文化人士、社会名流等做口译的译员都有相同的经验，就是这些名人在访问时常常在演讲中引用一些名家名言、经典诗句，以表达自己的感情、观点和立场，或赞赏对方国家的文化传统。

例如，2005年6月26日温家宝总理在第六次亚欧财长会议开幕式讲话时说："中国有句古话：相知无远近，万里尚为邻(Distance cannot separate true friends who feel so close even when they are thousands of miles apart.)。中国与亚洲各国山水相连，共同铸就了灿烂的亚洲文明。"

美国前总统克林顿1998年6月访华时在人民大会堂的国宴上致辞时引用了孟子的一句话，他说道："In so many different ways, we are upholding the teachings of Mencius, who said: 'A good citizen in one community will befriend the other citizens of the community; a good citizen of the world will befriend the other citizens of the world.' (一乡之善士斯友一乡之善士，天下之善士斯友天下之善士)"

时任中华人民共和国国务院总理的朱镕基在1999年春访美时，在一次记者招待会上回答某个记者提出的有关人权问题时引用了"民为贵，社稷次之，君为轻"(The people are the most important element in a state; next are the gods of land and grain; least is the ruler himself.) 这句古话表明中国政府十分重视人权问题。

又如，中国外交部长杨洁篪2007年12月在英国皇家国际问题研究所的演讲中说道：中国有句古话，叫做"同声相应，同气相投"(From China, it's an old saying: Things that accord in tone vibrate together.)，意思是：意见相同的人互相响应，志趣相投的人自然结合在一起。贵国著名诗人塞缪尔·约翰逊这样勉励我们："积极地去创造并抓住那些我们触手可及的好机会，这是人生最大的艺术。"(From Britain, it's a famous line from the great poet Samuel Johnson: To improve the golden moment of opportunity, and catch the good that is within our reach, is the great art of life.)

中国译协刘习良会长2008年8月在第18届世界翻译大会开幕式上的讲话中说："中国2000多年前的著名教育家孔子曾经说过：'有朋自远方来，不亦乐乎？'"(The ancient Chinese thinker and philosopher Confucius said, "How happy we are to meet friends from afar.")

习语是语言中的精华，大都富于形象色彩，通过形象词语比拟事物、说明道理。口译时若能处理得当，译文将会因之而色彩增辉，反之，就不免会显得平淡，有失原文的神韵和特色。因此在能够"移植"的情况下采用直译，不能"移植"的时候要采用融汇变通的方式，如意译、转换喻体形象、直译意译兼用以及加注等方法来灵活处理英汉习语的口译。

1. 直译

由于人们在感情、对客观事物的感受以及社会经历等方面有相似之处，英汉习语中有一些相同或相似的表达法，这些习语的字面意义和形象意义相同或相似，隐含意义也相同，也就是说这类习语的字面意义和形象意义传达出了相同的文化信息，可以相互转换。例如，"Easy come, easy go"(来得容易，去得快)；"Strike while the iron is hot"(趁热打铁)；"Practice makes perfect" (熟能生巧)；"as busy as bee" (像蜜蜂一样忙碌)；"as black as crow" (像乌鸦一般黑);"He who laughs last laughs best"(谁笑到最后,谁笑得最好);"A fall in the pit, a gain in your wit"(吃一堑,长一智);"a castle in the air"(空中楼阁);"to go through fire and water"(赴汤蹈火);"to turn a blind eye to"(熟视无睹);"heart and soul"(全心全意);"to turn a deaf ear to"(充耳不闻);"as easy as turning over one's head"(了如指掌)。汉语成语"雪中送炭"可译成"to offer fuel in snowy weather";"祸不单行"对应的英文是"Misfortunes never come single";"路遥知马力,日久见人心"对应的英文是"A long road tests a horse's strength and a long task proves a man's heart"。这类习语的直译做到了从字面意义、形象意义及隐含意义三个方面对原文的忠实,可以说是最佳的翻译。随着跨文化交际的深入发展,一些英语俗语如"crocodile tears"(鳄鱼的眼泪),"armed to teeth"(武装到牙齿),"Time is money"(时间就是金钱)等已逐渐为我国听众所接受。

2. 意译

在英汉习语的口译过程中,如果字面意义或形象意义与隐含意义因文化差异出现矛盾时,我们应舍弃前两者,而注重习语的隐含意义。我们知道"龙"在英汉两种文化中意义完全不同。"望子成龙"意指父母希望孩子长大后能有所作为。有人将其译作"hope one's child will become a dragon",西方人则很难接受,因为在他们看来,龙(dragon)是一种凶残、肆虐的怪物,是邪恶的象征,喻指凶恶的人、撒旦、魔王、严厉而有警觉性的女人。为了使西方人易于理解,最好译作"hope one's children will have a bright future"、"have great ambitions for one's child"、"hold high hopes for one's child"或"to expect one's son to become an outstanding person"。又如汉语俗语"天有不测风云",若把字面意义和形象意义毫无保留地译成英语,会使英文听众疑惑不解,因为汉语中"风云"的文化含义一般西方人很难理解,若把它的隐含意义"Something unexpected may happen any time"口译出来则利于听众理解和接受。英语俗语中"When in Rome, do as the Romans do"其真正含义即"入乡随俗"。字面意义和形象意义不同而隐含意义相同的英汉习语还有"He who lives with cripples learns to limp."(近朱者赤,近墨者黑);"to rain cats and dogs"(倾盆大雨);"hit the nail on the head"(说得中肯,一语道破);"to cast pearl before swine"(对牛弹琴);"You can't make bricks without straw."(巧妇难为无米之炊);"have an axe to grind"(别有用心);"talk through one's hat"(胡言乱语);"a fly in the ointment"(美中不足);"by the skin of one's teeth"(九死一生);"call a spade a spade"(直言不讳);"hang on sb's lips"(言听计从);"to be fall of beans"(精力充沛);"A quiet conscience sleeps in thunder."(不做亏心事,不怕鬼敲门);"Don't pat the cart before the horse."(切勿本末倒置);"It is no use crying over spilt milk."(覆水难收);"The leopard cannot change its spots."(本性难移;狗改不了吃屎)等。口译这样的习语时,译员应本着"功能对等"的原则,舍弃原文字面意义和形象意义,体现其隐含意义,才能使译文听众切实感受到原文的真正内涵。

3. 转换喻体形象

由于不同的历史渊源和两种文化间的差异,有些喻体形象在使用英语的民族心中的概念与使用汉语的民族的概念大相径庭,直译显得晦涩难懂,这时可以更换喻体形象,使译文听众获得与原文相似的感受。例如"Mary and her mother are as like as two peas."(玛丽和她的母亲长相酷似。)汉语听众可能不明白为什么把人喻为豌豆,甚至会认为这是不敬和轻视,而在英语里却给人以形象逼真的感觉,所以译成汉语时不得不放弃形式上的对等,译出符合汉语听众文化习俗的喻体。又如"He treated his daughter as the apple in the eye."(他把女儿视为掌上明珠。)"apple in the eye"在汉语中无比喻用法,因此汉语听众很难理解孩子怎么会是"眼睛里的苹果",其实"apple"在英语中指"瞳孔",套用汉语"眼里最重要的东西——掌上明珠"才能使中国听众了解其意。

英汉语义相同而喻体不同的习语还有"to spring up like mushroom"(雨后春笋);"as stubborn as a mule"(倔强如牛);英语谚语"kill two birds with one stone",有人直译成"一石二鸟",笔者认为此种译法远不及传统的汉语成语"一箭双雕"来得形象逼真,特别是"一箭"传神的动作,远非"一石"所能比拟。又如"like a rat in the hole"(瓮中之鳖),不能译成"洞中之鼠"。英语谚语"birds of a feather flock together"和"no smoke without fire"在汉语中可分别译成"物以类聚,人以群分"以及"无风不起浪"。尽管更换了喻体,但中国听众获得的感受与原文要传递的信息是相同的,达到了翻译的目的。类似的还有"to tread upon eggs"(如履薄冰);"as thin as a shadow"(瘦得像猴);"to fish in the air"(水中捞月)等。

4. 直译意译兼用

有时为了更确切地表达原意,译员可同时兼用直译和意译来口译习语。例如,"to spend money like water"(挥金如土),"like water"可意译为"如土";汉语俗语"不到黄河心不死"恰当的翻译是"until all is over ambition never dies","心不死"直译为"ambition never dies";"不到黄河"若直译为"until the Yellow River is reached",外国听众会听不懂,所以译成"until all is over"更好。

5. 加注法

严格地讲,加注不能算一种译法,注解多了,听起来往往会失去流畅感,但有的习语只有在说明历史背景和典籍出处后才能充分表达它的意义,所以译员有时必须酌情考虑利用注释法使习语的含义充分表达出来。例如,"to carry coal to Newcastle"的字面意思是"将煤运往纽卡斯尔(英国产煤中心)",隐含意义指"多此一举;背着石头上山";"守株待兔"有人翻译成"watching the stump and waiting for a hare"——see Chinese folklore, suggesting "waiting for gains without pains",这种加注是很得体的。这种处理方法既能使听众清楚地明白原习语的含义,又体现了它的文化特点。又如,"Don't be too proud of your premature success, as it always turns to be a Pandora's box."(切不可为过早的成功得意忘形,因为它常常会变成灾祸的根源)(Pandora's box 潘多拉的盒子,见希腊神话,用来比喻灾难、麻烦、祸害等的根源)。

综上所述,英语习语的口译是一个复杂的问题,既要尽量保持原文特色,又要尊重本国国情、民俗;既要引入异国情调,又要考虑听众的反映、感受;既要忠实地再现原文,又要符合译文语言规范。即使同一习语,其译法也常因上下文、语境及其本身用法和文体而异，译文能否为广大听众所接受是衡量翻译成功与否的关键，译员应灵活运用各种翻译手段，注重英汉习语反映出的文化差异及其隐含意义，努力提高翻译的准确性和生动性，使听众切实从中领悟到原文习语的真正内涵与魅力。

一个称职的译员必须准确、流利地将口译材料中出现的习语和引语译成目标语。这就要求译员掌握一定数量的习语、名人名言、经典诗句，尤其是中国古代思想家流传下来的一些名言佳句，如《四书》(《论语》、《孟子》、《中庸》、《大学》)语录、唐诗宋词等。对于不少译员来说，这是一道艰难但又必须逾越的难关。有着五千年文明史的中国，文化底蕴深厚，儒道墨法争鸣，哲人智者如云，传世绝句如林，都可以信手拈来，为我所用。因此，译员平时需要加强积累，做个有心人，博闻强记，收集古今名人的经典名言，以不断充实自己的语料库。

本书第四部分"时文语林——实用口译必备词汇"中，编者根据多年来的口译教学和口译实践的经验和体会，挑选了近百条最常用的汉语成语、谚语、典故、歇后语和《四书》语录的英译，供读者学习参考。

六、译前准备

在开始口译之前，译员需要进行有针对性的准备。前面也谈到，口译所涉及的内容包罗万象，服务的对象很可能是某个领域的专家。然而译员不可能成为无所不知的全才，因此需要对即将开展的口译服务做好准备。准备什么呢？一般情况下，译员都会事先得到客户方的一些资料，比如日程安排、技术资料，甚至是讲话者的发言稿等，但有时出于保密的考虑可能不会事先透漏，但至少要向客户方了解主题内容、行业、讲话人或会谈的意图、听众或会谈的双方等背景信息，越清楚、具体越好。可以从以下几个方面进行准备。

1. 长期准备

长期准备包括双语言准备，口译技能准备、跨文化敏感性、跨文化交际技能、主题知识和术语的准备。

2. 短期准备

短期准备是指本次口译任务的基本信息和情况，但准备时间可能只有一周或是几天甚至更短的时间，该从哪方面着手准备呢？译员需要达到与专家同样的知识水平吗？实际上，译员需要的不是最高深的专业知识，不需要也不可能掌握相关领域的所有知识。译员需要的是能够很好地处理信息的知识，简单一点来讲，是口译活动中可能涉及的主题知识和术语及其内涵的知识。当译员拿到客户方的资料后，应当认真阅读这些文件资料，找到其中的专业术语，通过查阅双语字典或是相关的专业词典，根据上下文确定术语的意义，将所有涉及的术语列一个术语双语对照表，最好单面书写，以便于口译中翻阅参考。仅仅知道术语的对应译法是很危险的，因为所要表达的意思要以术语和句子中其他的成分为基础，不能生硬地在口译时将一个术语用另一种语言替换。译员只有理解了术语的意思，才能很好地使它与其他的话语相互作用，融为一体，才能够清楚地表达讲话人的意思。必要的时候应当查阅百科全书，在网络上搜索相关的文章，甚至是查阅专业杂志、专业书籍来把握术语的含义以及同其他概念之间的关系，只有这样才能在具体语境中达到收放自如。

那么，哪些词汇或表达属于需要准备的术语呢？术语可分为三类。第一类是单一指向的术语，或称技术术语。这些术语可以在相关的专业词典或是综合技术类词典里查到(当然，技术类词典的作用也很有限，可以参考国际机构编纂的词汇表、术语库等)，比如在篮球比赛转播时进行口译解说中涉及投篮方式的术语就有"dunk(灌篮)，bank shot(擦板球)，fade-away shot(后仰式跳投)，set shot(立定投篮)"等。注意，某一个术语所使用的词汇在不同的行业里有不同的含义，不可混淆。某一缩略语在不同的行业里指代的内容不同。还有一些词汇表面看来没有什么特殊，但实际上却是一个技术词汇，这种情况也要留心，重要的是一定要通过上下文的理解来确定术语的含义，不可想当然。第二类是特种指向的术语，如人名、机构名称、作品或电影名称等。上述两类术语在翻译时必须使用另一种语言里现有的对应术语，不可随意杜撰。第三类是讲话人特意使用的一些词汇，要求翻译时做出相应的选择。

除了术语准备之外，还要进行主题知识准备。主题知识准备包括相关行业的现状，涉及主题的最新成果、相关数据。如果是产品设备，最好能见见实物，了解一下工作原理等。如果条件许可，在口译活动开始之前，最好能够与组织方和与会专家见面，与专家座谈可以比较详细地了解相关主题，请专家解答疑问，同时还能够了解讲话者的思路，讲话的口音、语速等。实在不行，也可以与了解相关行业的专家探讨一下相关的内容，这些准备工作都会对口译活动的开展有很大的益处。甚至在口译现场也可以利用会前时间或休息时间与主要发言人进行简短接触来进行准备。口译做完以后，短期准备的知识和术语一部分可能会变成今后的长期准备，另外一部分术语则永远忘记了。

短期准备还包括语言的准备，比如在西安的丝绸之路博览会，有很多不同国家参会，像尼泊尔等国，他们说话非常快，发音较难懂，口译准备时可以找音频或视频熟悉发音特点。另外，短期准备还包括服装的准备，笔和纸的准备，文件、交通状况的熟悉。充分的短期准备可以帮助译员克服心理上的紧张。

3. 最后准备

译员一定要比活动发生的时间提前半个小时到活动现场，同传提前到的时间应该更长，利用这段时间提前熟悉并适应环境和设备，比如笔记本放在什么地方，文件放在什么地方，有没有话筒，设备状况等。尽量早到还可以和主办者交流，了解到场嘉宾的座次、官位，领导是女性还是男性，某个发言人是否临时参会等。另外还可以和提前到的外国人交谈，熟悉他们的发音特点、口音等。提前到达有助于做好身体和心理的准备，这些很琐碎，但一定程度上会影响口译的质量和效果。

4. 应急技巧

不管译员精心做了多少译前准备，设想了各种问题和困难，做了语言、专业知识和百科知识的准备，依然会遇到问题，因为口译不只是语言现象，还是复杂的社会和文化现象，语言再好还有其他的问题出现。译员的角色不只是传话筒的角色，还扮演着文化协调员等多重角色，协商、协调不同国家的人之间的交流，有时候还是独立的交际者。

口译时如果有和语言相关的问题，如听不懂，翻译不出来，对有经验的译员不是问题，知道应该怎么处理，而学生译员则经常是不懂装懂，这是口译中的大忌。如果出现听不懂的情况，译员可以请发言人进行核对或者换个说法解释，向合作者和听众求助。对专业词汇，可带 e-词典，可做解释性的说明；还可以做合乎逻辑的猜测，作为自我保护；还可适当放弃一些东西。还有一种情况，比如刚开始丢掉或遗漏，或者理解有误，译错一些，后来随着听了更多，理解更多，可以补译，这是译员伦理的表现，但译员不要做过多解释和道歉。译员的底线和基本的准则是最大限度地帮助双方达成交际的目的，达到讲话人初始的本意，尽量花最少的代价做找补。

本章练习参考译文

4-1　In 1984, China sent a delegation of 350-plus to the 23rd Olympic Games held in Los Angeles, who returned in triumph with 15 gold, 8 silver and 9 bronze, thus ending China's history of never having won a gold medal at the Olympic Games.

4-2　周五以来，美国西海岸大部分港口一直很忙碌。谈判者在长达九个月之久的劳动纠纷和怠工之后达成初步解决方案。如今，码头货物又开始被卸下来，码头工人和雇主均表示可协商长期问题。

不少船只在 29 个西海岸港口停靠或在近海等待进港。港口官员称处理所有货物需要花上数月时间。许多码头工人已经重新开工，但是他们仍然必须就一项五年的初步合同进行投票。

美国劳工部长托马斯·佩雷斯前往旧金山督促双方尽快解决分歧。克雷格·梅瑞利斯就职于国际码头和仓库联盟，他表示协商一直很困难。"要知道在长达九个月的过程中存在不少棘手问题，其中一些难题影响着所有工作者，包括好工作外包。"

工人们称港口行政工作已经转到其他州和他国，同时他们也担心港口业务越来越自动化将减少对工作人员的需求。

运输货物进出该国的包括旧金山咖啡公司，艾琳·瑞纳第是公司老板。"我们依赖源源不断的咖啡到货，以便供应新鲜的咖啡。"

许多其他企业也依靠通过港口运输货物，比如使用进口啤酒花的制造商，需要运输作物的农民。一家加利福尼亚的童装公司一直在等待困在奥克兰港附近船只的货物。

汤姆·奥布赖恩是加利福尼亚州大学长滩分校的交通专家，他表示必须解决港口长期存在的问题。他也表示不仅仅是港口，道路、桥梁和铁路都亟待升级。

"现在我们需要更大的船只进港，这将使对劳动力和设备的需求达到顶峰，而这一事实将给我们的基础设施，不仅仅是港口，还有公路网、铁路运输承载力、物流中心和仓储业形成不少压力。"

劳动纠纷起始于去年 7 月的劳动协议到期，而这次罢工已经影响 29 个西海岸港口数月并延缓了美国同亚洲的贸易。这些港口要处理全美国 25% 以上的海上贸易及美国 70% 以上的亚洲进口贸易。

4-3 During the past year, China has, overall, achieved a stable performance while at the same time securing progress in its economic and social development. The main indication of this stable performance is that the economy operated within an appropriate range. The growth rate was steady China's GDP reached 63.6 trillion yuan, an increase of 7.4% over the previous year, making China one of the fastest-growing major economies in the world. Employment remained robust, with 13.22 million new urban jobs created, which is higher than the figure for the previous year. Prices were stable, with the CPI rising by 2%. The underlying feature demonstrating progress is that our development is becoming better coordinated and more sustainable. The economic structure was upgraded. Grain output reached 605 million metric tons; the contribution of consumption toward economic growth rose by three percentage points to 51.2%; the value added of the service sector increased from 46.9% to 48.2% of the GDP; and there was a constant stream of new industries, new types of business, and new business models. The central and western regions grew faster in economic terms than the eastern region. The quality of development was raised. Revenue in the general public budgets grew by 8.6%. Research and development spending accounted for more than 2% of the GDP. Energy intensity was cut by 4.8%, the biggest reduction made in recent years. People's lives were improved. Per capita disposable personal income increased by 8% in real terms nationwide, growing faster than the economy, and the per capita disposable income of rural residents grew by 9.2%, outpacing that of those living in urban areas. In rural areas, the number of people living in poverty was reduced by 12.32 million, and over 66 million more people gained access to safe drinking water. The number of outbound trips made by Chinese tourists exceeded 100 million. New breakthroughs were made in reform and opening up. A series of key tasks for comprehensively deepening reform were launched, and the goal of the current administration to cut the number of items that require government review by one third was achieved ahead of schedule.

第二部分 口译实践
Interpretation Practice

第五章 迎来送往口译
Reception of Foreign Guests

一、机场迎送

外宾来到中国，第一印象来自机场接待，因而机场接待工作水平的高低格外重要。这个时候译员往往首先就是接待员。

译员接待外宾应注意的事项有：预先取得航班时刻表，并且向有关部门确认所要迎接的外宾是否在飞机上，如果航班因天气等因素晚点，还需要了解延误多久，以便适时调整接机计划。如果接待重要宾客，译员最好在接机之前先行办理礼遇通关手续，这样贵宾抵达机场后，就可以经由特别的礼遇通道入境。可安排献花仪式，宾主互相介绍后，可进入机场、港口、车站的贵宾接待室，请贵宾稍事休息，也可请来宾直接乘坐事先安排好的交通工具，前往住宿处。如接待普通宾客，在接机时，由于机场人较多，应事先约定好出海关后碰面的地点，或留下联络方式，以避免到时错过。在接机时，用看板书写姓名供外宾辨识是一种好方法。看板要高举过头，使其在拥挤的人流中突出醒目。如果是接待代表团等群体贵宾，译员可以准备大型旗帜等明显标志物，以便外宾容易辨认。

外宾抵达机场后，应先帮助客人确认行李、机票和护照等物品是否均已妥善处理，然后译员帮助主人与外宾相互见面和介绍。一般由礼宾人员或中方迎候人员中身份最高者率先将中方迎候人员按一定顺序一一介绍给客人，然后再由客人中身份最高者将客人按一定顺序一一介绍给主人。

通常译员应陪同外宾一同前往住宿处。到达后，要给外宾留下充足的洗澡、更衣、休息的时间。译员可暂时离去，但走前应告诉外宾下一步的活动计划，并征得其同意。应当为外宾留下中方联系人员及自己的电话号码，以便为之提供及时的帮助。

随同译员往往要到机场把外宾送走，其工作才算真正意义上的完成。作为译员，要尽早了解客人的航班信息，查询路上交通情况，提醒客人早点出发，以免贻误航班。

机场接送工作看起来很具体烦琐，但这项工作十分重要，不得有半点闪失，所以准备工作要特别仔细周全。

对话口译/Dialogue Interpretation

Dialogue 1

Interpret the following dialogues alternatively into English and Chinese.

5-1.mp3

A: 先生，请问您是从美国来的约翰逊先生吗？

B: Yes, I am David Johnson. And you must be Mr. Zhang.

A: 是的，我叫张明。约翰逊先生，我一直在此恭候您的到来。

B: Thank you for coming to meet me. Just call me David. First name is more friendly than last name.

A: 好的，欢迎您来到上海，旅途可好？

B: Not too bad. But we were later than expected. Our plane delayed taking off as we ran into a storm. We were held up for several hours at the airport, waiting for the storm to clear up.

A: 嗯，您也安全无恙地到达了。经过这么久的旅行您肯定很累了，我们直接开车送您去宾馆吧。

B: Yes, I am rather tired. But I'll be all right by tomorrow.

A: 但愿如此，我们明天晚上为您安排了一个宴会。

B: You're very kind, indeed. I'll be glad to come.

A: 好的，我们王总要我向您问好，遗憾的是他不能亲自来接您。

B: It doesn't matter at all.

A: 我祝您在此过得愉快。有什么需要，请跟我说。我去推行李车，您到行李台那里等我吧。

B: Thank you so much. You take the traveling-bag and I can manage the cases.

A: 都齐了，我们的车等在外面，我们走吧。

B: Yes. Let's go.

二、住宿接待

陪同国外客户或友人入住宾馆也是随同译员经常需要做的事。为了使行程更顺利，译员最好事先询问客户对宾馆的地理位置、内部环境、硬件设施(包括上网)等有何要求，以便事先选择好宾馆，并与宾馆预约。此外，客户也许对房间还有一定的讲究，比如不喜欢朝阴面的房间，或者因为过敏不能在房间里摆放鲜花等。这就要求译员与客户充分沟通相关细节，然后再准确地传达给宾馆相关负责人。

在入住宾馆期间，万一客户对房间或某些设施有任何疑问和不满，译员必须随时在场协助其顺利解决问题。因此这也往往要求译员需要同客户入住同一宾馆，或至少要在客户入住宾馆当天陪同客户至宾馆。若是国外客户邀请译员聊天解闷，译员必须注意尽量选择公开场合，不可随意进入客户的房间。

为了更好地完成在宾馆的随同口译任务，译员需要对酒店里最常用的一些表达有所了解。比如，在和外国客户沟通好之后，译员需要和酒店的前台(front desk)联系，帮助其预定好(book or reserve)合适的房间。在接到客户之后，要带着客户到前台进行住宿登记(check-in)，并将酒店相关服务介绍给客户，以便客户需要时可以及时得到帮助，比如洗衣服务(laundry service)、叫醒业务(wake-up service)、餐桌预订(table reservation)、票务服务(ticket service)等。

译员在酒店的主要任务就是做好客户和酒店方面的联系沟通工作，避免一些不愉快的事情发生，影响到客户的工作和酒店的声誉等，这些都需要译员在口译过程中对各种事务加以灵活有效的处理。

Dialogue 2

Interpret the following dialogues alternatively into English and Chinese.

5-2.mp3

A: Hello! Is this room service?
B: 您好！这里是客服部。请问有什么可以为您效劳的？
A: I'd like to order some food, a bottle of Budweiser and a beef sandwich, please.
B: 请问您的姓名和房间号码？
A: This is Michael in Room 629.
B: 好的，我们稍后就会为您送上来。
A: By the way, I want my shirts washed and the overcoat dry-cleaned. How long will it take to get them done?
B: 衬衣明天上午就可以洗好，但干洗的外套需要等到大后天，不知道这样行不行？
A: That's all right. I'm not in such a hurry.
B: 好的，如果您还有别的衣服需要清洗，把它们放在卫生间门后的袋子里就行了，每天上午都会有服务员来收的。
A: I get it. Thank you very much.
B: 如需加急服务，拨打号码5就可以了，洗衣部的人会马上来取您的衣服。您还有别的需要吗？
A: One more thing, how do I arrange for a wake-up call? I have an important appointment tomorrow morning.
B: 您可以直接打电话给接线生，告诉他几点钟来叫醒您就好了。
A: OK, I get it. Thanks a lot. Bye-bye.
B: 不用谢，再见！

三、宴会饮食

在译员的职业生涯中，经常需要做的一件事就是陪外国朋友参加各种酒席宴会。因此译员必须熟知中西宴会的一些基本礼仪。

首先，赴宴前的准备工作：应注意仪表整洁、穿戴大方，最好稍作打扮。忌穿工作服、满脸倦容或一身灰尘。在高档餐厅就餐时，男译员要穿着整洁的衣服和皮鞋；女译员则要穿套装和有跟的鞋子。如果指定要穿正式服装的话，男译员必须穿西装打领带。另外，男译员要注意刮净胡须，如有时间还应理发。注意鞋子是否干净、光亮，以免临时尴尬。其次，宴会入席：一般宴会都会事先安排好座次。通常以主人的座位为中心，如果女主人参加时，则以主人和女主人为基准，近高远低，右上左下，依次排列。主宾安排在最尊贵的位置，即主人的右手位置，主宾夫人安排在女主人的右手位置。而随同译员的座位一般都安排在外宾右侧。就座时要注意由椅子的左侧入座。当椅子被拉开后，身体在几乎要碰到桌子的距离站直。领位者会把椅子推进来，腿弯碰到后面的椅子时，就可以坐下来。用餐时，上臂和背部要靠到椅背，腹部和桌子保持约一个拳头的距离，最好避免两脚交叉的坐姿。

中式宴会基本用餐礼仪：译员入席后，不要立即动手取食。而应待主人打招呼，由主人举杯示意开始时，才能开始用餐。并且通常情况下，主人会在开始用餐前向来宾提议，提出某个事由或为当时的宴会而发表一篇专门的祝酒词。因此译员在此时应该做好准备为外宾翻译祝酒词的内容。中餐宴席进餐伊始，服务员送上的第一道湿毛巾是擦手的，不要用它去擦脸。上龙虾、鸡、水果时，会送上一只小小水盂，其中飘着柠檬片或玫瑰花瓣，它不是饮料，而是洗手用的。用餐的动作要文雅，夹菜时不要碰到邻座，不要把盘里的菜拨到桌上，不要把汤泼翻。译员应选择恰当的时机进餐和口译，切忌一边吃东西，一边进行翻译。要学会既把翻译工作做好，又把肚子填饱，这也是译员口译工作能力的一部分。用餐结束后，可以用餐巾纸或服务员送来的小毛巾擦擦嘴，但不宜擦头颈或胸脯。在主人还没示意结束及外宾未准备离席时，译员不能先离席。

西式宴会基本用餐礼仪：餐巾在用餐前就可以打开。在前菜送来前的这段时间把餐巾打开，如果餐巾较大，应双叠放在腿上；如果较小，可以全部打开。餐巾虽然也可以围在颈上或系在胸前，但显得不大方，所以最好不这样做。可用餐巾的一角擦去嘴上或手指上的油渍，但绝不可用餐巾揩拭餐具。使用刀叉时，应右手用刀，左手用叉。只用叉时，可用右手拿。使用刀时，不要将刀刃向外。更不要用刀送食物入口。若有两把以上的刀叉，应由最外面的一把依次向内取用。切肉应避免刀切在瓷盘上发出响声。吃面条时，可以用叉卷起来吃，不要挑。中途放下刀叉，应将刀叉呈"八"字形分别放在盘子上。如果把刀叉放在一起，表示用餐完毕。和中式宴会相同，切忌在咀嚼食物时进行口译。即使在进餐时突然要求口译，也应咽下口中食物后再进行。口译时可以不放下刀叉，但不可拿着刀叉在空中挥舞。

宴会口译中的要点：酒宴中经常出现的就是祝酒词及关于餐桌上的种种美味佳肴。在此类场合做随同口译，可以避免用长句或结构复杂的句子，尽量表达得简短、通俗、易懂，令双方放松地交谈，还要注意选择需要翻译的对话内容。随同口译并不是演员，很多语气词之类的词语在不影响双方交谈气氛的情况下可以省略。

最后，要提醒一下，不同民族的饮食中有一些必需和禁忌。比如穆斯林的饮食中，就不能出现猪肉和猪肉制品；很多国家的人，比如美国和英国等，不吃狗肉。在接待不同国家不同信仰的外宾时，随同口译员需要事先了解到这些人的信仰和禁忌等，安排好相应的饮食。很多外宾习惯了每天饮用咖啡，所以周到的口译员会把这一点考虑进去。如果能有现磨的咖啡提供，那最理想；如果无法做到的话，至少准备一点速溶咖啡。你的服务对象会很感谢你的细心周到，他对你的信任和赏识会大大有利于沟通和合作的进行，方便你更加出色地完成口译任务。

Dialogue 3

Interpret the following dialogues alternatively into English and Chinese.

5-3.mp3

A: Mr. Luther, since it is your first visit to Beijing, do you want to taste real Beijing food?

B: 当然啦！现在英国可流行吃中国菜了。

A: Wow. You know, China is a country with a splendid food culture. You can have nice food with different styles. This time, let's try Beijing food, is that all right?

B: 太好了，既然到了北京，就得入乡随俗嘛。

A: This restaurant *Quanjude* is a famous one with hundreds of years of history. There are over a hundred chain stores all over China.

B: 那这家饭店的特色菜有哪些呢？

A: The most well-known dish is roast duck. Besides, sauteed duck hearts, marinated duck wings, and duck feet with mustard are also very popular.

B: 太好了！看来您对这个饭店了如指掌啊。

A: I come here very often. I take every foreign friend here when they come to China for the first time. I suggest we start with a cold dish as an appetizer, then a roast duck, and dry-braised duck feet with duck meat and bamboo shoots. What kind of sweet food do you like?

B: 这里有水果做的甜食吗？

A: Yes, then I'd like you to try toffee apples. It tastes very nice.

B: 听着就挺诱人的。

A: Would you like to try some drinks?

B: 可以，我听说中国的茅台酒很有名，能尝尝那种酒吗？

A: That is what I am thinking. Let's wait for a second, and soon you will taste some really tasty Chinese food and wine.

B: 真是太好了。

篇章口译/Passage Interpretation

Passage 1

相关词语/Related Words and Expressions

on behalf of	代表
extend our sincere thanks	表达真挚的感谢

strengthen the friendship	加强友谊
consolidate	巩固
promote mutual understanding	促进相互理解
joint effort	共同努力
propose a toast to	提议祝酒

Interpret the following speech from English into Chinese.

 5-4.mp3

Ladies and Gentlemen:

I feel greatly honored to come here on my first visit to this beautiful city. On behalf of all the members of the delegation, I'd like to take this opportunity to extend our sincere thanks to our hosts for their earnest invitation and the gracious hospitality we have received here.

China and America have been enjoying good relations for a long time, both politically and economically. As far as our two companies are concerned, I am pleased to see that trade cooperation between us has been more consolidated since we started trading with each other 15 years ago. I am sure that the present cooperation will strengthen the friendship between us, and promote mutual understanding. I hope that our joint effort will expand future trade between us even further, and I am confident that it will.

Finally, on the occasion of this reception, I'd like to propose a toast to our friendship and cooperation, to the good health of everyone present here tonight. Cheers!

Passage 2

相关词语/Related Words and Expressions

West Lake	西湖
guest rooms	客房
hustle	喧嚣
central service desk	前台
check-in and check-out service	入住和退房业务
microwave oven	微波炉
safety deposit box	保险箱
fitness center	健身中心

Interpret the following speech from English into Chinese.

 5-5.mp3

Distinguished guests:

On behalf of the staff of our hotel, I'd like to extend our warm welcome to you.

Since it is probably your first time here, I will give you a brief introduction to our hotel. I would be delighted to make your stay pleasant and comfortable.

You may have already heard that West Lake is one of the most beautiful places in Hangzhou, where hundreds and thousands of people visit every day. Our hotel is located on the bank of the lake. It owns over 200 comfortable guest rooms with simple and graceful designs that bring a relaxing space to our customers to get away from the city hustle.

The central service desk on the first floor mainly deals with check-in and check-out service. Of course, you can also book plane tickets, rent a conference room or ask for taxi hiring service.

The restaurant on the second floor provides you with fine Chinese and Western Cuisines. This floor is also equipped with the large banquet hall, which can provide food for over 100 guests at the same time.

Recreation centers are on the third and fourth floor, where you can drink coffee and enjoy some nice wines, drinks and snacks. Besides, there is also a fitness center on this floor where you can do exercises for free.

The hotel facilities also include laundry room, microwave oven and safety deposit box, etc. To make your stay happy here with our best services is our ultimate goal. Finally, I wish you a pleasant stay in our hotel! Thank you.

参考译文/Reference Version

对话口译/Dialogue Interpretation

Dialogue 1

A: Excuse me, sir, are you Mr. Johnson from the United States?

B: 是的,我是大卫·约翰逊,你一定是张先生了。

A: Yes, I'm Zhang Ming. Mr. Johnson, I have been expecting you here. (提示:注意时态的用法。)

B: 谢谢你来接我,就叫我大卫吧,称呼名字要比称呼姓更亲切一些。

A: OK. Welcome to Shanghai. Did you enjoy your trip?

B: 还可以,但是比预期晚到了。碰上下大雨,我们的班机推迟起飞。我们在机场耽搁了几个小时等天放晴。

A: Well, you arrived safe and sound. I suppose you must be very tired after the long trip. We will drive you directly to the hotel.

B: 是的,我是很累了。但我明天就好了。

A: I hope so. We shall give you a dinner party tomorrow evening.

B: 你们真好,我很乐意前往。

A: Good, Mr. Wang, our general manager, sends his greetings to you but regrets that he is unable to come to meet you personally.

B: 没关系的。

A: I hope you'll have a pleasant stay. If there's anything you need, please let me know. I'll get a luggage cart and meet you over there at the carrousel.

B: 非常感谢。你帮我拿旅行包，我自己拿皮箱。

A: We have got everything. Our car is waiting outside. Let's go.

B: 好的，我们走吧。

Dialogue 2

A: 喂，您好！请问是客房服务部吗？

B: Hello, room service, what can I do for you?

A: 请您送点吃的到我房间。我要一瓶百威啤酒和一份牛肉汉堡。

B: May I have your name and room number?

A: 迈克，629房间。

B: OK, we will bring it right up.

A: 对了，我想拿几件衬衣去洗，还有一件外套要干洗，要多久才能洗好？

B: Your shirts can be cleaned by tomorrow morning. But the coat can't be ready till the day after tomorrow. Is this all right with you?

A: 没问题，我也不是很急。

B: OK, if you have more laundry, just put your clothes into the bag behind the bathroom door. We will collect them every morning.

A: 我知道了，谢谢！

B: If you need a quick service, just dial 5. Staff in the room service will take your clothes right away. Is there anything else I can do for you?

A: 还有一件事，你们这儿的叫醒业务如何办理？明天早上我有个重要的约会。

B: Just call the operator and tell him what time to ring you.

A: 我明白了，谢谢！再见！

B: You're welcome. Bye!

Dialogue 3

A: 路德先生，初到北京，想不想尝尝地道的北京风味？

B: Sure, Chinese food is very popular in Britain now.

A: 是吗？中国是个饮食文化十分丰富的国家，在这里，你可以品尝到各种口味的佳肴。这回我先带你尝尝北京菜，怎么样？

B: That is nice, when in Beijing, do as Beijing people do, right?

A: 现在我们来到的是一家老字号，叫全聚德，在全国各地有上百个连锁店，名气很大的。

B: Then what are the specialties in this restaurant?

A: 全聚德最有名的菜非烤鸭莫属了，此外还有火燎鸭心、卤水鸭膀、芥末鸭掌等一系列的特色菜。

B: It sounds fantastic. It seems that you are very familiar with this restaurant.

A: 是的，我可是这里的常客啊。有外国客人第一次来中国时，我就会带他们来这里。我们先来盘凉菜开胃，然后是北京烤鸭、干烧四鲜。您想吃点什么甜食呢？

B: Is there any sweet food made by fruit?

A: 那您就尝尝这里做的拔丝苹果吧，味道相当的地道。

B: OK, that sounds nice.

A: 咱们要不要喝点酒？

B: Oh, yes, I heard that Maotai is very popular in China. Could we try some?

A: 咱们想到一块儿去了。请稍等片刻，您马上就可以品尝到中国的美食和美酒了。

B: Good.

篇章口译/Passage Interpretation

Passage 1

女士们，先生们：

第一次来中国，我就来到了一座如此美丽的城市，深感荣幸。我谨代表代表团的全体成员，借这次机会，向在座的各位表示衷心的感谢！感谢你们的盛情款待。

无论是在政治上还是在经济上，中美两国长期以来一直都保持着友好的关系。就我们两个公司而言，我很高兴地看到，自从15年前我们开始建立贸易关系以来，双方在贸易领域的合作一直在不断加强和巩固。我相信，双方本次的合作将进一步加深我们之间的友谊，并推进双方的理解。我希望，而且我也相信，我们的共同努力将进一步拓展彼此的合作领域。

最后，借招待会之机，让我们举起手中的酒杯，为了两国之间的友谊，为了我们之间的合作和诸位的健康，干杯！

Passage 2

各位尊敬的来宾：

我谨代表本酒店的全体员工，热烈欢迎你们下榻本酒店。

由于可能这是你们第一次来到这里，所以我将首先向你们简略介绍一下本酒店的基本情况，希望能使你们在这里过得愉快舒心。

你们也许听说过，西湖是杭州市景色最为优美的地方之一。每天都有成千上万的游客慕名前来旅游，而本酒店就位于西子湖畔。我们拥有200多间客房，房间的装饰简约而不失典雅，安静的环境让您远离城市的喧嚣，是住宿的理想场所。

酒店一楼是前台，主要办理入住和退房等业务。当然，你们也可以在这里预订机票，办理租赁会议室或者出租车业务,等等。

　　酒店二楼为你们提供可口的中西餐。在这一层,我们还提供大型的宴会厅,能容纳上百名宾客同时用餐。

　　我们的康体娱乐中心位于酒店的三楼和四楼。在这里,你们可以享用咖啡、饮料、各种零食和名酒。此外,你们可以在此楼的健身中心免费锻炼身体。

　　而且,本酒店同时还配备有洗衣房、微波炉以及保险箱,等等。您在本酒店住得开心舒适就是我们最大的目标。最后,我衷心祝愿各位在此住得开心!谢谢!

第六章 礼仪讲话口译
Ceremonial Speech

一、热身阅读材料/Warming-up Reading Material

第一篇/Passage 1

Your Excellencies, distinguished guests, my lords, ladies and gentlemen,

It is with my great pleasure that I welcome you tonight to this magnificent castle. We warmly welcome you and your distinguished delegation to Wales. Wales is a small country compared with China. However, the Welsh people have made a significant contribution to the development of the United Kingdom and to the part the UK has played throughout the world.

I would like to ask you, Mr. Chairman, to help increase the awareness of Wales among Chinese companies that are considering their first move into Europe. For many years, Wales has been one of the most popular destinations for foreign investment in Europe. Investors in Wales have brought over £12 billion into the country and continue to reinvest once established.

Investors are not limited to US and Europe. Many companies from the Far East have chosen to establish their European operations here. Our Welsh Development Agency has set up an office in China. It demonstrates our commitment to your country. Welsh companies are increasingly focused on outward investment and establishing joint ventures with partners in China. China's accession to the World Trade Organization will present new opportunities for both our economies.

Developing special relationships with China is something to which we attach great importance, not only through trade but also in other areas such as science, education and justice. Recently, the Welsh Science Mission visited China. The visit raised Wales's profile in the Chinese scientific community. It also established an exchange scheme from which Welsh scientists will benefit.

Mr. Chairman, as you are aware, there has been contact at ministerial level. Not long ago, we were delighted to receive a visit from his Excellency Mr. Wen Jiabao. As you know already, his visit was a great success. In return, our Deputy First Minister has just accepted a generous invitation to lead a delegation to China later this year. They will be visiting Beijing, Shanghai and Guangzhou. They are looking forward to the visit.

These visits are clear signals of the highly productive relationship which Wales and China have developed. Judging by the crowd that have gathered here tonight, I'm very confident that the relationship will continue to grow. Thank you for taking the time to pay a visit to Wales in your busy and demanding program. We are honored by your presence here this evening and would ask you to take back with you the warmest good wishes from the people of Wales and the United Kingdom. May I propose a toast now?

课文词语/Words and Expressions from the Text

Your Excellencies	诸位阁下
first move into Europe	首次打入欧洲
Welsh Development Agency	威尔士经济发展署
Deputy First Minister	副首席部长
Welsh Science Mission	威尔士科学考察团
contact at ministerial level	部长级接触
busy and demanding program	紧张、繁忙的日程
propose a toast	举杯

第二篇/Passage 2

Looking Ahead

Mr. Chairman,

Ladies and gentlemen,

Today, we leaders of Asian and European countries meet here again. We will exchange views on cooperation in a wide range of areas and on the building of a new Asia-Europe partnership on the basis of equality and in a friendly manner. I wish to take this opportunity to express my heartfelt thanks to the host for the successful organization of this meeting.

This year marks the 10th anniversary of the Asia-Europe Summit. The last decade has witnessed the growth of Asia, profound changes in the international relations, and a growing trend toward multi-polarity.

Over the past decade, guided by the principles of mutual respect, conducting dialogue on an equal footing, making gradual progress and building consensus through consultation, Asia and Europe have carried out extensive and diversified cooperation and intensified political dialogue. We enjoy closer economic links, rapidly growing cooperation in social areas and expanding cultural and people-to-people exchanges. The Asia-Europe Summit has become a strategic platform for Asia and Europe to strengthen coordination, promote cooperation and pursue common development.

Facing the new development, people naturally place higher expectations on the Asia-Europe Summit, and it is imperative that we adopt a long-term strategy to plan our future cooperation. We should set the following goals for the Asia-Europe Summit:

We should make Asia and Europe more influential in addressing major global issues through expanding dialogues and cooperation.

We should promote diversified development of culture and civilization through enhanced mutual political trust.

We should further economic cooperation in substantive terms on the basis of equality and mutual benefit.

We should advance institutional building for cooperation that meets long-term needs as called for.

We should maintain the openness of the Asia-Europe Summit by increasing its outreach.

And we should consolidate and further develop the new Asia-Europe partnership in the interest of global peace and prosperity.

To build a new Asia-Europe partnership calls for new concepts and new methodology. When we look back on the past experiences and look into the future, I believe that a new partnership between Asia and Europe should be constructed on the basis of mutual respect, equality and mutual benefit. We should seek common ground while putting aside differences, enhance mutual understanding and trust, eliminate trade discrimination, oppose imposition of trade sanctions, and enhance technical exchanges and cooperation.

China attaches great importance to and has taken an active part in the process of Asia-Europe cooperation. Over the past 10 years, China has carried out many follow-up activities in counter-terrorism, the judicial sector, economy and trade, finance, science and technology, customs, environment and cultural exchanges. We have actively promoted multilateral cooperation, economic exchanges and dialogue between different cultures and civilizations.

We have carried out a major reform in foreign trade and formulated a set of related laws. We have reduced our tariffs to the average level of the developing countries. I am convinced that China's reform, opening-up and stability will provide the business community of Asian and European countries with tremendous investment and trade opportunities, thus making positive contributions to peace, stability and prosperity in Asia and the world at large.

We will continue to develop friendly relations and cooperation with our Asian and European partners and other countries in the world and work with them to build a world of harmony, durable peace and common prosperity. Let us join hands in building a new Asia-Europe partnership and shaping a more splendid future for our two continents and the world at large.

China will host a new Asia-Europe Summit next year. I look forward to meeting you again at the Summit in Beijing.

Thank you, Mr. Chairman.

课文词语/Words and Expressions from the Text

Asia-Europe partnership	亚欧伙伴关系
Asia-Europe Summit	亚欧首脑会议
multi-polarity	多极化

mutual political trust	政治互信
in substantive terms	以实质性的方式
outreach	超出范围、领域
equality and mutual benefit	平等互利
seek common ground while putting aside differences	求同存异
eliminate trade discrimination	消除贸易歧视
oppose imposition of trade sanctions	反对贸易制裁
follow-up activities	持续不断的行动
reduce tariffs	降低关税

二、口译实践/Interpretation Practice

句子口译/Sentence Interpretation

(一)英译汉/E-C

Interpret the following sentences into Chinese.

6-1.mp3

1. President Xi, thank you very much for your kind and generous remarks.

2. On behalf of the faculty and the staff and the students of the Harvard Business School I welcome all of you to our campus.

3. It is a great honor to have Professor and Mrs. Gao with us today.

4. I wish the first round of China-US Strategic and Economic Dialogues a crowning success.

5. My wife and I are privileged to have the opportunity once again to travel in China. We are grateful for the welcome we have received, especially for the kind of reception here at Fudan University.

(二)汉译英/C-E

Interpret the following sentences into English.

6-2.mp3

1. 您旅途辛苦了。
2. 久仰。
3. 我代表市政府欢迎各位朋友访问我市。
4. 对您的大力协助，我谨代表市政府表示衷心的感谢。
5. 请代我问候……先生。
6. 我一定向他转达您的问候和邀请。
7. 欢迎多提宝贵意见。

8. 请入席。
9. 晚上好，女士们、先生们。招待会很快就要开始了，请尽快就座。谢谢!
10. 招待会现在开始。
11. 全体起立，奏国歌。
12. 出席今天招待会的贵宾有……
13. 现在请……讲话。
14. 请允许我向远道而来的贵宾表示热烈的欢迎和亲切的问候。
15. 我们在此受到了隆重的接待和盛情的款待，我再次非常愉快地向我们的东道主表达深深的谢意。

对话口译/Dialogue Interpretation

Interpret the following dialogues alternatively into English and Chinese.

 6-3.mp3

A: 史密斯省长，史密斯夫人，欢迎你们访问广州，贵省与广东省一直有着密切的联系，去年两省更是建立了姐妹省的关系，让我们为两省间的友谊干杯!

B: Governor Huang, thank you very much for inviting us to this beautiful dinner, I feel much honored. This is my second visit to Guangdong and I feel that we are old friends already. I want to propose a toast to our host! Thank you for your hospitality. Let's drink to the great province — Guangdong! Cheers!

A: 自从我们建立了姐妹省关系以来，两省人民一直有着友好的往来，双边的贸易额也有大幅度的上升。相信史密斯省长此次的访问能进一步促进两省之间的友好关系。希望您此次在广东访问愉快。

B: Thank you! It's a very precious trip to me. I am very impressed with the rapid growth of Guangdong since my last visit here. I visited the New Baiyun International Airport and the Metro Station yesterday, which are among the best in the world. It's very amazing.

A: 谢谢您的称赞，广东省是中国率先实现现代化的几个省份之一，但广东的发展还有很长的路，我们希望能够向您以及您所率领的代表团学习宝贵的经验。

B: Our delegation has also learned a lot from our visit this time.

段落口译/Short Passage Interpretation

(一)英译汉/E-C

Interpret the following short passages into Chinese.

 6-4.mp3

Thank you, Director General Han, for those opening remarks. It's an honor to be co-hosting with you the "First US-China Forum on Sustainable Energy and the Environment". This meeting, which we hope is the first of many discussions between US and Chinese government and business officials, is a unique opportunity to exchange ideas and discuss areas of cooperation in the fields of energy and the environment, the two biggest challenges facing our countries in the 21 century.

6-5.mp3

Good morning.

It is a privilege to open this inaugural meeting of the Strategic and Economic Dialogue between the United States and China. I am especially pleased to join my co-chair, Secretary Geithner, and to welcome State Councilor Dai and Vice Premier Wang. I look forward to resuming the productive discussions I had with Councilor Dai, President Hu, and Premier Wen on my trip to China in February, and to build on President Obama and President Hu's meeting in London.

This is both a culmination, and a beginning. A culmination of actions taken by our predecessors 30 years ago, when the United States and China established formal diplomatic relations, and Deng Xiaoping launched China's economic reform and opening to the world. What followed was a blossoming of Chinese economic growth and diplomatic engagement that has allowed our nations to reach this place of opportunity today.

This dialogue also marks a beginning — the beginning of an unprecedented effort to lay the foundation for a positive, cooperative, and comprehensive U.S.-Chinese relationship for the 21st century.

(选自 Remarks at plenary session of the U.S-China Strategic and Economic Dialogue, Hillary Rodham Clinton, Secretary of State, Washington. DC. July 29, 2009.

(二)汉译英/C-E

Interpret the following short passages into English.

6-6.mp3

女士们，先生们：

早上好！

首先，请允许我代表清华大学计算机科学系06级一班全体同学对各位表示最衷心的感谢。很长时间以来，我们一直期望见到你们。今天正是一个不错的日子。

现在，我简单地介绍一下我的学校，因为我想把最精彩的部分留给各位去挖掘。清华大学闻名国内外。假如你想遇见最令人敬仰的学者，请你来清华。假如你想遇见最勤奋刻苦的学生，请你来清华。假如你想发现最迷人的校园，请你来清华。我衷心希望各位在清华过得愉快。

谢谢各位！

6-7.mp3

各位嘉宾,女士们,先生们:

我感到非常地荣幸和高兴能受邀为第三届中欧投资贸易洽谈会作总结。首先,我要祝贺本次洽谈会在上海的胜利召开,并对组委会全体成员为此次洽谈会付出的大量辛勤劳动,表示衷心的感谢。

当今世界,没有国家能够在闭关自守的状态下得到发展。中国的开放政策不仅对中国的经济发展起到了有力的推动作用,同时也为世界各国的企业到中国寻找商机、进行合作创造了有利条件。

篇章口译/Passage Interpretation

Passage 1

相关词语/Related Words and Expressions

国际译联	International Federation of Translators (FIT)
中国翻译协会	Translators Association of China (TAC)
第18届世界翻译大会	The XVIII FIT World Congress
有朋自远方来,不亦乐乎?	How happy we are to meet friends from afar.
四川5·12大地震	the earthquake in China's Sichuan Province on May 12
国际译联亚洲翻译家论坛	the FIT Asian Translators Forum
联合国教科文组织	United Nations Educational, Scientific and Cultural Organization (UNESCO)

Interpret the following passage into English.

6-8.mp3

刘习良会长在第18届世界翻译大会开幕式上的讲话

三年前,在芬兰坦佩雷市,国际译联宣布中国翻译协会为第18届世界翻译大会的主办组织,中国翻译协会从芬兰翻译协会手中接过了国际译联会旗。这将是首次在亚洲也是在中国举办的世界翻译界的盛会。我们深深感到,我们接过来的不仅仅是信任与荣誉,更是沉甸甸的责任。

为了做好东道主,中国翻译协会申办成功后,立即开始着手为第三年的大会做准备。在大会组委会的领导下,从国内外的宣传,到1500多篇学术论文摘要的评审,到会务细节的落实,到资金的筹措,我们尽了最大的努力。今天,我们高兴地迎来了来自70多个国家和地区的1500余名与会者。中国2000多年前的著名教育家孔子曾经说过:"有朋自远方来,不亦乐乎?"我们衷心希望,国际翻译界的同仁们通过这次大会互相交流,互相促进,增进彼此之间的友谊。在大会筹备过程中,我们就感受到了这种友谊。四川5·12汶川大地震后,国际译联以及芬兰、挪威、黎巴嫩、阿联酋、日本、加拿大、尼日利亚、阿尔巴尼亚等国的翻译工作者纷纷来函表示慰问，对此我们深表感谢。

中国翻译协会自1987年加入国际译联以后，一直积极参与国际译界的活动，其多名代表先后当选国际译联理事。1995年，中国译协发起组织了首届国际译联亚洲翻译家论坛，迄今已经举办5届，成为亚洲翻译界最重要的活动之一。过去三年，在筹办第18届世界翻译大会期间，中国译协广泛与国际翻译组织和机构建立了联系，进一步加强了沟通与合作。我们深切地感觉到，既然翻译工作是不同文化之间的桥梁，翻译工作者首先必须加强交流与沟通。我们知道，要切实提高全世界翻译工作者的地位，保障翻译工作者的权益，我们还有很多的工作要做。我们愿意与热心翻译事业的相关组织机构和广大翻译工作者一起，在国际译联的旗帜下共同努力，让翻译工作得到应有的尊重，让翻译的价值得到普遍的认可。

在世界翻译大会筹备过程中，联合国和联合国教科文组织等国内外众多机构和组织给予了高度关注，中国政府和上海市政府给予了大力支持，北京元培世纪翻译有限公司和上海东方翻译中心等业界企业给予了热情赞助。我谨在此对他们表示真诚的感谢。我也代表中国翻译协会感谢所有前来参加大会的同仁们，正是你们的到来让会议变得精彩。

愿4天的会议让大家不虚此行，祝国际翻译界大家庭三年一次的聚会圆满成功！

刘习良
中国翻译协会会长

Passage 2

相关词语/Related Words and Expressions

达沃斯	Davos
头脑风暴	brain-storm
盘尼西林	Penicillin
赢者通吃	winner takes all
面对改革之风，有人砌围墙，有人转风车	when the wind of change blows, some build walls, while others build windmills
双引擎	both the traditional and new engines of growth

Interpret the following passage into English.

6-9.mp3

维护和平稳定　推动结构改革　增强发展新动能
李克强2015年冬季达沃斯世界经济论坛特别致辞(节选)
2015年1月21日，达沃斯

尊敬的施瓦布主席，尊敬的索马鲁加主席，尊敬的各位贵宾，女士们，先生们，朋友们：

很高兴时隔5年再次来到达沃斯，出席世界经济论坛2015年年会。达沃斯小镇十分宁静祥和，但我们所处的世界却并不平静，国际社会需要应对新局势。我还听说，达沃斯曾经是治疗肺病的疗养地，因为盘尼西林的发明而转型。时至今日，达沃斯已经成为"头脑风暴"的智力中心，世界也需要新的"盘尼西林"来应对新挑战。

毋庸讳言，当今世界远非太平，地区热点、局部冲突以及恐怖袭击等此起彼伏，对人类社会构成现实威胁；全球经济又复苏乏力，主要经济体走势分化，大宗商品价格反复波动，通货紧缩迹象更雪上加霜。不少人对世界前景抱有悲观情绪，认为不仅和平与安宁出了问题，发展也难见曙光。

有哲人说过，当问题出现的时候，不能用曾经制造问题的办法去解决它。老问题的解决，不能再从对抗、仇恨、封闭中谋答案；新问题的应对，更要在对话、协商、合作中找出路。我们要吸取历史经验，运用时代智慧，寻求各方利益的最大公约数。人类在艰难时刻，总是能激起突破困境的勇气，迸发出变革创新的力量。

面对复杂的国际局势，我们主张要坚定维护和平稳定。今年是世界反法西斯战争胜利70周年。保持世界和平稳定，符合各国人民共同利益。二战后形成的国际秩序和普遍公认的国际关系准则，必须维护而不能打破，否则繁荣和发展也就无从谈起。国家间应摒弃冷战思维与零和游戏，"赢者通吃"是行不通的。任何地区热点和地缘冲突，都应坚持通过政治手段、以和平方式寻求解决。我们反对一切形式的恐怖主义。中国将继续走和平发展道路，维护地区稳定，无意与任何国家一争高下。世界各国都要像爱护自己的眼睛一样爱护和平，让文明理性正义之花开遍世界。

面对多元的世界文明，我们主张要共同促进和谐相处。文化多样性与生物多样性一样，是我们这个星球最值得珍视的天然宝藏。人类社会是各种文明都能盛开的百花园，不同文化之间、不同宗教之间，都应相互尊重、和睦共处。同可相亲，异宜相敬。国际社会应以海纳百川的胸怀，求同存异、包容互鉴、合作共赢。

面对多变的经济形势，我们主张要大力推动开放创新。国际金融危机爆发7年来的实践证明，唯有同舟共济，才能度过难关。在相互依存的世界里，各国有权根据自己的国情制定经济政策，但是也应加强同其他国家的宏观政策协调，扩大利益汇合点，实现共同发展。欧洲有谚语讲："面对变革之风，有人砌围墙，有人转风车。"我们倡导顺势而为，坚定不移推进自由贸易，旗帜鲜明反对保护主义，积极扩大区域经济合作，打造全球价值链，迎接新科技革命的到来。宏观政策固然重要，但结构性改革势在必行，这是国际社会的共识。尽管难度很大，但也应该坚持去做，这样才能形成全球创新合力，增强世界发展的新动能。

女士们，先生们，我知道，与会者对中国经济前景很关注，或许有人担忧受到中国经济速度放缓的拖累，还有人担忧受到中国经济转型的冲击。因此，我想多介绍中国的情况。

当前，中国经济发展进入新常态，经济由高速增长转为中高速增长，发展必须由中低端水平迈向中高端水平，为此要坚定不移地推动结构性改革。

应当看到，中国经济增速有所放缓，既有世界经济深度调整的大背景，也是内在的经济规律。现在，中国经济规模已居世界第二，基数增大，即使是7%的增长，年度现价增量也达到8000多亿美元，比5年前增长10%的数量还要大。经济运行处在合理区间，不一味追求速度了，紧绷的供求关系变得舒缓，重荷的资源环境得以减负，可以腾出手来推进结构性改革，向形态更高级、分工更复杂、结构更合理的发展阶段演进。这样，中国经济的"列车"不仅不会掉档失速，反而会跑得更稳健有力，带来新机遇，形成新动能。

刚刚过去的2014年，我们就是按照这个思路做的。面对下行压力，我们没有采取强刺激，而是强力推进改革，尤其是政府带头改革，大力简政放权，激发市场和企业的活力。全年GDP增长7.4%，在世界主要经济体中是最高的；城镇新增就业1300多万人，在经济放缓情况下不减反增，登记失业率、调查失业率都是下降的；CPI上涨2%，低于年初预期目标。事实说明，我们出台的一系列宏观调控政策是正确的、有效的。更重要的是结构性改革迈出新步伐。

不可否认，2015年，中国经济仍面临较大下行压力。在这种情况下如何选择？追求短期更高增长，还是着眼长期中高速增长，提升发展质量？答案是后者。我们将继续保持战略定力，实施积极的财政政策和稳健的货币政策，不会搞"大水漫灌"，而是更加注重预调微调，更好实行定向调控，确保经济运行在合理区间，同时着力提升经济发展的质量和效益。

我们正在采取有效措施防范债务、金融等潜在风险。中国储蓄率高达50%，能够为经济增长提供充裕资金。地方性债务70%以上用于基础设施建设，是有资产保障的。金融体制改革也正在推进。我在这里要向大家传递的信息是，中国不会发生区域性、系统性金融风险，中国经济不会出现"硬着陆"。

要看到，中国还是一个发展中国家，实现现代化还有很长的路要走。和平是中国发展的基础条件，改革开放和人民对幸福美好生活的追求是发展的最大动力。中国城乡和区域发展空间广阔，国内需求潜力巨大。以中高速再发展一、二十年，中国的面貌就会持续改善，也会给世界带来更多发展机遇。

中国经济要顶住下行压力，实现"双中高"，就需要对传统思维"说不"，为创新体制"叫好"，下决心推进结构性改革。要创新宏观调控，增添微观活力，调整城乡、区域和产业结构，促进比较充分的就业特别是年轻人的就业，改善收入分配和民生福祉。这需要付出艰辛努力，但是我们将不畏困难。只有沿着促改革、调结构的路子坚定走下去，才能使中国经济长期保持中高速增长，发展迈向中高端水平。

中国经济要行稳致远，必须全面深化改革。用好政府和市场这"两只手"，形成"双引擎"。一方面要使市场在资源配置中起决定性作用，培育打造新引擎；另一方面要更好发挥政府作用，改造升级传统引擎。

参考译文/Reference Version

句子口译/Sentence Interpretation

(一)英译汉/E-C

1. 习主席，感谢您热情洋溢的致辞。
2. 我谨代表哈佛大学商学院全体师生，向您表示热忱的欢迎。

3. 今天我们很荣幸地邀请到了高教授及夫人。

4. 祝第一轮中美战略与经济对话取得圆满成功。

5. 能再次来中国，我和夫人感到非常荣幸。感谢你们的热情欢迎，尤其感谢复旦大学对我们的盛情款待。

(二)汉译英/C-E

1. How is your journey/flight?

2. I've heard so much about you.

3. On behalf of the Municipal Government, I wish to extend our warm welcome to the friends who have come to visit our city.

4. On behalf of the Municipal Government, I wish to express our heartfelt thanks to you for your gracious assistance.

5. Please remember me to Mr....

6. I'll surely remember you and your invitation to him.

7. Your valuable advice is most welcome.

8. Please take your seat.

9. Ladies and gentlemen, good evening. The reception will start soon. Please get yourself seated. Thank you!

10. The reception will now begin.

11. All rise please, for the P.R.C. National Anthem.

12. The distinguished guests participating the reception are...

13. I have the honor to call upon...to make a speech.

14. Allow me to express my warm welcome and gracious greetings to our distinguished guests coming from afar.

15. It gives me great pleasure to express once again to our host my deep appreciation for the grand reception and generous hospitality we enjoy here.

对话口译/Dialogue Interpretation

A：Governor Smith, Mrs. Smith, welcome to Guangzhou. Your province and Guangdong has always enjoyed a close relationship. Last year, we became Sister Provinces. Here I propose，let's drink to the friendship between our two provinces!

B：黄省长，谢谢您邀请我们来参加这么美好的晚宴，我感到十分的荣幸。这已经是我第二次访问广东省，我感觉我们已经是老朋友了。让我们为主人干一杯！谢谢你们的热情款待；让我们为伟大的广东省干杯！干杯！

A：Since the establishment of the relationship of Sister Provinces, people of the two provinces have enjoyed friendly relations and the bilateral trade has increased greatly. I believe your visit this time will further promote our friendship. Wish you a very pleasant visit.

B: 谢谢！对我来说这是一次非常珍贵的访问。自我上次访问以来，广州的快速发展让我印象深刻。昨天，我参观了新白云国际机场和地铁站，它们都达到了世界上数一数二的水平。非常棒！

A: Thank you for your compliments. Guangdong Province is one of the first provinces that realized modernization in China, yet we still have a long way to go. We want to learn the precious experience from you and your delegation.

B: 我们的代表团在此次的访问中也学到了很多。

段落口译/Short Passage Interpretation

(一)英译汉/E-C

6-4 谢谢韩司长的开幕词。能够和您共同主持"第一届美中可持续能源与环境论坛"，我感到非常荣幸。我们希望这次会议会激发美中两国政府和商界领导人之间更多的讨论。这次会议将在能源和环境方面为我们提供独特的机会来交流想法、讨论合作的领域。能源和环境正是美中两国在21世纪面临的两个最大的挑战。

6-5 早上好！

十分荣幸能在美中两国之间的战略与经济对话首次会议开幕式上致辞。我特别高兴能与盖特纳部长共同主持会议，并欢迎王岐山副总理和戴秉国国务委员。我期待着继续我2月访华期间与戴秉国国务委员、胡锦涛主席和温家宝总理进行的富有成果的讨论，并在奥巴马总统和胡锦涛主席伦敦会晤的基础上取得更多成果。

这一对话既是一个结果又是一个开端。作为结果，它源于我们的前任们30年前所采取的行动。那时，中美两国建立了正式外交关系，邓小平发起了中国的经济改革并实行对外开放。随之而来的是中国经济的蓬勃发展和频繁的外交接触使我们两国到达今天的地步。

这一对话也标志着一个开端——一个为建立21世纪积极、合作、全面的美中关系奠定基础而做出前所未有的努力的开端。

(二)汉译英/C-E

6-6 Ladies and Gentlemen,

Good Morning!

First of all, please allow me to express the most heartfelt welcome to all of you on behalf of Class One, Grade 2006 in the Computer Science Department of Tsinghua University. We have been looking forward to seeing you for long. It is a wonderful day today.

Now I would like to brief my university to you since I want to leave the most wonderful for you to discover. Tsinghua University is well-known both at home and abroad. If you want to meet respectable scholars, please come to Tsinghua. If you want to meet the most industrious students, please come to Tsinghua. If you want to discover the most attractive campus, please come to Tsinghua. I do hope that you will enjoy your stay in Tsinghua.

Thank you!

6-7 Distinguished Guests, Ladies and Gentlemen,

It is my honor and pleasure to be invited to give the concluding remarks of the Third China-Europe Investment and Trade Fair. First of all, I would like to express my congratulations to the successful holding of the fair in Shanghai, and give my heartfelt thanks to all the members of the organizing committee for their hard word, which has made this fair possible.

In today's world, no country can possibly develop in isolation. China's opening-up policy has not only given a strong boost to China's economy, but also created favorable conditions for enterprises from all over the world to seek business opportunities in China and cooperate with Chinese enterprise.

篇章口译/Passage Interpretation

Passage 1

Speech of President Liu Xiliang at the Opening Ceremony of the 18th FIT World Congress

Three years ago, the FIT World Congress held in Tampere, Finland, voted Translators Association of China (TAC) as its host for the 18th FIT World Congress. This is the first time in its history that FIT decides to host a congress in Asia. Accepting the FIT flag from our Finnish colleagues, we felt both a great honor and a heavy responsibility.

TAC began preparations for the event immediately after the Tampere Congress. Under the leadership of the local organizing committee of the Congress, we have put all our efforts into promoting the Congress at home and abroad, assessing the 1,500-plus abstracts submitted, arranging financing for the Congress and making logistical arrangements. Now, we are happy to welcome more than 1,500 participants from over 70 countries and regions to the Congress. The ancient Chinese thinker and philosopher Confucius said, "How happy we are to meet friends from afar." We sincerely hope that this Congress will facilitate communication and exchanges among our translator and interpreter colleagues worldwide, and increase our friendship. Such friendship was felt during the preparation for this Congress. After the devastating earthquake in China's Sichuan Province on May 12, we received letters of condolences from the FIT and our colleagues from Finland, Norway, Lebanon, the United Arab Emirates, Japan, Canada, Nigeria, Albania and more. We appreciate your kind concerns very much.

Since TAC joined FIT in 1987, it has actively participated in international translation activities, and a number of its representatives have been elected Council Members of FIT. In 1995 TAC hosted the first FIT Asian Translators Forum. So far, the forum has been held five times in different countries and regions in Asia, and has become one of the most important regional activities in the translation field. In preparation for the Congress over the past three years, TAC has made wide contacts with translation organizations and institutions around the world, and increased its communication and coordination with them. We have the strong feeling that, as a bridge connecting different cultures, we translators and interpreters should first of all increase communications and exchanges among ourselves. We all know that a great deal needs to be done to enhance the status of translators and to uphold their intellectual and material interests. Under the guidance of FIT, we will work closely with other translation organizations and language workers to promote the recognition of translation as a profession, and further public appreciation of the value of translation.

Many domestic and international organizations, including the United Nations and UNESCO, have paid great attention to the Congress in the preparation process of FIT World Congress. The Chinese government and Shanghai Municipality have supported the event, and many enterprises, institutions and individuals, including the Beijing Yuanpei Century Translation Co. Ltd and the Shanghai Oriental Translation Center, have generously sponsored the Congress. I wish to express our sincere gratitude for their support. I would also like to thank, on behalf of the Translators Association of China, all Congress participants for coming to the event. Your presence makes the event more wonderful!

I sincerely believe that this four-day gathering of the international translation community will be crowned with success.

Liu Xiliang
President of Translators Association of China

Passage 2

Uphold Peace and Stability, Advance Structural Reform and Generate New Momentum for Development
Special Address by Chinese Premier Li Keqiang
At the World Economic Forum Annual Meeting 2015
Davos, 21 January 2015 (excerpted)

Professor Klaus Schwab,

President Simonetta Sommaruga,

Distinguished Guests,

Ladies and Gentlemen,

Dear Friends,

It gives me great pleasure to come to Davos again after five years to attend the World Economic Forum Annual Meeting 2015. Davos is a town of peace and serenity, yet the world outside is not tranquil. We need to work together to shape the world in a new global context. I was told that Davos used to be a resort for recuperation from lung diseases, and the later discovery of Penicillin changed that. Now it is a place for people to gather and pool their wisdom for "brain-storm". Personally, I find this more than relevant, because our world also needs new forms of "Penicillin" to tackle new challenges that have emerged.

Admittedly, the world today is by no means trouble-free. Regional hotspots, local conflicts and terrorist attacks continue to flare up, posing immediate threats to humanity. Global economic recovery lacks speed and momentum. Major economies are performing unevenly. Commodity prices are going through frequent fluctuations. And signs of deflation have made the situation even worse. In fact, many people are quite pessimistic about the future of the world. They believe that the guarantee of peace is weak, and the prospect of development is elusive.

A philosopher once observed that we cannot solve problems by using the same kind of thinking we used when we created them. Indeed, old problems can no longer be solved by clinging to the outdated mindset of confrontation, hatred and isolation. Dialogue, consultation and cooperation must be explored to find solutions to new problems. It is important that we draw lessons from history, and pool our collective wisdom to maximize the convergence of interests among countries. Fortunately, in time of hardship and trial, mankind have always been able to find the courage to get out of the predicament and move ahead through change and innovation.

In a world facing complex international situation, we should all work together to uphold peace and stability. This year marks the 70th anniversary of the victory of the world's anti-Fascist war. To uphold peace and stability serves the interests of all people in the world. The world order established after World War II as well as generally recognized norms governing international relations must be maintained not overturned. Otherwise, prosperity and development could be jeopardized. The Cold War and zero-sum mentalities must be abandoned. The "winner takes all" approach will not work. Regional hotspots and geopolitical conflicts must be resolved peacefully through political means. Terrorism, in all its manifestations, must be opposed. China remains committed to peaceful development and regional stability. And China has no intention to compete with other countries for supremacy. Peace in the world must be cherished the same as we cherish our eyes, so that the achievements and benefits of civilization, including reason and justice, will prevail.

In a world of diverse civilizations, we should all seek to live in harmony. Cultural diversity, like biodiversity, is a most precious treasure endowed to us on this planet. And human society is like a garden where all human civilizations blossom. Different cultures and religions need to respect and live in harmony with each other. While maintaining the natural close ties among those with whom we see eye to eye, we also need to respect those with whom we disagree. Like the vast ocean admitting all rivers that run into it, members of the international community need to work together to expand common ground while accepting differences, and seek win-win progress through inclusive cooperation and mutual learning.

In a world facing volatile economic situation, we should all work to promote opening-up and innovation. What has happened since the outbreak of the international financial crisis seven years ago proves that to work in unity is the surest way for countries to get over the difficulties. We are all interdependent in this world. While we each have the right to adopt economic policies in line with national conditions, we need to strengthen macro-policy coordination to expand the convergence of interests and achieve common development. A European proverb says, "When the wind of change blows, some build walls, while others build windmills." We need to act along the trend of our time, firmly advance free trade, resolutely reject protectionism, and actively expand regional economic cooperation. We need to build global value chains, and seize the opportunity of a new technological revolution. While the international community agrees on the importance of macro-policies to the economy, they also recognize the urgency to go ahead with structural reform. Structural reform must be carried through no matter how difficult it is, as it is an effective way to foster conditions conducive to global innovation and bring about new momentum for global development.

Ladies and Gentlemen, I know you are all interested in the outlook of the Chinese economy. Some of you may even worry about the possible potential impact of China's economic slowdown and transition. To ease your concerns, let me spend more time today on what is really happening in China.

The Chinese economy has entered a state of new normal. The gear of growth is shifting from high speed to medium-to-high speed, and development needs to move from low-to-medium level to medium-to-high level. This has made it all the more necessary for us to press ahead with structural reform.

It must be noted that the moderation of growth speed in China reflects both profound adjustments in the world economy as well as the law of economics. The Chinese economy is now the second largest in the world. With a larger base figure, a growth even at 7% will produce an annual increase of more than 800 billion US dollars at current price, larger than a 10% growth five years ago. With the economy performing within the reasonable range and the speed of growth no longer taken as the sole yardstick, the strained supply-demand relationship will be eased, the pressure on resources and the environment will be lowered, and more time and energy will be devoted to push forward structural reform. That means, the economy will enter a more advanced stage of development, with more sophisticated division of labor and a more optimized structure. If I could compare the Chinese economy to a running train, what I want you to know is that this train will not lose speed or momentum. It will only be powered by stronger dynamo and run with greater steadiness, bringing along new opportunities and new momentum of growth.

In 2014, we followed exactly the afore-mentioned approach. In the face of downward pressure, we did not resort to strong stimulus; instead, we vigorously pursued reforms, and the government in fact led these reforms by streamlining administration and delegating power. This has motivated both the market and the business sector. GDP grew by 7.4% for the whole year, the best among major economies in the world. Over 13 million new jobs were created in cities, with both registered and surveyed unemployment rates lower than the previous year. That is, we achieved growth in employment despite the economic slowdown. CPI was kept at 2%, lower than the target set at the beginning of the year. These outcomes prove that the host of macro-regulation measures China adopted has been right and effective. More importantly, new progress has been made in advancing structural reform.

Needless to say, the Chinese economy will continue to face substantial downward pressure in 2015. What shall we choose to do under such circumstances? Shall we go for even higher growth for the short term, or for medium-to-high growth and a higher quality of development over the long run? The answer is definitely the latter. We will maintain our strategic focus and continue to pursue a proactive fiscal policy and a prudent monetary policy. We will avoid adopting indiscriminate policies. Instead, we will put more emphasis on anticipatory adjustment and fine-tuning, do an even better job with targeted macro-regulation to keep the economy operating within the reasonable range, and raise the quality and performance of the economy.

We are taking effective measures to fend off debt, financial and other potential risks. China's high savings rate, which now stands at 50%, generates sufficient funds for sustaining economic growth. Besides, China's local debt, over 70% of which was incurred for infrastructure development, is backed by assets. And reform of the financial system is making progress. What I want to emphasize is that regional or systemic financial crisis will not happen in China, and the Chinese economy will not head for a hard landing.

It must be pointed out that China is still a developing country and still has a long way to go before achieving modernization. While peace is the basic condition for China's development, reform and opening-up along with our people's desire for a happy life constitute the strongest impetus propelling development. The space of development in China's rural and urban areas and various regions is enormous, and the country's domestic demand will simply generate great potential of growth. Development at medium-to-high speed for another ten to twenty years will bring even bigger changes to China and create more development opportunities for the world.

For the Chinese economy to withstand downward pressure, and to maintain medium-to-high speed of growth and achieve medium-to-high level of development, we need to say "no" to traditional mindset. We must encourage innovative institutions, and press ahead with structural reform. We need to adopt more innovative macro-regulation policies and develop a more vigorous micro economy. We need to promote more balanced development of industries, between rural and urban areas and among regions. We need to ensure relatively high employment rate, especially sufficient employment for the young people. And we need to optimize income distribution and raise the people's welfare. All this certainly calls for tremendous efforts. Yet we will stay undaunted in the face of difficulties. We will unswervingly press ahead with reform and restructuring to ensure that our economy maintains medium-to-high speed of growth and achieves medium-to-high level of development.

To ensure long-term and steady growth of the Chinese economy, we need to comprehensively deepen reforms. We need to properly use both the hand of the government and the hand of the market, and rely on both the traditional and new engines of growth. We will let the market play a decisive role in resource allocation to foster a new engine of growth. At the same time, we will give better scope to the role of the government to transform and upgrade the traditional engine of growth.

第七章 旅游观光口译
Tour and Sightseeing

一、热身阅读材料/Warming-up Reading Material

第一篇/Passage 1

The Statue of Liberty standing at the entrance to New York Harbor is a gift given by the people of France to the people of the United States over one hundred years ago in recognition of the friendship of the two nations established during the American Revolution. Over the years, the Statue of Liberty has become a representative of freedom and democracy of people everywhere.

To commemorate the centennial of the American Declaration of Independence, sculptor Frederic Auguste Bartholdi was commissioned by the French government to design a sculpture in 1876. The Statue was a joint effort between America and France and it was agreed upon that the American people were to build the pedestal, and the French people were responsible for the Statue and its assembly here in the United States. However, lacking of funds was a problem on both sides of the Atlantic Ocean.

In France, public fees, various forms of entertainment, and a lottery were among the methods used to raise funds. In the United States, benefit theatrical events, art exhibitions, auctions and prizefights assisted in providing needed funds. However, fund raising for the pedestal was going particularly slowly, so Joseph Pulitzer (noted for the Pulitzer Prize) opened up the editorial pages of his newspaper, *The World*, to support the fund raising effort. Pulitzer used his newspaper to criticize both the rich who had failed to finance the pedestal construction and the middle class who were content to rely upon the wealthy to provide the funds. Pulitzer's campaign of harsh criticism was successful in motivating the people of America to donate.

Financing for the pedestal was completed in August 1885, and pedestal construction was finished in April of 1886. The Statue was completed in France in July 1884. In transit, the Statue was reduced to 350 individual pieces and packed in 214 crates. The Statue arrived in New York Harbor in June of 1885 and was reassembled on her new pedestal in four months time. The pedestal was designed by architect Richard Morris Hunt and built on Bedloe's Island. The Statue's framework was engineered by Gustave Eiffel who later designed the famous tower in Paris, which bears his name. On October 28, 1886, in front of thousands of spectators, President Grover Cleveland dedicated the Statue of Liberty, which was officially titled Liberty Enlightening the World. Since then millions have made pilgrimage to visit her. She was a centennial gift ten years late.

Over the years, Americans shortened the name of the statue. They called it the Statue of Liberty, or Miss Liberty. The care and the administration of the statue changed several times. In 1956, the name of Bedloe's Island was changed to Liberty Island and became part of the Statue of Liberty National Monument.

The statue wears a loose robe. Her right hand holds a torch — a golden light. Her left hand holds a tablet which shows the date of the American Declaration of Independence — July 4th, 1776. The statue wears a crown on her head. The crown has 7 points, each of these rays representing the light of freedom. A chain representing oppression lies broken at her feet. The height from base to torch is 151 feet. The height from the foundation of the pedestal to the torch is 305 feet. She weighs 225 tons (100 tons of copper and 125 tons structural steel). Visitors may climb into her head for a spectacular view of New York Harbor. At night the statue is floodlighted, and the lights that shine from her torch can be seen for miles.

By the 1980, the statue badly needed repairs. Again people on both sides of the Atlantic Ocean cooperated to raise money. In May of 1982, President Ronald Reagan appointed Lee Iacocca to head up a private sector effort to restore the Statue of Liberty. Fund raising began for the $87 million restoration under a public/private partnership between the National Park Service and the Statue of Liberty-Ellis Island Foundation, Inc.. In 1984, at the start of the Statue's restoration, the United Nations designated the Statue of Liberty as a World Heritage Site. On July 5, 1986 the newly restored Statue re-opened to the public during Liberty Weekend, which celebrated her centennial. Today thousands of people still visit the statue every day. They reach the statue by boat. Many people climb the 354 steps to the crown. Or they ride up to observation areas in an elevator. Or they study the story of the statue in a museum in the monument.

课文词语/Words and Expressions from the Text

centennial	百年纪念
be commissioned(to)	受委托做某事
pedestal	(纪念碑)底座
auction	拍卖
prizefight	悬赏拳击
secondary skeletal framework	辅助框架
editorial pages	(报纸)社论版
centennial gift	百年庆典的礼物
National Park Service	国家公园管理处
World Heritage Site	世界遗产
restoration	修复

第二篇/Passage 2

Sightseeing in Beijing

A Modern Look for an Ancient City

Beijing, the Capital of the People's Republic of China, has a history of thousands of years and previously served as the capital of the Jin (1115 — 1234), Yuan (1271 — 1368), Ming (1368 — 1644), and Qing (1644 — 1911) dynasties. Beijing has many ancient architectural complexes such as the 600-year-old Imperial Palace; the Summer Palace, which is China's largest imperial garden; famous institutions of higher learning such as Peking and Tsinghua Universities; and National Library of China, China's largest library, with a collection of paintings, calligraphy, classical books, periodicals and materials going back through the ages.

Beijing today covers an area of 16,808 square kilometers, 23 times that of 50 years ago. Roads have been widened and high buildings have been built in the city. Beijing has become an international metropolis with a population of 13.82 million.

The central north-south axis of Beijing was determined according to the principles of traditional architecture 700 years ago, when the city, then known as Dadu (the Great Capital) was built by Kublai Khan, the founding emperor of the Yuan Dynasty. In the 16th century, many structures were built along the 7.8-kilometer central axis, including *Yongdingmen* Gate, the Forbidden City, and the Drum and Bell Towers. Ten years ago, the International Olympic Sports Center and Asian Games Village were built on the northern section of the axis, which by that time had been extended to 13 kilometers.

In the 1970s, Beijing's first Underground Railroad line was completed. When the *Fuxingmen* Overpass was built, Beijingers had their first look at a clover-leaf overpass. Since then, 124 overpasses have been built in Beijing, and the overpasses at *Sanyuan*, *Siyuan*, and *Tianningsi* compete for magnificence.

The second and third ring roads have been turned into high-speed highways, and the Beijing-Shijiazhuang, Beijing-Tongzhou, Capital Airport, and Badaling Expressways have now opened to traffic. The total length of highways and expressways in Beijing has reached 3,800 kilometers.

Twenty years ago, Beijing built 4.11 million square meters of housing a year, but housing was still a problem for many. Some people lived in compounds occupied by many families or in simple dwellings. Since the implementation of the reform and opening policies, great changes have taken place with each passing day.

In 1981, construction began on the Great Wall Sheraton Hotel, designed by Beckert International, an American company, and during the following decade, a series of hotels, covering a total of five million square meters of ground space was completed by introducing foreign funds and encouraging organizations and individuals to develop the service industry in

Beijing. In addition to the major downtown business centers such as *Wangfujing, Xidan*, and Qianmen, there are 80 modern shopping centers, each having a commercial floor space of 10,000 square meters.

Over the past 20 years, the municipal government of Beijing has invested 100 billion *yuan* in water, power, central heating, roads, and telecommunications. Beijing now has 14 satellite towns and 371 residential areas. The annual completion of housing area exceeds 15 million square meters, and the average living space per person has increased from six square meters 20 years ago to 14.85 square meters.

Although Beijing has been modernized, it still retains its historical and cultural aspects. The unique features of 25 protected historical and cultural areas in Beijing have long attracted tourists from home and abroad.

In and around Beijing there are 30 rivers and 26 lakes that not only supply water for the city but also serve as scenic spots. In order to protect and recreate the look of the ancient capital, a large sewage-treatment project is now under way, using an investment of 1 billion *yuan*, on the city's major rivers and lakes, including the city's Moat, *Changhe* and *Tongzi* River, and *Yuyuantan* and *Beihai* Lakes.

Some 62 percent of the Beijing area is hilly. Twenty years ago, Beijing suffered from dust pollution, but great changes have taken place since the forestation project started in and around Beijing and Tianjin in 1986. At the end of 1998, 39 percent of the urban area of Beijing was covered with trees and flowers. The green space in Beijing now averages 8.18 square meters per person, and the dust has decreased from 21 tons per square kilometer per month to 16.5 tons per square kilometer in the center of the city. The Miyun Reservoir, one of the major water supplies of Beijing, has 60.4 percent forest coverage.

Some Major Places of Interest in Beijing

The Great Wall

Known as the fourth wonder of the world, the Great Wall runs from Shanhaiguan Pass on the shores of Bohai Bay at the east end to Jiayuguan Pass in Gansu Province at the west end. It rises and falls, twists and turns along the ridges of mountain chains in northern China, stretching for 12,000 *li* (6,000km) across seven provinces. Therefore, it is known in China as the "Ten-Thousand-*Li* Great Wall".

The construction of the Wall began during the Warring States Period in the 5th century B.C. At that time, some ducal states in north China began to build defense walls in their own land in order to ward off the nomadic tribes further north. In the 3rd century B.C. when Emperor *Qin Shihuang* conquered all the other states and became the first emperor of a unified China, he had these walls linked up and extended. Reinforcement and renovations were carried out during successive dynasties. In the Ming times (14th~17th century) the Wall underwent major repairs and became what it is today.

The section best preserved and most often visited is the Great Wall at Badaling. Built solidly with regular lath stone and large-sized bricks, the Wall at Badaling is 8.5 meters high and 5.7 meters broad. Five horses or ten people can walk along it abreast. There are ramparts, embrasures, peepholes and apertures for shooting. Two-storied watchtowers were built in at 100-meter intervals. The top-story watchtowers were designed for observing enemy movements.

It is estimated that some 180 million cubic meters of tamped earth and 60 million cubic meters of stone and bricks must have been used to build the Great Wall. So it was an immense engineering project to obtain, transport the building material and construct the Great Wall.

Today, as the most important historical monument in China and one of the world's famous architectural wonders, the Great Wall attracts large number of tourists from home and abroad each year.

Tian'anmen Square

Tian'anmen Square is located right in front of the Imperial Palace in the center of Beijing. It is one of the largest squares in the world and its 440,000-square-meter area can accommodate half a million people at one time. To the north of the square is the magnificent Tian'anmen Gate-tower. At the south is *Qianmen* or "Front Gate". Both these gate-towers date back to the 17th century and typify classical Chinese Architecture. Now the square is flanked by massive modern buildings, the Great Hall of the People on the west, and the Museum of Chinese History and the Museum of Chinese Revolution on the east. At the center of the square stands the Monument to the People's Heroes. To the south of the Monument lies Chairman Mao Memorial Hall. The bright Five-star red flag flies high on the square.

On the white marble base with fine bas-reliefs and 10-meter high red walls stands the splendid double-eaves and yellow-glaze-tiled Tian'anmen Gate-tower. The gate used to be the outer entrance to the Imperial Palace. It has five archways with the central one used exclusively by the emperor. A moat named Golden Water River flows along the foot of the Gate-tower and spanned by five carved marble bridges, one for each archway. Each of the bridge is guarded by two stone lions and two towering stone pillars carved with cloud and dragon motifs. All these match perfectly and form a single unit of masterpiece of art signifying power and beauty.

During the Ming (1368 — 1644) and Qing (1644 — 1911) dynasties, Tian'anmen Gate was where the emperors issued imperial edict and held grand celebrations. In modern Chinese history, many important historical events took place on Tian'anmen Square. For example, the well-known May Fourth Movement in 1919, the December Ninth Patriotic Students Movement in 1935, the grand ceremony to celebrate the founding of the People's Republic of China on October 1, 1949 are all associated with the name of Tian'anmen.

The Summer Palace

The Summer Palace is situated 15 kilometers northwest of Beijing. It is the largest and best-preserved imperial Chinese gardens.

The Summer Palace is famous not only for its beautiful scenery but also for its long history. Originally, it was a natural lake formed by spring water and surrounded by a hill called the Jar Hill. In 1153, Wanyan Liang, an emperor of the Jin Period, made it an imperial palace for short stays when he was away from the capital. In the Yuan Dynasty, the lake was enlarged and became a reservoir providing water for the court and the capital. In the Ming Dynasty, the royal family had a temple built on the hill, which was named the Perfect and Quiet Temple. In 1750, in the celebration of the 60th anniversary of his mother's birthday, Emperor Qianlong, the fourth emperor of the Qing Dynasty, had the Perfect and Quiet Temple rebuilt. He renamed the hill the Longevity Hill and the reconstructed garden the Clear Ripples Garden. In 1860 the garden was burned down by Anglo-French invasion forces. In 1888, when Emperor Guangxu was in reign, Dowager Cixi had it reconstructed by embezzling the navy funds under the pretext of building a navy training site, but it was never once used for that purpose. Cixi renamed it Summer Palace and made it her residence for the greater part of the year. In 1900, the palace garden was again badly damaged by the allied forces of the eight imperialist powers. It was reconstructed in 1903 and opened as a public park in 1924 — 13 years after the overthrow of the last imperial dynasty.

The palace garden covers an area of 290 hectares, three-fourths of which is water, mainly Kunming Lake at the foot of the Longevity Hill. It has more than 3,000 halls, mansions, towers, pavilions, corridors, walkways, bridges and other structures, each having its unique style, but they all bend harmoniously with the landscape. They are many tourist attractions in the garden.

The Hall of Benevolence and Longevity was where the Empress Dowager and Emperor Guangxu handled court affairs, received government officials and foreign diplomatic envoys.

The Hall of Happiness and Longevity was where Cixi lived during her stay at the Summer Palace.

One of the marvels of the Summer Palace is the Long Corridor which runs for 728 meters along the northern shore of the Kunming Lake and connects with the buildings at the southern foot of the Longevity Hill. It is the longest garden corridor in China consisting of 273 sections. On its cross-beams, the ceiling and side pillars are all paintings of historical and legendary figures, famous Chinese landscapes, flowers and birds, and there are more than 14,000 pieces of pictures in all. So it is actually an art gallery.

At the west end of the long corridor is the Marble Boat. The 36-meter long "boat" was carved out of a piece of huge marble. It is where Cixi relaxed in mid-summer.

The first attraction on entering the park is the marble Seventeen-arch Bridge spanning the blue-green waters of the lake in a pleasant curve. All the 500 balusters along its 150-meter length are topped by more than 540 carved lions, each in a different pose. The bridgeheads are guarded by pairs of legendary formidable animals.

With the background of the Jade Spring Hill and the Western Hill in the distance and the Longevity Hill, the Kunming Lake and numerous graceful garden buildings, flowers and trees inside the garden, the Summer Palace has the poetic touch of a traditional Chinese painting. It is a classic example Chinese Garden-building art.

The Temple of Heaven

Located in southeast Beijing and built in 1420 during the Ming Dynasty, the Temple of Heaven used to be the place where the emperors of Ming and Qing Dynasties worshiped heaven for good harvest and performed sacrificial rituals. It is now one of the largest public parks in the capital.

The Temple of Heaven covers an area of 273 hectares. It consists of three main structures on a north-south axis: the Hall of Prayer for Good Harvest in the north, the Imperial Vault of Heaven in the center and the Circular Mound Altar in the south.

The Temple of Heaven is mostly sky blue in color. It has two surrounding walls, both of which are round to the north and square to the south. Such a pattern symbolizes the ancient belief that the heaven is round and the earth square.

The main temple, the Hall of Prayer for Good Harvest, is a lofty cone-shaped wooden structure joined together entirely by wooden bars, laths, rafters, and brackets without the use of iron or bronze. This brilliant example of ancient Chinese architecture measures 38 meters in height and 30 meters in diameter. Set with deep blue glazed tiles, the roof is crowned at the top with a huge golden ball. The triple-eaves of the roof are supported by 28 massive wooden pillars. The four central columns, called the "Dragon-Well Pillar", represent the four seasons. Surrounding these four columns, there are 2 rings, one inside the other, of 12 columns each: the inner ring symbolizes the 12 months and the outer, the 12 divisions of day and night; the pillars of the inner and the outer rings together stand for the 24 solar terms or the 24 divisions of the solar year in the traditional Chinese calendar. It was in this hall that the emperors of Ming and Qing Dynasties prayed for good harvest every year on the 15th of the first month of the lunar year.

The Imperial Vault of Heaven, circular structure with deep blue glazed tiles, was used to house the memorial tablets of the "Supreme Ruler of Heaven". Around it is the Echo Wall, where the acoustic effects are such that a whisper at one end of the wall can be heard at some distance at the other end.

The Circular Mound Altar is a 3-tiered circular marble terrace enclosed by marble balustrades on each tier. The platform is laid with marble stones in nine concentric circles, and everything is arranged in multiples of the number 9. Every year on the winter solstice sacrifices were offered at the altar by the emperor who, surrounded first by the circles of the terrace and their railings and then by the horizon, seemed to be in the center of the universe.

课文词语/Words and Expressions from the Text

ancient architectural complexes	古建筑群
overpass	高架道路；天桥
clover-leaf overpass	四通八达的立交桥
compound	这里指北京的"四合院"
sewage-treatment	污水处理
forestation	造林
moat	护城河
reinforcement	加固
renovation	修复
lath stone	条石
rampart	城墙
embrasures	垛口
apertures for shooting	射击孔
historical monument	历史名胜
accommodate	容纳
the Great Hall of the People	人民大会堂
the Museum of Chinese History	中国历史博物馆
the Military Museum of the Chinese People's Revolution	中国人民革命军事博物馆
the Monument to the People's Heroes	人民英雄纪念碑
Chairman Mao Memorial Hall	毛主席纪念堂
double-eaves	重檐的
glaze-tiled	琉璃瓦的
imperial edict	诏令
the Perfect and Quiet Temple	圆静寺
the Longevity Hill	万寿山
the Clear Ripples Garden	清漪园
embezzling the navy funds	挪用海军军费
the allied forces of the eight imperialist powers	八国联军
the Hall of Benevolence and Longevity	仁寿殿
the Hall of Happiness and Longevity	乐寿堂
the Marble Boat	石舫
the Seventeen-arch Bridge	十七孔桥
legendary formidable animals	传说中的怪兽
the Jade Spring Hill	玉泉山

the Hall of Prayer for Good Harvest	祈年殿
the Imperial Vault of Heaven	皇穹宇
the Circular Mound Altar	环丘坛
wooden bars, laths, rafters and brackets	木条、板条、椽和斗拱
24 solar terms	24 个节气
solar/lunar year	阳历/阴历年
memorial tablet	牌位
the triple eaves of the roof	三重檐屋顶
Supreme Ruler of Heaven	皇天上帝
the Echo Wall	回音壁
marble balustrade	大理石栏杆
winter solstice	冬至
offer sacrifices to	祭祀
railing	栏杆；围栏；扶手

二、口译实践/Interpretation Practice

句子口译/Sentence Interpretation

(一)英译汉/E-C

Interpret the following sentences into Chinese.

 7-1.mp3

1. Many islands succumb to tourism overkill and have lost its natural beauty.

2. The seascape is one reason the islands tied for the third place in a new ranking of the world's best-kept island destinations.

3. A cool climate and remote location have kept many tourists away, leaving "lovely, unspoiled islands" that are "a delight to the traveler".

4. The islands have spectacular sea cliffs; pristine beaches; fascinating geology; over a million breeding seabirds; regular sightings of killer whales.

5. The park abounds in wildlife and its features appeal to the naturalists, the plant lovers or those who would do nothing more than relax in beautiful surroundings.

(二)汉译英/C-E

Interpret the following sentences into English.

7-2.mp3

1. 旅游业是现代发展最快的行业之一，它的发展速度已经超过世界经济发展的水平。
2. 旅游业不仅让服务行业受益，而且对旅游商品的制造业有利。它不是一个单一的行业，而是包含了交通业、住宿业、餐饮业、导游服务、银行业、制造业、教育等多种行业。
3. 上海被誉为"万国建筑博览会"，最吸引人的建筑作品是外滩的高楼大厦，黄埔江畔的东方明珠也是游客常去的地方。登上观光层眺望，无限风光，尽收眼底。
4. 该宾馆是一家四星级涉外宾馆。它提供许多精致舒适的房间，都装有闭路卫星电视和中央空调。它还提供多功能厅、会议室、华丽的宴会厅以及娱乐中心和商务中心。
5. 这些旅游项目集观光、度假和文化娱乐于一体，使游客有机会了解中国文化，尽情观赏所游之地的风土人情，尤其是当地的历史名胜和人文景观。

对话口译/Dialogue Interpretation

Interpret the following dialogues alternatively into English and Chinese.

7-3.mp3

A: 杰克逊先生，今天天气不错，对吧？这几天我们一直在谈判，都没有空出来转转，今天我带你去西湖看看怎么样？

B: That's a good idea. I heard that West Lake is a very famous scenic spot in China and there are many scenic spots around it, right?

A: 是的，西湖是浙江最著名的旅游景点之一，每天都有成千上万的游客前来观光旅游。

B: Is it far away from here?

A: 不是很远，我们驱车半小时就到了。

B: OK, let's go now. I can't wait any more.

(Half an hour later)

A: 你看，前面就是著名的西湖了。很多人把西湖比作"人间天堂"，这足以让人想象它有多美了。

B: I see. It is definitely a very nice lake. "The Paradise on Earth" is a good way of putting it. May I ask how large is this lake?

A: 西湖南北长3.3公里，东西宽2.8公里，面积大约为5.66平方公里。

B: What is this long path in the middle of the lake?

A: 那就是著名的白堤。由唐代大诗人白居易在公元821年修建而成。那边一条是苏堤，由北宋时期著名诗人苏东坡修建而成。

B: I notice that there are many pavilions, bridges, flowerbeds, and mountains. They compose a really beautiful picture.

A: 西湖边上有十大著名景点，比如说"花港观鱼"、"苏堤春晓"等。

B: They are fascinating names, poetic and picturesque.
A: 没错，我们一个一个参观吧。
B: OK, I think it will be an unforgettable trip.

段落口译/Short Passage Interpretation

(一)英译汉/E-C

Passage 1

Interpret the following short passages into Chinese.

7-4.mp3

Wangfujing, located in the *Dongcheng* District of Beijing, is one of the Chinese capital's most famous shopping streets. Much of the road is off-limits to cars and other motor vehicles, and it is not rare to see the entire street full of people. Since the middle of the Ming Dynasty there have been commercial activities in this place. In the Qing Dynasty, eight aristocratic estates and princess residence were built here, soon after that a well full of sweet water was discovered, thereby giving the street its name "Wang Fu" (means aristocratic residence), "Jing"(means well).

Wangfujing is now home to around 280 famous brands of Beijing, such as *Shengxifu* hat store, *Tongshenghe* shoe shop. A photo studio which took formal photos for the first leadership of new China is also located on the street.

The Wangfujing Night Market has a selection of exotic street food on the Snack Street. Deep fried insects, scorpions, and sea creatures can be found, along with other animals and animal parts not ordinarily consumed as food in the west. But while these exotic snacks can be found, other more common foods, such as *Tanghulu*(sugar-coated haws), or other candied fruits make up the majority of the food sold on the street.

Passage 2

7-5.mp3

In Provence, you will find dishes made with garlic, sweet tomatoes, and olive oil. Provence is also famous all over France for its delicious wine. People there are well-known for keeping their traditions alive. They hold many celebrations, dances, and festivals. You can even see a bullfight in the towns of Arles and Nimes, or enjoy poetry at Orange's ancient Roman Theater with the stars shining above you. Although Paris is the usual destination for travelers in France, you would be making a good choice by heading down south to Provence.

(二)汉译英/C-E

Interpret the following short passages into English.

🎵 **7-6.mp3**

1. 黄果树大瀑布非常耐看，无论本地人或是外地来宾共同的体会便是：此瀑布百看不厌，它那变化多端的景色，往往因观赏的方位、角度相异而起变化。任何角度都可呈现一幅独特的画面。大瀑布组成的特大水帘的气势，令人惊心动魄而萌生一种崇高而壮丽之美感。

🎵 **7-7.mp3**

文武庙位于潭北山腰上，因供奉孔子(文圣)、岳飞及关羽(武圣)而得名。殿宇沿山势而建，分前、中、后三殿，占地广阔，色彩以黄金色为主，为中国宫殿式庙宇，气势雄伟。孔雀园位于环湖公路北侧，园内分三个区：孔雀园、瑞鸟园和蝴蝶博物馆。园内饲养400多只孔雀，各类飞禽及标本20万只。然后是光华岛。光华岛位于日月潭中心，为日月潭分界。岛上有座月下老人亭，为旅客必游之地。

篇章口译/Passage Interpretation

Interpret the following passage into English.

🎵 **7-8.mp3**

秦始皇兵马俑是当地村民1974年3月在田里打井时偶然发现的。经考古学家探测，认定为秦代兵马俑坑。后经勘探和试掘，共发现三处兵马俑坑，按发现时间把它们分别定名为兵马俑一号、二号、三号坑。三个坑总面积为22,780平方米。

这一发现震惊中外。为了保护这些罕见的历史文物，1975年，国务院批准在一号坑原址上建一座占地16,300平方米的博物馆。1979年国庆节，博物馆正式对外开放。此后，兵马俑3号坑、2号坑展厅和铜车马馆也陆续建成，并对外开放。现在，秦始皇兵马俑博物馆被列为中国十大名胜之一，被联合国教科文组织列为世界文化遗产。

一号坑呈长方形，东西长230米，南北宽62米，深5米，面积16,620平方米。一号坑内的兵马俑完全按当时的实战军阵排列。坑道的东端长廊里站立着三排武士俑，每排70，共210件。这些武士身着战袍，脚打绑腿，手持弓弩，面向东方，是整个军阵的前锋部队。其后是十道土夯的隔墙隔成的11个过道，里面排列着步兵与车兵相间的38路纵队。兵俑全部身穿盔甲，手持长兵器。他们是整个军阵的主力部队。另外，在主力部队的南北和西头，分别有一排武士俑，他们都面朝外，分别是主力部队的左后翼和后卫部队。在试掘的960平方米范围内，出土武士俑500多个，战车4辆，挽马24匹。据测量，一号坑共有兵马俑6,000多件。

二号坑呈曲尺形，面积6,000平方米，是一个由四个独立的单元、四个不同的兵种编制而成的混合军阵。第一单元是由334个弩兵组成的小方阵。第二单元是由64乘战车组成的方阵。每乘战车有三个军士。第三单元是由19乘战车和100个兵俑组成的方阵。第四单元是由6乘战车、124个骑兵和鞍马组成的方阵。四个单元既是一个互相紧密相连的大军阵，又是四个独立的、灵活机动的、能攻能守的小军阵。据估计，二号坑可出土兵马俑1,500多件。

三号呈凹字形，面积520平方米，仅有4马1车和68尊陶俑。三号坑内的兵俑是环绕周壁面对面夹道排列。他们手持一种专门用于仪仗的无刃长兵器。同时，坑内还发现有用于战前占卜和祈祷的动物骨头和鹿角残迹。因此，考古学家认为3号坑可能是整个军阵的指挥部。

三个坑呈"品"字形排列，形成一个庞大的军事场面：8,000兵马，浩浩荡荡，待命征战，显示出一幅气势磅礴、雄伟壮观的动人场面。这是秦始皇为自己所造的一支守陵的卫戍部队。

三个坑内的陶俑都仿真人塑造，全身彩绘。兵俑的队列布局按将军、武官、武士等不同级别和步兵、车兵、骑兵等不同兵种有序排列，他们容貌各异，个个神态逼真、栩栩如生，显示了中国古代雕塑艺术的高超技艺和民族风格。

除了数以千计的兵马俑外，三个坑内出土了数以万计的各种青铜武器，主要有刀、剑、矛、戈、戟、弓、箭、弩、镞。特别引人注目的是一把青铜剑，虽在地下埋藏了2,000多年，仍不生锈，至今光亮如新，锋利无比，一次能划透20张纸。经检测，这把剑为铜、锡合金，并含有十多种稀有金属，表面经过铬的处理，能防锈防腐。这表明2,000多年前中国的铸造工艺和冶金技术已达到惊人的高度。

1980年12月，考古工作者在秦始皇陵西侧20米处发现了两组大型彩绘铜车马，更是给博物馆增添了新的光彩。根据发现顺序，把这两组铜车马分别命名为一号和二号车。两组铜车均为单辕车，各配四匹马。一号车为"高车"，驭手和乘车的人均站立车上。二号车叫"安车"，分前后两乘室，中间相隔。驭手坐前乘室，主人坐后乘室。后乘室前面及左右两侧各有一车窗，后面留门，可能是供秦始皇灵魂出游时乘坐的。铜车马为真人、真马二分之一大小，由3,400多个零件组成，并有1,720件金银饰品，显得华丽富贵。据初步研究，铜车马的制造采用了铸、焊、铆、镶、刻等多种工艺。

铜车马的制作工艺高超，造型艺术逼真，是我国历史上最早、制作最精美的青铜珍品，也是世界考古发现的最大青铜器，证明秦代的工艺已经达到了很高的水平。

课文词语/ Words and Expressions from the Text

兵马俑	Terra-cotta Warriors And Horses
考古探测	archeological exploration
试掘	test excavation
军阵	battle array/battle formation
穿着战袍、打着绑腿	wear battle tunics and puttee
前锋	vanguard
主力部队	main body
后卫	rear guard
两翼	flank guard

战车	chariot
挽马	drafting horse
铠甲	armor
卫戍部队	garrison army
步兵	foot solider/infantry man
骑兵	cavalryman
青铜武器	bronze weapons
长兵器	long shaft-weapon
剑、矛、戈、戟	sward, spear, dagger-ax, halberd
弩、箭、簇	crossbow, arrow, arrowhead
铜锡合金	an alloy of copper and tin
稀有金属	rare metal
经过铬处理	coated with chromium
防腐防锈	prevent corrosion and rust
冶金技术	metallurgical technique
单辕车	single-shaft chariot
前乘室	the front compartment
后乘室	the rear compartment
华丽富贵	luxurious and graceful
铸、焊、铆	casting, welding, riveting
镶、刻	embedding, chiseling

参考译文/Reference Version

句子口译/Sentence Interpretation

(一)英译汉/E-C

1. 很多岛屿都因为旅游破坏过重而失去了自然美。

2. 海景是该岛名列最新榜单"世界保存最完好的岛屿"季军的原因之一。

3. 这里的凉爽气候以及偏远的位置让很多游客无法亲近,反而成为让"游客们十分欢喜"的"孤独、完整的岛屿"。

4. 此岛拥有壮观的海崖,质朴的海滩,迷人的地理景色,上百万只饲养的海鸟,而且虎鲸时常出没。

5. 公园里有大量的野生动物,公园的特色吸引着博物学家、植物热爱者,以及那些只是到这优美环境中休闲放松的人们。

(二)汉译英/C-E

1. Tourist industry is one of the fastest growing industries in modern times. Its growth rate has exceeded that of the worldwide economy.

2. Tourism benefits not only the service sector, but also manufacture of tourist commodities. It is not a single trade, but a comprehensive one of consisting of many enterprises such as transportation, accommodation, guiding service, banking, manufacturing, education and so on.

3. Shanghai is crowned as the exhibition of world architecture. The most attractive architecture works are the high buildings in the Bund. The Oriental Pearl TV Tower standing by Huangpu River is also a frequent tourist destination. When standing in its sightseeing floor and looking around in a distance, you will enjoy the charming styling of the city and admire the endless smoothing beauty of the city, which you'll find hard to turn away from.

4. This hotel is a four-star hotel authorized to accommodate foreign guests. It has many elegant and comfortable rooms all equipped with close-circuit satellite TV and central air-conditioner. It also has multifunctional halls, conference rooms, splendid banquet halls as well as recreation centers and business service centers.

5. All these tourist programs have been designed to incorporate sightseeing, vacationing and cultural activities, thus providing tourists with an opportunity to learn about Chinese culture and to enjoy the local customs and scenery, particularly the places of historic interest and cultural heritage.

对话口译/Dialogue Interpretation

A: Mr. Jackson, it is a nice day, isn't it? We have been negotiating over the past few days. We didn't have time to do some sightseeing. How about taking you to the West Lake today?

B: 太好了！我早就听说西湖是中国非常著名的旅游景点，而且湖周围有很多景点呢，对吗？

A: That's right. West Lake is one of the best-known scenic spots in Zhejiang Province. Thousands of tourists come here every day.

B: 西湖离这儿远吗？

A: Not far away. It is about half an hour's ride from here.

B: 好的，那我们赶快走吧，我已经等不及了。

(半小时后)

A: Look. That is the West Lake. Many people call it Paradise on Earth. You can imagine how beautiful it is.

B: 是的。真是一个非常漂亮的湖。"人间天堂"是个再好不过的比喻了。那西湖有多大呢？

A: The distance from north to south is about 3.2 kilometers, and east to west, 2.8 kilometers, with an area of around 5.66 square kilometers.

B: 湖中那条长长的道路是什么呢？

A: That is called Bai Dike, built by the great poet Bai Juyi in Tang Dynasty in 821. And that one over there is Su Dike, built by Su Dongpo, a famous poet in North Song Dynasty.

B: 我注意到那边有很多亭子、小桥、花坛和山水。看上去就像是一幅美丽的风景画。

A: There are ten famous scenic spots around the West Lake, such as Viewing Fish at Flower Harbor, Spring Dawn by Su Dike, et..

B: 这些名字都太美了，非常富有诗情画意。

A: That's true. Let's visit these spots one by one.

B: 好的，这次旅游肯定难以忘怀。

段落口译/Short Passage Interpretation

(一)英译汉/E-C

7-4 王府井位于北京东城区，是中国首都最著名的商业街之一。这条街基本上不允许机动车通行，而且经常能见到街头人头攒动。自明朝中期以来，这里就是商业活动的主要场所。清朝年间，贵族和皇室成员在这里建了八处房产，之后又发现了一眼甜井，故取名为王府井。

目前，王府井聚集了280多家北京著名的品牌，比如像盛锡福的帽子店、同升和的鞋店等。曾为新中国第一代领导人照过相的照相馆也坐落在这条街上。

王府井夜市的小吃街上有各式各样奇异的小吃，比如油炸昆虫、蝎子、海鲜等，还有其他在西方很少食用的肉和动物内脏等。除了这些奇异的小吃外，还有更多的各种常见的小吃，比如说糖葫芦或者是其他由水果制成的甜食。

7-5 在普罗旺斯你会找到用大蒜、甜西红柿和橄榄油调制而成的佳肴，这儿的美酒在法国也很有名。当地居民以维护自己的传统闻名，他们经常举办许多舞会和庆典活动。你甚至可以在名为阿尔勒和尼姆的小镇里观赏斗牛表演，或在奥朗日的古罗马剧场中，伴着闪耀星空聆听诗词诵读。虽然旅客前往法国的目的地通常是巴黎，但如果南下到普罗旺斯也是个不错的选择。

(二)汉译英/C-E

7-6 Huangguoshu Grand Waterfall is, at all times, a great pleasure to see. All the people there, whether the locals or the visitors, share a common experience: one can never get bored with its view, which is constantly changing in accordance with the different viewing angles. It may present a unique picture at any angle, and the gigantic water curtain of the waterfall can always create an imposing and lofty beauty.

7-7 Wenwu Temple is located at the mountain slope of Tanpeishan. This temple is devoted to Confucius, a great scholar in ancient China, you know, and Yue Fei and Guan Yu, great warriors in ancient China. The temple consists of three sections, the front, the middle and back chambers. It is specious and decorated with multiple colors with gold as the main color. The architecture is of traditional Chinese palace style. It is majestic and grand-looking. Peacock Park stands at the north flank of Huanhu Road. The park is divided into three sections: the Peacock Park, Rui Bird Park and the butterfly Museum. Inside the park, there are more than 400 peacocks and a variety of birds and samples amounting to more than 200,000 of them. Then Guanghua Island is at the center of Sun Moon Lake. On the island is a popular shed named "Yashialaulen" meaning "Old Man under the Moon." This island is a must-visit spot.

篇章口译/Passage Interpretation

Emperor *Qin Shihuang*'s Terra-cotta Warriors and Horses were discovered accidentally in March 1974 when the local farmers were digging a well in the fields. Archeologists believed that the terra-cotta warriors and horses were from the Qin Dynasty. After many explorations and test excavation, three pits have been discovered, covering an area of 22,780 square meters.

This discovery created a world sensation. In order to protect these rare historical relics, in 1975, the State Council granted permission to construct a 16,300-square-meter museum over the site of Pit No.1. The museum was officially open to the public on the National Day, October 1, 1979. Later, exhibition halls housing Pit No. 3, No. 2 and the Bronze Chariots and Horses were built and open to the public in succession. The Museum and the Mausoleum of Emperor *Qin Shihuang* have been listed as one of the country's ten great historical sites and designated by the UNESCO as a World Culture Heritage Site.

Pit No.1 is rectangular in shape. It is 230 meters from east to west, 62 meters from north to south, 5 meters deep, and covers an area of 16,620 square meters. Warriors and horses in this pit are arranged in a practical battle array. In the long corridor at the east end of the pit stand three rows of terra-cotta warriors, 70 in each, 210 in all. Armed with bows and arrows, the soldiers are wearing battle tunics and puttees, and facing east. They are regarded as the vanguard of the battle formation. These are followed by 38 columns of troops, consisting of infantrymen and charioteers that are arranged in 11 corridors separated by 10 earth-rammed walls. The warriors all wear armors and carry long-shaft weapons. They make up the main body of the battle formation. Furthermore, at the north, south, and west end, there is one row of terra-cotta warriors respectively, all facing outward. They are the flanks and rear guards of the entire battle formation. From the 960 square meters testing trenches, some 500 warriors, 4 chariots, and 24 drafting horses have been unearthed. According to the density, 6,000 pieces in all can be excavated from Pit No.1.

Pit No.2 is "L"- shaped, covering an area of 6,000 square meters. It is actually a mixed battle formation consisting of military forces in four separate arrays. The first array is composed of 334 archers, the second of 64 chariots with three warriors on each. The third array includes 19 chariots and 100 warriors. The fourth array consists of 6 chariots, 124 cavalrymen and saddled horses. Together, the four arrays constitute a large battle formation, closely connected with one another. At the same time, each of the four arrays is an independent division, flexible and capable of both attacking and defending. It is estimated that altogether 1,500 pieces are expected to be excavated from Pit No.2.

Pit No.3 is "U"-shaped, taking up 520 square meters with only 4 terra-cotta horses, one chariot and 68 armored warriors discovered. Warriors here stand in two rows, opposite to each other along the wall. They carry a kind of long weapon, which has no blades and are believed to be used by the guards of honor. Remains of animal bones and deer horns probably used for sacrificial offerings and war praying are found in this pit. So archeologists believe it is the headquarters of the underground army.

The three pits are arranged in a triangle and form an enormous battle array, consisting of 8,000 warriors and horses. Vast and powerful, they give us a grand view of a mighty army in full battle array. They are the garrison army molded to guard Emperor *Qin Shihuang* tomb.

All the pottery figures were modeled life-size and were originally all color-painted. The warriors in the formation are arranged in accordance with their ranks-generals, officers and soldiers, and their functions-foot soldiers, charioteers and cavalrymen. The warriors vary from one another in feature and facial expressions, looking lifelike and vivid. They reveal the high artistic skill and national style of the group sculpture of ancient China.

Together with the warriors and horses are thousands of bronze weapons, including broad knives, swords, spears, dagger-axes, halberds, crossbows, arrows and arrowheads. The most eye-catching among the weapons is a bronze sword. Though buried under ground for over two thousand years, the sword is rustproof, still bright and sharp, and it can cut through 20 sheets of paper piled together. Technical examination reveals that the sword has been cast of an alloy of copper and tin. It also contains more than ten other rare metals. The surface was coated with chromium that has prevented corrosion and rust. This shows that 2,000 years ago China's technique of casting and metallurgy reached an amazingly high level.

In December 1980, archeologists discovered two teams of color-painted bronze chariots 20 meters to the west of *Qin Shihuang*'s mausoleum. This has added more splendors to the museum. They are listed as No.1 and No. 2 chariot respectively according to the order of their discovery. Both chariots are single-shaft and drafted by four horses. No.1 chariot was named High Chariot. The charioteers and the passengers all stood in it. No.2 chariot was named Security Chariot, which has two cabins; the front compartment is for the charioteer and the rear one is for the emperor. The rear compartment has a window on both sides as well as in the front and a door at the back. It is said that the chariots are used to hold the emperor's soul for inspection. The chariots and horses are half life-size, consisting of more than 3,400 component parts and 1,720 pieces of gold and silver decorations and ornaments. They are luxurious and graceful. Test studies have revealed that the making of the bronze chariots and horses involve such techniques as casting, welding, riveting, embedding, and chiseling.

The bronze chariots and horses were manufactured with high technology and modeled vividly. They are the earliest and most exquisite bronze treasures made in Chinese history and the largest bronze ware ever discovered in the history of world archaeology. They prove that the technique of chariot manufacture during the Qin period was undoubtedly advanced.

第八章　商贸洽谈口译
Business Negotiation Interpretation

一、热身阅读材料/Warming-up Reading Material

第一篇/Passage 1

1. Amway Products — Value for Money

New customers are occasionally surprised at the price of AMWAY products. Some people expect products offered by direct sale to be low-priced, inferior copies of the goods they can buy in stores. Amway has never built its business on that concept. From its beginning in the late 1950s, Amway's focus has been on quality products that deliver exceptional performance at competitive prices.

This commitment to quality is reflected in the intensive research and development that goes into AMWAY products. What other company can boast:

- A development and manufacturing facility more than a mile (1.6 km) long
- Organic farms in two hemispheres
- Research partnerships with leading international universities
- Facilities to replicate the water quality in countries around the world
- A list of parents related to products for everything from water treatment to hair repair

Despite this huge investment in product development, AMWAY products, in general, are price-competitive and good value for the money. Research shows that some products are less expensive than their counterparts, others are more expensive, and most are competitively priced.

Products that are more expensive usually have greater features and benefits over competitive products.

Many products, such as L.O.C.™ Multi-Purpose Cleaner, are highly concentrated, meaning a single purchase lasts longer. On a cost-per-use basis, these products are priced very competitively.

Product is delivered directly to the consumer and backed by a Satisfaction Guarantee.

2. New Digital Talking Book

A model for a new digital talking book that could take the place of the cassette-based players in use today was made known to the public October 21 by the library of National Library Service for the Blind. The book-like model is called a Dook (digital book) by its designer Lachezar Tsvetanov, a 23-year-old student of industrial design at the University of

Bridgeport, Connecticut.

Tsvetanov, who won $5,000 for the design in an Industrial Designers competition in June, said he wanted the player to resemble a book because "a high percentage of talking-book readers are older. And young people who use the Dook will feel they don't stand out in a crowd because it looks like a book".

The Dook has no moving parts and reads a book using a digital card. It resembles an open book with two thick pages divided by a metal string; buttons along the edge allow for page-turning, bookmarks, and searching. Its sound system will benefit older readers who cannot read Braille.

课文词语/Words and Expressions from the Text

Amway product	安利产品
organic farm	有机农场
water treatment	水处理
Satisfaction Guarantee	顾客服务保证
Braille	布莱叶盲文，点字法

第二篇/Passage 2

Foreign-Capital Enterprises

I'd like to take this opportunity to introduce China's laws and regulations concerning foreign-capital enterprises.

To expand economic cooperation and technological exchanges with foreign countries and promote the development of China's national economy, the People's Republic of China permits foreign enterprises, other foreign economic organizations and individuals to set up enterprises with foreign capital in China and protects the legitimate rights and interests of such enterprises.

Foreign-capital enterprises shall be established in such a manner as to help the development of China's national economy. The State shall encourage the establishment of export-oriented and technologically advanced foreign-capital enterprises. The investments of foreign investors in China, the profits they earn and their other lawful rights and interests are protected by Chinese laws.

The application to establish a foreign-capital enterprise shall be submitted for examination and approval to the department under the State Council which is in charge of foreign economic relations and trade, or to another agency authorized by the State Council. After an application for the establishment of a foreign-capital enterprise has been approved, the foreign investor shall, within 30 days from the date of receiving a certificate of approval, apply to the industry and commerce administrative authorities for registration and obtain a business license. A foreign-capital enterprise that meets the requirements for being a legal entity under Chinese law shall acquire the status of a Chinese legal entity, in accordance with the law.

A foreign-capital enterprise shall make investments in China within the period approved by the authorities in charge of examination and approval. If it fails to do so, the industry and commerce administrative authorities may cancel its business license.

In the event of separation, merger or other major changes, a foreign-capital enterprise shall report to and seek approval from the authorities in charge of examination and approval, and register the change with industry and commerce administrative authorities.

When employing Chinese workers and staff, a foreign-capital enterprise shall sign contracts with them according to law, which shall clearly prescribe matters concerning employment, dismissal, remuneration, welfare benefits, labor protection and labor insurance, etc. Workers and staff of foreign-capital enterprises may organize trade unions in accordance with the law to conduct trade union activities and protect their lawful rights and interests. Foreign-capital enterprises shall provide necessary conditions for the activities of the trade unions in their respective enterprises.

A foreign-capital enterprise must set up account books in China, conduct independent accounting, submit the accounting statements as required and accept supervision by the financial and tax authorities.

Foreign-capital enterprises shall pay taxes in accordance with relevant state provision, and may enjoy preferential treatment for tax reduction or exemption. An enterprise that reinvests its profits in China after paying income tax may, in accordance with relevant state provisions, apply for a refund of the portion of the income tax already paid on the reinvested amount.

The foreign investor may remit abroad profits that are lawfully earned from a foreign-capital enterprise, as well as other lawful earnings and any funds remaining after the enterprise is liquidated. Foreign employees in a foreign-capital enterprise may remit abroad their wages, salaries and other legitimate income after the payment of individual income tax in accordance with the law.

When terminating its operation, a foreign-capital enterprise shall promptly issue a public notice and proceed with liquidation in accordance with legal procedures. At the termination, the foreign-capital enterprise shall nullify its registration with the industry and commerce administrative authorities and hand in its business license for cancellation.

Thank you for your attention.

课文词语/Words and Expressions from the Text

foreign-capital enterprise	外资企业
laws and regulations	法律法规
legitimate rights and interests	合法权益
State Council	国务院

legal entity	法人
industry and commerce administrative authorities	工商行政管理机关
remuneration	酬劳；赔偿
cancel business license	吊销营业执照
set up account books	设置会计账簿
submit the accounting statements	报送会计报表
financial and tax authorities	财政税务机关
preferential treatment for tax reduction or exemption	减免税优惠待遇
pay income tax	缴纳所得税
apply for a refund	申请退税
remit abroad profits	把利润汇寄国外
liquidate	清理，清算(破产企业)
terminate the operation	终止经营
nullify the registration	取消注册

二、口译实践/Interpretation Practice

句子口译/Sentence Interpretation

(一)英译汉/E-C

Interpret the following sentences into Chinese.

 8-1.mp3

1. In order to extend our export business to your country, we wish to enter into direct business relations with you.

2. Our hope is to establish mutually beneficial trading relations between us.

3. It is hoped that you would seriously take this matter into consideration and let us have your reply soon.

4. We hope that this dispute can be settled through friendly negotiation without its being submitted for arbitration.

5. This machine will pay back your investment in six months.

(二)汉译英/C-E

Interpret the following sentences into English.

 8-2.mp3

1. 我们认为我们的产品在亚洲是最好的，在价格上完全可以和日本竞争。

2. 我们的产品因其优秀的品质，在很多地区经常脱销。

3. 在我们的市场上，这种玩具的需求一直很稳定。

4. 我们是一家国营公司，专营轻工产品。

5. 我们专营餐布的出口业务。

对话口译/Dialogue Interpretation

Dialogue 1

Interpret the following dialogues alternatively into English and Chinese.

🔘 8-3.mp3

A: I understand the farmers were the first group who benefited from China's reform started in 1979. Now is there so much talk about farmers being poor?

B: 对，因为改革是从农村先开始的，而且农民收入很快得到了提高。改革进一步深入以后，尤其是这几年来，随着城市化的进程逐渐加快，城市经济发展很快，大大超过了农村。

A: But there has been a lot of news about some state-owned enterprises going bankrupt too. What is the situation now? How has life changed?

B: 这几年来，大多数中小型国有亏损企业已经基本脱困。很多企业职工的工资也有很大地提高。离退休职工由于社会保障体系的完善，也增加了收入。教师、医务人员的工资有了较大的涨幅，国家公务员差不多增加了一倍的工资。而平均物价指数稳定。但是相对而言，就是农民的收入增加得不快，有些地区的农民尤其如此。不过南方的农村发展比较快，农民生活还不错。

A: What is the main reason for some rural areas lagging behind?

B: 主要是因为目前农业发展滞后，造成农民收入增长缓慢。所以我们要推进农村改革。近几年来，我国政府在这方面做了很多工作。今后，我们要努力解决"三农"问题，在农村发展多种经营、取消农业税，在粮食购销体制改革和农村医疗制度改革等方面做更大的努力。

A: Oh, I see. Thanks for the information. Now I have a better picture.

Dialogue 2

Interpret the following dialogues alternatively into English and Chinese.

🔘 8-4.mp3

A: 谢谢你把可行性报告的修改稿传真给我们。我们为即将开始的技术转让项目感到非常激动，认为这个项目是我们现在的合同的副产品或者是这个合同的继续。

B: We feel the same way, so let's have a separate contract for this project. This will make things easier for both of us. During the negotiation in Houston last December, we agree on all the particular details, except royalty rate.

A: 对，我们今天来这里就是为了这个问题。从我们的角度来看，先进的技术是极其重要的。对你们这样的制造公司来说，先进的技术就是生命线。你们是生产商，也有进出口权。如果你们的技术改进了，产品的质量就会更好，更有竞争性。你们的出口量就更大，在国际市场上的份额也会更大。

B: We fully understand this. These years we have been doing our best in technology innovations. But you must realize that at the beginning of our operation, there may be some unpredictable risks: the quality of the products may not be consistent and the production level may be lower than anticipated.

A: 嗯，我承认你说的也有道理，但是你们必须认识到技术本身是有价的。我们在开发新技术的过程中花费了不少钱。所以，恐怕提成率是不能降低的。

B: If the company has such a burden at the very beginning, we will have many difficulties in operation; so, at our board meeting, a suggestion was put forward: We will pay the royalty rate at the level you requested starting from the third production year. We will appreciate it very much if you would consider our position.

段落口译/Short Passage Interpretation

(一)英译汉/E-C

Interpret the following short passages into Chinese.

8-5.mp3

China is now the world's second largest economy. Its contribution to prosperity in the UK is becoming increasingly important. That is why we have come to China as the strongest ministerial delegation ever to visit from the UK. We look forward to this afternoon, when the Prime Minister David Cameron and Premier Wen will take part in the UK-China Summit.

8-6.mp3

We also discussed the trade links between our countries. It is worth remembering that China is the world's largest exporter of goods and the UK is the world's second largest exporter of services. This complementarity in our relationship will provide a strong foundation to strengthen our trade and investment links. Both sides will uphold the principles of free trade and resist all forms of protectionism. We will work together to achieve Doha — the UK sees 2011 as a key window of opportunity for achieving this, and I hope China will take a leading role in driving this agenda forward at the G20 Summit in Seoul.

(二)汉译英/C-E

Interpret the following short passages into English.

🔊 8-7.mp3

中国改革开放的26年，也是积极吸收外资扩大开放促进发展的26年。26年来，中国吸收外商投资从无到有，从小到大，从东部到中西部，从单一方式到多元化，产业结构和区域结构不断优化，水平不断提高，形成了全方位、多层次、宽领域的格局，取得了举世瞩目的成绩。

🔊 8-8.mp3

截至2004年7月底，外商在华投资累计设立企业49万余家，实际投入的金额近5,400亿美元。外商投资已遍及制造业、服务业、农业、基础设施等诸多领域。目前，来华投资的国家和地区近190个，全球最大的500家跨国公司已有400多家在华投资，其中30多家设立了地区总部，外商投资设立的研发中心超过600家，高新技术产业已成为外商投资的热点。

篇章口译/Passage Interpretation

Passage 1

相关词语/Related Words and Expressions

The Bloomberg news service	彭博社
United Aryan Limited	联合雅利安有限公司
the African Growth and Opportunity Act	非洲增长与机会法案

Interpret the following passage into Chinese.

🔊 8-9.mp3

The Significance of Continuing American Trade Agreement in Kenya

The Bloomberg news service recently published a list of the 20 fastest-growing economies. Bloomberg rated a total of 57 countries. China received the top rating, with the Philippines in second place. Kenya and Nigeria were the only African countries on the list.

Unemployment in Kenya remains high. And some industries in the East African nation may be hurt if the United States fails to extend a trade agreement.

That is the sound of an industrial sewing machine at a textiles factory near the Kenyan capital, Nairobi. The factory belongs to United Aryan Limited. The company was formed 13 years ago. It employs about 10,000 people. Workers earn an average of $150 in wages a month.

United Aryan Limited exports most of the goods it makes. Each month, it sends products worth $100 million to buyers in the United States. The company has been grown partly because of the African Growth and Opportunity Act. The United States Congress approved the act to permit import of some products from Africa without the payment of duties or taxes. The U.S.

trade program is set to end in September.

...

Bloomberg predicts Kenya's economy will grow six percent this year. If it does, it would join China, India, the Philippines and Indonesia as the only economies with a growth rate of five percent or more.

But unemployment in Kenya remains high, and 40 percent of Kenyans are very poor. In Kenya, political unrest, water shortages and terrorist attacks have all slowed efforts to help the country's economy. If the trade agreement is not renewed, many Kenyans would suffer.

...

Passage 2

相关词语/Related Words and Expressions

硬着陆	a hard landing
结构改革	structural reforms
工业模式	industrial model
由科技和创新驱动的模式	a model powered by science and innovation

Interpret the following passage into English.

8-10.mp3

国务院总理李克强表示，中国经济能够避免硬着陆。李克强在夏季达沃斯论坛上发表讲话时表示，中国的结构改革已经减少风险，中国经济从工业模式向由科技和创新驱动的模式转变过程中可以避免急剧下滑。

李克强同时表示，经济发展方式不转变不行，经济发展是就业和收入增加、节能环保的发展。

中国经济在2014年经历了一些困难，今年第一季度的经济增长率为7.4%，这是18个月以来的最低值。今年第二季度的经济增长率小幅攀升至7.5%。

今天，国家主席习近平将启程前往塔吉克斯坦参加上海合作组织峰会并对塔吉克斯坦进行国事访问。

在出发前，主席在塔吉克斯坦《人民报》发表文章，承诺进一步加强中塔关系并推动上合组织的发展。他表示塔吉克斯坦是重要的合作伙伴，中国将致力于促进贸易畅通、实现道路联通、推动货币流通、扩大民心相通。

习近平主席还称赞了上合组织过去13年的发展。他表示，成员国开创了结伴而不结盟的国际关系新模式。上海合作组织峰会将于今天和明天在塔吉克斯坦首都杜尚别举行。

参考译文/Reference Version

句子口译/Sentence Interpretation

(一)英译汉/E-C

1. 为了能在贵国拓宽我方的出口业务,我们希望能与你们直接建立业务关系。
2. 我们希望双方能建立互惠的贸易关系。
3. 希望你方能认真考虑这件事,并尽快答复我们。
4. 我们希望通过友好谈判加以解决,而不要仲裁。
5. 该机器半年就可收回投资成本。

(二)汉译英/C-E

1. We feel that our product is the best kind in Asia and we can very well compete against Japan in price.

2. By virtue of this superior quality, this product is often sold out in many areas.

3. There has been a steady demand in our market for this kind of toy.

4. We wish to introduce ourselves to you as a state-owned corporation dealing exclusively in light industrial goods.

5. We specialize in the export of table-cloth.

对话口译/Dialogue Interpretation

Dialogue 1

A: 我知道中国1979年开始改革,第一批受益的是农民。但为什么现在大家都在说农民贫穷呢?

B: Right, the reform started in the rural areas. And the framers' income was greatly increased. With the reform progressing, especially with the rapid increase in urbanization during these years, the development of cities has been fast and has left rural areas behind.

A: 但是,我也听到很多有关国有企业破产的消息。现在情况怎样了?人们的生活有什么变化?

B: In recent years, we have managed to turn around most of the small and medium-sized state-owned enterprises. As a result, many employees have seen their salaries go up significantly. And thanks to the improvement of the social security system, the retirees are also getting more benefits. Teachers and medical workers have seen their salary rise by a rather big margin, and civil servants have nearly doubled their salary. Meanwhile, the mean price index remains more or less stable. But by comparison, China's rural population is not seeing a rapid increase in their income, especially in some areas. But rural areas in the south are generally more developed and farmers there enjoy a fairly comfortable life.

A: 是什么原因造成农村发展滞后呢?

B: The main problem is the slow and backward development of agriculture; that has prevented a rapid increase of farmers' income. So we should push rural reform. Over the past few years, the central government has been making tremendous efforts in this area. In the future, we will do our best to solve the problem in agriculture production and rural area development and improve the life of the farmers. We will do more to diversify production, do away with agricultural taxes and carry out grain-distribution system reform and medi-care system reform and so on.

A: 噢,是这样的。谢谢你的介绍。我现在比较清楚了。

Dialogue 2

A: Thank you for faxing us the revised version of the feasibility report. We are excited about the upcoming technology transfer project, which we consider a positive add-on or continuation of our present contract.

B: 我们也有同感,让我们就这个项目另签一个独立的合同,这样对咱们双方都方便一些。去年12月我们在休斯顿谈判,除了提成率这一项,其他细节基本上都达成了一致。

A: Yes, that's why we are here today. From our point of view, advanced technology is extremely important, a lifeline for manufacturing companies like yours, which have the right to import and export. If your technology is upgraded, your products will be better in quality and more competitive. Your export volume will be greater and so will your share of the international market.

B: 这一点我们很清楚。这些年来我们在技术革新方面一直在做最大的努力。但是,你们一定要认识到在我们运营初期,可能有些不可预知的风险:产品质量可能会不稳定,产量也可能会比我们预期的低。

A: Well, I admit you have a point there, but you must realize technology itself has a price. During the development process, we spent a lot of money. I am afraid the royalty rate cannot be lowered.

B: 如果公司一开始就负担那么重,经营会有很多困难的。所以,我们在董事会上提了这样的建议:我们从第三个生产年头开始按你们的要求支付提成。如果你们能考虑我们的建议,我们将非常感谢。

段落口译/Short Passage Interpretation

(一)英译汉/E-C

8-5 中国现在是世界上第二大经济体。它对于英国经济繁荣的贡献日益重要。这也是我们此次作为英国有史以来最强大的部长级代表团到中国访问的原因。我们期待着今天下午戴维·卡梅伦首相和温家宝总理共同出席的英中峰会。

8-6 我们也探讨了两国间的贸易关系。值得一提的是，中国是世界上最大的商品出口国，而英国是世界上第二大服务出口国。两国的这一互补关系将为加强双方的贸易和投资关系提供强有力的基础。双方都坚持自由贸易的原则，抵制各种形式的贸易保护主义。我们将协同努力，实现多哈回合成果。英国认为2011年是实现这一目标的关键机会期，我希望中国在首尔召开的G20国峰会上可以发挥领导作用，推动此项议程的开展。

(二)汉译英/C-E

8-7 The 26 years of China's reform and opening up are 26 years when China has promoted its development through positively absorbing foreign direct investment and opening up wider to the outside world. Over the 26years, foreign direct investment attraction in China has started from scratch, grown from strength to strength, expanded from the east to the central and western regions and continuously diversified in modality, optimized in industrial structure and regional distribution and improved in level. By forming an all-directional, multi-layered and wide-ranging pattern of foreign direct investment utilization, China has scored achievements that attract world wide attention.

8-8 By the end of July 2004, foreign investors had altogether established over 490,000 enterprises in China with an actually placed investment volume of nearly USD 540 billion. Foreign investment is now widely seen in numerous areas including manufacturing, service, agriculture and infrastructure. Today, there are almost 190 countries and regions having investment in China and of the world's top 500 multinational companies, more than 400 have invested in China and among them, 30 plus have located their regional headquarters in this country together with 600 odd foreign funded R&D centers. High-tech has turned out to be a highlight of foreign direct investment.

篇章口译/Passage Interpretation

Passage 1

延续美国贸易协定对肯尼亚的意义

彭博社最近公布了20个发展最快经济体名单，该社对57个国家进行了排名。中国名列前茅，其次是菲律宾。非洲只有肯尼亚和尼日利亚上榜。

肯尼亚的失业率仍很高，如果美国未能延长一项贸易协议，非洲东部国家的一些产业可能会受损。

这是肯尼亚首都内罗毕附近一家纺织厂的工业缝纫机发出的声音，该工厂属于联合雅利安有限公司。这家公司成立于13年前，雇佣了大约一万人。工人们平均每月薪水150美元。

联合雅利安有限公司大部分产品都用于出口,每月向美国的买主发出价值 1 亿美元的产品。这家公司的发展部分得益于《非洲增长与机会法案》。美国国会批准了该法案,对从非洲进口的部分商品免税。美国的这项贸易协议将于 9 月份到期。

……

彭博社预测肯尼亚经济今年将增长 6%,一旦如此,该国将能跻身于中国、印度、菲律宾和印尼之列,成为少数几个经济发展在 5% 及以上的经济体。

但肯尼亚的失业率仍很高,有 40% 的肯尼亚人非常贫困。在肯尼亚,政治动荡、缺水和恐怖袭击一直阻碍了该国经济的发展,如果这项贸易协议到此为止,那么很多肯尼亚人会遭殃。

……

Passage 2

Premier Li Keqiang says the Chinese economy can avoid a hard landing. Speaking at the World Economic Forum, or Summer Davos, the premier said that China's structural reforms have reduced risk, and the economy will be able to avoid a steep drop in growth as it switches from an industrial model to a model powered by science and innovation.

He added that the country cannot advance without changing the growth model, and that development should promote employment, improve incomes, boost energy conservation, and environmental protection.

China's economy has experienced a tricky year in 2014, with growth hitting an 18-month low of 7.4% in the first quarter. The number rose slightly to 7.5% in the second three months period this year.

Chinese President Xi Jinping is traveling to Tajikistan today for a summit of the Shanghai Cooperation Organization and a state visit.

Ahead of his departure, the president wrote in Tajikistan's People's Gazette newspaper, pledging to further enhance bilateral ties as well as the development of the Shanghai Cooperation Organization. He calls Tajikistan an important cooperation partner, saying China will work for trade facilitation, for the development of road links, for pushing for the use of each other's currencies in trade, and for strengthening people-to-people contacts.

Xi Jinping also hailed the Shanghai Cooperation Organization's development over the past 13 years, saying member countries have created a new model of international relations — partnership instead of alliance. The Shanghai Cooperation Organization summit runs today and tomorrow in Dushanbe, Tajikistan.

第九章　环境保护口译
Environmental Protection Interpretation

一、热身阅读材料/Warming-up Reading Material

第一篇/Passage 1

UK research shows that without active mitigation against the current level of emissions, the world's temperature will rise by 4 degrees by the end of the century compared to the pre-industrial level. That would mean 23% of China's population deprived of the dry season glacier melt, making water scarcity far more severe than it is even today. It would mean a decrease in rice yield of up to 30% would be likely. Sea levels could rise by 0.9 metres.

The UK, starting from the Industrial Revolution, pursued rapid development. It was only later that we turned to sustainable development. China, now the world's biggest emitter, is working on both in parallel. This is to be praised.

Developed countries recognize their historic responsibility and need to take the lead in combating climate change. The UK was the first country to introduce legally-binding carbon budgets. These commit us to carbon savings of 34% by 2020 and at least 80% by 2050 against a 1990 baseline. The UK's per capita emissions, now 10 tonnes per annum, may fall below China's, now 6 tonnes per annum but rising, by around 2016. Our policies and work to combat climate change in the UK are transforming how we generate power and use it in our homes, businesses, transport and public services, and are creating new jobs and industries for a low carbon economy.

Unlike Europe, most of the homes, offices, power stations and infrastructure that will exist in China in 2030 have not yet been built. This means China's capacity for green growth and innovation is potentially enormous.

China has adopted a stretching target between 2006-2010 to improve energy intensity by 20%. By 2020 it plans for 15% of its total energy mix to come from renewables and nuclear. Its solar, wind, hydro and nuclear industries are developing rapidly. Forest cover is to be 20% by 2010 and 23% by 2020 (from just 9% in 1949). In 2008 President Hu committed China to a low carbon economy. China's leaders see the harmful economic effects of climate change. China's middle class, now about 80 million, want a better city environment. In July this year, China agreed at an international meeting that it would take action between 2005 and 2020 to ensure a meaningful deviation from business as usual in its emissions and committed to the goal of limiting global temperature increases to no more than 2 degrees from pre-industrial levels.

课文词语/Words and Expressions from the Text

mitigation	减轻，缓和
level of emission	排放量
glacier melt	冰川融水
take the lead in	起带头作用
introduce legally-binding carbon budgets	将碳预算写入法律
tonne	公吨
low carbon economy	低碳经济
green growth	绿色经济
a stretching target	一个雄心勃勃的目标
forest cover	森林覆盖率

第二篇/Passage 2

The UK and China share many pressing challenges such as climate change, environmental degradation and poverty. We agreed to work together towards achieving the United Nations Millennium Development Goals and the commitments made at the Johannesburg World Summit on Sustainable Development. I hope my visit to China this week will help increase this momentum and deepen our partnership.

The challenges we face are enormous. In 1950, there were about 2.5 billion people on the planet. Since then, our numbers have swelled to 6 billion. More then 1 billion of those people do not have access to safe drinking water and over 2 billion lack sanitation.

There are estimated to be 5 to 15 million species of plants, animals, and microorganisms on the Earth today. Only about 1.5 million of these have been identified. Because of the loss of natural habitat, many will be extinct before they could be discovered.

We continue to lose around 17 million hectares of forest each year, an area two thirds the size of the UK. Over 30% of our coral reefs have been lost and fish stocks continue to dwindle. I could go on.

Why is this happening? Largely because of the pressures of economic development. Quite rightly, governments, businesses and communities strive to build a prosperous economy, which can support a viable society. But gradually over the last few decades I think we have all come to realize that, for long-term prosperity and stability, economies must be based on sustainability. Economic growth that doesn't integrate environmental and social factors is not sustainable development.

China has made an impressive start. GDP has increased from $362 billion to nearly $12 trillion since 1979, growing last year alone by over 9%.

The number of the poor is estimated to have dropped from 49% of the population in 1981 less than 7% in 2002.

Between 1990 and 2000 your economy grew by over 60% but emissions intensity fell by nearly 50%. You can? Indeed must — have sustainability and environmental good practice alongside greater economic prosperity.

But when we look at the global picture — at the threat of climate change, at our unsustainable patterns of production and consumption, and at the chronic poverty that still exists, particularly in Africa for example — we see that much more needs to be done.

In the UK we've just started to take a fresh look at our sustainable development strategy.

Our last such strategy, *A Better Quality of Life* — was published in 1999. It set out guiding principles for achieving sustainable development as well as broad areas of action and a set of 15 headline indicators against which to measure our progress. A lot has happened since 1999. There are new international commitments — notably from the World Summit on Sustainable Development. There have also been changes in patterns of government and economic activity within the UK. We want to have a new strategy in place early next year that reflects these and other changes in the past five years.

So, in April I launched a consultation to help us shape the UK's future strategy. Right now there are events being planned and taking place across the UK where people look at what our new aims and priorities should be, what more we need to do at home and in our work with other countries to make progress, and how we are going to measure and monitor that progress.

But we in the UK cannot improve our own quality of life at the expense of the quality of people's lives elsewhere. So the consultation on our future strategy will also look at how we can better incorporate into our own strategy the international dimension of sustainable development. International action sets the wider context for our own actions and policies, and will have a critical impact on our own chances of success.

Achieving sustainability is not just about what the UK can do. This challenge is truly global and everyone has a part to play. I believe that sustainable development worldwide is essential to ensure long-term peace and security, and tackle the underlying causes of instability, such as poverty and environmental degradation.

To illustrate the global nature of challenge, I would like to pick out just three of the key global threats we face, namely climate change, sustainable consumption and production and the WTO negotiations on trade.

Our priority internationally must be action to tackle climate change. Prime Minister Tony Blair has called this the "single most important issue that we face as a global community." He is determined to make this a priority during the UK's Presidencies of the G8 and European Union next year.

We believe that the UK must show leadership among the world's developed economies. That is why we have committed the UK to the goal of reducing our carbon dioxide emissions by 60% by 2050 as a core objective of our new energy policy.

And we believe that this can be achieved at the same time as healthy economic growth. We have made a good start. Between 1990 and 2002 the UK economy grew by 36% while our greenhouse gas emissions fell by 15.3%.

China too has an impressive record in improving the emissions intensity of its economy. And I strongly congratulate China on its foresightedness in preparing a long term national strategy on climate change. China is setting a real leadership example by showing how a fast developing economy should plan to tackle climate change.

The UK and China are already working in cooperation on a project to understanding the impacts of climate change for agriculture in China. I very much hope that our two leading countries can work together in other ways too to set an example in meeting the challenge of climate change.

But this is only a start. We must also look hard at our patterns of production and consumption. This is certainly one of the main domestic challenges for the UK. We have to put our own house in order.

课文词语/Words and Expressions from the Text

Millennium Development Goals	千年发展目标
the Johannesburg World Summit	约翰内斯堡世界首脑会议
coral reefs	珊瑚礁
A Better Quality of Life	更好的生活质量
headline indicators	主要指标
at the expense of	以……为代价，由……支付
underlying causes of instability	不稳定隐患
emissions intensity	排放浓度

二、口译实践/Interpretation Practice

句子口译/Sentence Interpretation

(一)英译汉/E-C

Interpret the following sentences into Chinese.

9-1.mp3

1. Respiratory illness from air pollution is now China's number one health problem.
2. Every major body of water is polluted.
3. Climate change is a real and growing issue.
4. We have examples of countries whose economies are doing well as they adopt more sensible environmental and energy practices, and many companies are making a significant share of profits, through conservation and the implementation of new technologies.
5. An energy revolution should be set out.

(二)汉译英/C-E

Interpret the following sentences into English.

9-2.mp3

1. 人们一直以为，发展中国家经济增长的唯一办法就是使用工业时代的能源使用模式，我们必须打破这一偏见。
2. 沙漠正以惊人的速度向我们逼近。
3. 风暴毫不费力就可以将光秃秃的河床吹得面目全非。
4. 导致春季沙尘暴的部分原因是土地过度开垦、放牧以及伐木。
5. 对于全球变暖问题，全世界的科学家都在进行理论上的探讨。

对话口译/Dialogue Interpretation

第一篇/Dialogue 1

Interpret the following dialogues alternatively into English and Chinese.

9-3.mp3

A: I think the biggest environment problem in my country is air pollution.

B: 我同意。这里的空气污染比我们国家严重多了。当然，我们国家农业比重比较大，工业比重比较小。

A: We have reduced emission of air pollutants in recent years, but cars are still a major source of them. Factories have become cleaner as stricter environment pollution law has been introduced.

B: 现在的问题是个全球性问题。我认为单凭一个国家的力量无法解决问题。

A: I think you're right. There needs to be an international response to this problem.

第二篇/Dialogue 2

Interpret the following dialogues alternatively into English and Chinese.

9-4.mp3

A: 这个周末你都干什么了?

B: I went to a global warming rally in London. It was fantastic to be around so many people who care about the environment.

A: 你觉得要想逆转目前我们对环境的破坏我们有什么能做的吗?

B: It might not be possible to fix the problems that we've created for ourselves, but there are lots of things we can do to prevent more damages from happening.

A: 比如哪些?

B: Well, we can use public transport instead of taking our cars for a start.

A: 想要保护环境还有什么可以做的?

B: If you do have to drive, you should make sure that your car runs on unleaded petrol. Also, your home should use sources of renewable energy.

A: 废物回收呢?这有帮助吗?

B: Yes. You should take your glass, paper, plastic, cardboard, and tin cans to a recycling center.

A: 那你觉得未来最令人担忧的是什么问题?

B: I think that the issue of greatest concern is having enough sources of clean water for everyone.

A: 我以前还真不知道你是个环保主义者。

B: To be honest, in order for the earth to continue to be a habitable place, we're all going to have to become more interested in the environment.

段落口译/Short Passage Interpretation

(一)英译汉/E-C

Interpret the following short passages into Chinese.

 9-5.mp3

And without common action extreme temperatures will create a new generation of poor with climate change refugees driven from their homes by droughts, climate change evacuees fleeing the threat of drowning, the climate change hungry desperate for lack of food.

 9-6.mp3

In recognition of their common but differentiated responsibilities, developing countries commit to nationally appropriate mitigation actions at their highest possible level of ambition, achieving a significant reduction from business as usual and standing behind their actions as developed countries must stand behind their emissions cuts.

(二)汉译英/C-E

Interpret the following short passages into English.

9-7.mp3

大气无国界,合作无边界。预防和减轻气象灾害、适应和减缓气候变化、开发和利用气候资源,不仅是中国也是全世界关注的重大问题,迫切需要各国之间在更大范围、更深层次、更广领域加强合作。中国政府将同国际社会一起,采取切实可行的措施和行动,密切合作,推进多方面的气候服务,使气候服务更好地造福全人类,为人类社会可持续发展做出新贡献。

9-8.mp3

第五,我们知道要切实实现减排的宏伟目标,唯一的手段是通过发展科学和技术,这就是为什么中国加大了应对气候变化的科研投入。中国已成为各种新能源技术的巨大实验基地。

篇章口译/Passage Interpretation

Passage 1

相关词语/Related Words and Expressions

electric-powered stoves	电力炉
clean fuels	清洁能源
LPG (liquified petroleum gas)	液化石油气
the ethanol	乙醇
crop waste	庄稼秸秆

Interpret the following passage into Chinese.

9-9.mp3

The way we cook is important. In many countries, the two choices are natural gas or electric-powered stoves.

The World Health Organization warns that millions of people are dying every year from indoor air pollution.

Indoor air pollution results from the use of dangerous fuels and cook-stoves in the home. To help fight the problem, the WHO announced new guidelines aimed at reducing household pollutants.

WHO officials say nearly three billion people are unable to use clean fuels and technologies for cooking, heating and lighting. And they say more than seven million people die from exposure to indoor or outdoor air pollution each year. Of that number, the WHO says about 4.3 million people die from household air pollution given off by simple biomass and coal cook-stoves.

Most of the deaths are in developing countries.

The WHO's plan of action for reducing indoor pollutants is based on new findings. These findings show that the use of toxic fuels in inefficient stoves, space heaters or lights is to blame for many of these deaths.

Carlos Dora is a Coordinator in the WHO's Department of Public Health, Environmental and Social Determinants of Health. He says people should not use unprocessed coal and kerosene fuel indoors. He says opening a window or door to let out the harmful air will not correct the situation. It will only pollute the outdoors.

"You cannot expect that a bit of ventilation is going to get rid of this. It is really about very clean technologies and clean fuels. And, the fuel story has not been stressed enough so far in the global debate. So, that is the new thing. We should be going for clean fuels. We should be avoiding coal. We should be avoiding kerosene and we should be going for the solar, the LPG (liquified petroleum gas), the ethanol ... the solutions that we know exist that can address a big proportion of this issue."

WHO officials say indoor pollution leads to early deaths from stroke, heart and lung disease, childhood pneumonia and lung cancer. Women and girls are the main victims.

The WHO says these diseases can often result from high levels of fine particulate matter and carbon monoxide released by the burning of solid fuels. These fuels include wood, coal, animal waste, crop waste and charcoal.

The United Nations found that more than 95 percent of households in sub-Saharan Africa depend on solid fuels for cooking. It says huge populations in India, China and Latin American countries, such as Guatemala and Peru, also are at risk.

Nigel Bruce is a professor of Public Health at the University of Liverpool. He says researchers are developing good cook-stoves and other equipment to burn fuels in a more efficient way.

"There are already multiple technologies available for use in clean fuels. There is really quite an effective and reasonably low-cost ethanol stove that is made by Dometic (a Sweden-based company) that is now being tested out. It has been tested out in a number of African countries and we do report results from that in the guidelines. LPG cook is obviously widely available and efforts are under way to make those efficient. Another interesting development is electric induction stoves."

WHO experts note some new, safe and low-cost technologies that could help are already available. In India, you can buy an induction stove for about $8.00. And in Africa you can buy a solar lamp for less than $1.00.

But, this, the agency says, is just a start. It is urging developing countries to use cleaner fuels and increase access to cleaner and more modern cooking and heating appliances.

Passage 2

相关词语/Related Words and Expressions

佩特拉诺项目	the Petra Novo project
碳捕捉技术	carbon capture technology
化石能源资源	fossil energy resources
百万瓦特	megawatts

Interpret the following passage into English.

 9-10.mp3

德克萨斯州一家火电厂正在捕捉排放到大气中的140万吨二氧化碳。这个佩特拉诺项目并没有建造完全新的工厂,而是将碳捕捉技术应用到现有的火电厂,帮助其改进技术,使其从化石能源资源中获得更清洁的产品,同时减少温室气体排放。

这个总部在休斯顿的项目是9月15日创立的,美国能源部对该项目提供1,670万美元的补贴,帮助其从60百万瓦特的产能中捕捉碳排放。项目赞助者NRG能源公司和新日本石油及能源公司认为自己可以做得更好,他们将项目规模扩大四倍,希望能捕捉240百万瓦特的产能,同时不需要联邦资助。一旦建成,该项目每年捕捉的二氧化碳量相当于25万辆汽车在道路上排放的二氧化碳量。

该项目使用之前在阿拉巴马州经过三年小规模试验的程序,将捕捉发电厂90%的二氧化碳。被捕捉的二氧化碳将被压缩、干燥并运输到一个油田,油田使用这样的二氧化碳来获得之前无法获得的石油,这个过程就叫做提高原油采收率。

能源部化石能源办公室支持许多有前途的碳捕捉和使用项目,佩特拉诺项目就是其中之一。这些项目的目的是想办法让美国各种能源变得更清洁。

25年来,美国能源部化石能源办公室所有并运作的国家能源技术实验室一直联合资助重大清洁碳技术展示项目,来加快这些技术在商业市场上的应用。联邦政府的资金支持将帮助减少这种首类项目的内在风险。

碳捕捉只是奥巴马总统减少美国温室气体排放并解决气候变化计划的一部分,促进可再生能源生产、提高能效、提高汽车燃油效率和建筑能效也是政府要采取的重大步骤。

由于对能源的需求在增加,而解决气候变化也越发迫切,美国正与政府和企业合作者一起来减少二氧化碳排放,从而促成更清洁的环境。

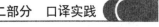

参考译文/Reference Version

句子口译/Sentence Interpretation

(一)英译汉/E-C

1. 大气污染引起的呼吸系统疾病是中国的头号健康杀手。
2. 所有主要水体均被污染。
3. 气候变化是千真万确的,是一个越来越严重的问题。
4. 比如有很多国家在经济健康发展的同时,采取了更为合理的环境和能源措施,有很多公司通过资源保护及采用新技术,将相当可观的利润分流。
5. 能源革命势在必行。

(二)汉译英/C-E

1. But we have to do something to break the idea in people's mind that the only way to grow the economy of a developing country is to adopt industrial age energy use patterns.
2. Deserts are approaching us at a frightening pace.
3. It is rather easy for windstorms to blow away the bare riverbeds.
4. Excessive land cultivation, grazing and lumbering are some of the reasons for sandstorm in spring.
5. Global warming is a problem for theoretical discussion among scientists all over the world.

对话口译/Dialogue Interpretation

第一篇/Dialogue 1

A: 我觉得我们国家最大的环境问题是空气污染。

B: Yes, I agree. The air here is much more polluted than in my country. Of course, my country is more agricultural and has much less industry.

A: 我们这些年也在减少有害气体排放量,但是汽车废气排放依然是空气污染的主要原因。随着更加严格的环境保护法的颁布,工业废气排放没有以前严重了。

B: The problem is now on a truly global scale. I don't believe that any single country can do anything about it.

A: 你说得对。环境问题需要全世界的国家负起责任来共同合作解决。

第二篇/Dialogue 2

A: What did you do over the weekend?

B: 我到伦敦去参加了一个有关全球变暖的集会。周围有那么多人都在关注环境问题,可真是好事!

A: Do you think there's anything we can do to reverse the damage that's been done already?

B: 我们自己酿成的恶果已经不大可能解决了，但是为了防止情况继续恶化下去我们还是有很多事情可以做的。

A: Like what?

B: 嗯,大家可以乘坐公共交通设施代替自驾车。

A: What else can we do to protect the environment?

B: 如果非开车不可，那一定要用无铅汽油。而且，家里一定要坚持使用可持续能源。

A: How about recycling? Does that actually help?

B: 是的。玻璃、纸张、塑料、硬板、纸盒、罐头盒都可以送进回收中心。

A: What do you think is the biggest worry for our future?

B: 我觉得最大的问题是是否有足够的水资源够每个人使用。

A: I had no idea you were such an environmentalist before!

B: 坦白说，为了让地球能够一直适合人类居住，我们都应该多关注环保问题。

段落口译/Short Passage Interpretation

(一)英译汉/E-C

9-5 如果不采取共同的行动，极端的气温将会酿成新的贫穷一代——他们因气候变化所致的干旱，被迫离开自己的家园，另觅居所；他们因气候变化而被迫撤离，以躲避溺死的威胁，也因气候变化而饥肠辘辘。

9-6 发展中国家负有共同但有区别的责任，因此发展中国家须最大限度地在国内推行适当的减排行动，在"照常发展情景"(BAU)下实现显著的减排。发展中国家必须履行诺言，一如发达国家也须履行减排的承诺那样。

(二)汉译英/C-E

9-7 Atmosphere recognizes no borders, and international cooperation transcends boundaries. Preparedness for and reduction of meteorological disasters, adaptation to and mitigation of climate change, exploration and utilization of climate resources are not only major issues of concern for China, but also for the world. It is imperative for all countries to strengthen cooperation in wider range, greater depth and broader areas. Together with the international community, the Chinese government will take practical and feasible measures and actions, conduct close cooperation, and promote the climate services in multiple aspects, so as to provide better climate services for the benefit of the mankind, and to make new contributions to the sustainable development of the human society.

9-8 Last but not least, the only means for China to really achieve its ambitious plan is through science and technology. This is why China is investing heavily in research and development. The country has become a giant laboratory for testing all kinds of clean energy technologies.

篇章口译/Passage Interpretation

Passage 1

我们做饭的方式非常重要。在许多国家,两大选择是天然气或电力炉。

世界卫生组织警告说,每年有数百万人死于室内空气污染。

室内空气污染来源于在室内使用危险的燃料和灶具。为了帮助解决这一问题,世界卫生组织宣布了旨在减少家庭污染物的新准则。

世界卫生组织官员最近表示,将近30亿人无法使用清洁能源和技术做饭、取暖和照明。他们还表示,每年超过7百万人死于室内外的空气污染,其中大约430万人死于生物燃料和煤炉释放出的室内空气污染。

大部分死者都是在发展中国家。

世界卫生组织减少室内污染物的行动计划是基于多项新的研究。这些研究结果表明,其中多数死亡归咎于在低效炉灶、取暖器或照明工具中使用有毒燃料。

卡洛斯·多拉是世界卫生组织公共卫生及健康问题,环境和社会决定因素司的协调员。他说,人们不应该在室内使用未经处理的煤或煤油燃料。他说,打开门窗让有害气体排出无法扭转这一局面。它只会继续污染室外环境。

"你不能指望通风就能摆脱污染,只能通过使用清洁技术和清洁燃料。而且,燃料一说在全球辩论中至今强调得还不够。因此这是一种新说法。我们应该采用清洁燃料,避免使用煤和煤油。我们应该采用太阳能,液化石油气和乙醇等。这些我们知道的现有解决方案可以解决很大一部分问题。"

世界卫生组织官员表示,室内污染会导致中风、心脏和肺部疾病、儿童肺炎和肺癌等早逝疾病。妇女儿童是主要受害者。

世界卫生组织表示,这些疾病通常源自固体燃料燃烧时释放的高浓度细颗粒物和一氧化碳。这些燃料包括木柴、煤炭、动物排泄物、庄稼秸秆和木炭。

联合国发现,撒哈拉以南非洲地区超过95%的家庭依靠固体燃料做饭。联合国称,人口众多的印度、中国,以及危地马拉和秘鲁等拉美国家也存在风险。

奈杰尔·布鲁斯是利物浦大学的公共健康教授。他说,研究人员正在研发让燃料燃烧更有效的炉具和其他设备。

布鲁斯说,"现在已经有可用于清洁燃料的多种技术。一种非常有效、成本合理的瑞典多美达公司生产的乙醇炉现在也正在接受测试。它已经在一些非洲国家经过测试,我们对此结果做了报告。液化石油气做饭显然已经得到广泛使用,并且采取了多种措施使其高效。另一种有趣的发展是电磁炉。"

世界卫生组织专家指出,一些可能有帮助的安全、低成本的新技术已经面世。在印度,8美元就能买到一个电磁炉。而在非洲,不到1美元就能买到一盏太阳能灯。

但是世界卫生组织表示,这仅仅是个开始。该机构正在督促发展中国家使用清洁能源,并提供更多途径来获得更清洁、更现代的烹饪和取暖设备。

Passage 2

A coal-fired power plant in Texas is on its way to capturing 1.4 million tons of carbon dioxide, or CO_2 that previously would have been released into the air. Rather than building an entirely new facility, the Petra Novo project will apply carbon capture technology to an existing coal-fired power plant helping to advance the technologies that help enable cleaner energy production from fossil energy resources and reduce greenhouse gas emissions.

The Houston-area project, which was founded on September 15th, was awarded $167 million from the U.S. Department of Energy to capture emissions from 60 megawatts of generation. Project sponsor NRG Energy Inc. and JX Nippon decided they could do better than that. They quadrupled the size of the project — expanding the design to capture the emissions from 240 megawatts of generation — with no additional federal funding. When completed, the project has the potential to capture the same amount of CO_2 each year as taking 250,000 cars off the road.

Using a process previously tested in a three-year pilot scale test in Alabama, the project will capture up to 90 percent of CO_2 from the power plant. The captured carbon dioxide will then be compressed, dried and transported to an oil field where it will be used to recover previously unreachable oil — a process known as Enhanced Oil Recovery or EOR.

Petra Nova is one of many promising carbon capture and use projects supported by the Energy Department's Office of Fossil Energy that aim to find ways to make American energy from all sources cleaner.

For over 25 years, The National Energy Technology Laboratory, an energy research laboratory owned and operated by the U.S. Department of Energy's Office of Fossil Energy, has been co-funding major demonstrations of clean coal technologies to hasten their adoption into the commercial marketplace. The federal government's financial support helps reduce the risks inherent in these first-of-a-kind projects.

Carbon capture is just one piece of President Obama's plan to reduce U.S. greenhouse gas emissions and tackle climate change. Boosting renewable energy production, advancing energy efficiency, improving the fuel efficiency of our cars and making our buildings more energy efficient are also important steps the Administration is taking.

As both demand for energy and the urgency to address climate change continues to increase, the United States is working with government and with private sector partners to reduce carbon dioxide emissions for a cleaner environment.

第十章 政治和外事口译
Interpretation of Politics and Diplomacy

一、热身阅读材料/Warming-up Reading Material

第一篇/Passage 1

A Decade of Bilateral Magic

—— An exclusive interview with *Beijing Review* reporter Ni Yanshuo, Dave Malcomson, Minister Plenipotentiary of the South African Embassy to China, spoke about the evolution of bilateral ties between the two nations.

Beijing Review(B): Would you please comment on the 10-year development of the bilateral relations between China and South Africa?

Dave Malcomson(D): I think it's wonderful that at the end of September we held the third meeting of the Bi-National Commission between South Africa and China since we established diplomatic relations.

Our delegation was led by our deputy president and was met by your vice president. We had about 150 people who came with the deputy president.

During the discussions in the Bi-National Commission, it was agreed by both sides that our bilateral relationship has been developing very well. Both sides expressed satisfaction with the bilateral relationship, which covers all sectors. So we have a sound political and economic relationship, as well as in other sectors — culture, sport affairs, forestry, science, technology, etc. — covering the full spectrum of activities between our countries.

Obviously, there are some pragmatic ways that we can deepen our bilateral relationship. In 2004, we identified each other as strategic partners, and we are looking at how to go forward in the next 10 years and see how to deepen our strategic relationship.

There are three things that the South African cabinet has taken a decision on, in terms of marketing South Africa in China for the next three years. The first is to have a comprehensive program in China from the beginning to the end of next year to celebrate the 10th anniversary of our diplomatic relations. Secondary, we've announced that we will participate in the Shanghai 2010 World Expo, making sure we will represent South Africa perfectly as a business partner to the Chinese people and showing that South Africa has a modern and vibrant economy that China can do business with. In terms of the third area, we agreed we will establish something called the Partnership for Growth and Development, which will take our economic relationship to a much higher level. At the moment, the trade balance between our two countries is in favor of China. The investment was in favor of South Africa's investment into China. That investment pattern changed recently when the Industrial and Commercial Bank of China (ICBC) invested in [South Africa] Standard Bank — the 20 percent stock they bought for $5.5 billion.

Now, obviously China is the greater investor. But actually, what the partnership should do is to look into the Chinese economy: what needs of the Chinese economy can the South African economy fulfill, and what can South Africa supply to the Chinese economy? At the moment we may be exporting raw materials and commodities to China, so we would look to higher value-added commodities, and to work with China, both in manufacturing and beneficiation. So it's quite an extensive program that we are looking at — matching the needs of the Chinese economy with what the South African economy can currently supply, and working together to ensure that South Africa can also add value to the products coming to China and put them at the higher end.

So we are happy with our relationship with China. We are happy that China has paid a number of high-level visits to South Africa. The Chinese president, premier, a number of ministers and delegations have been to South Africa. Similarly, the South African President [Thabo] Mbeki, deputy presidents and other ministers have also been to China. At the political level, we are doing very well. Moreover, the party-to-party level exchanges are satisfying. Politically and in any other way, I think the relationship can be seen as a strategic partnership and is mutually beneficial to both sides.

B: What are your expectations for the future cooperation between the two countries in the economic and trade sectors?

D: Clearly, the trade relationship is healthy, and has growth from almost a zero base 10 years ago to over 60 billion rand (about $8.55 billion) in 2006. But as I've said, that has been from quite a narrow base of what South Africa exports to China, mainly in the areas of minerals and commodities. So what we are trying to do is to broaden that base to make it also include high value-added products, and for China to assist us in beneficiating products in South Africa, so that they can be sold on to China.

Equally I think that it is in accordance with the thrust of China to look at your overall trade imbalances and try to make sure that you import more from your partners like South Africa. Certainly, the key factors there will be the Partnership for Growth and Development.

B: What sectors do you think need improving?

D: In the Bi-National Commission, they specifically identified energy, infrastructure, machinery, home appliances, agro-processing, tourism and finance. The South African cabinet also listed the following priority sectors for investment, such as chemicals, mineral beneficiation, agro-processing, business process outsourcing, tourism, arts and crafts, automobile, aerospace, marine and rail transport. So there are a number of sectors that we are exploring.

Your Ministry of Commerce and our Department of Trade and Industry are working hard together to make sure that we have some growth in those sectors, both in terms of Chinese investment in these sectors of South Africa, as well as Chinese procurement of those types of high-end products from South Africa.

B: How does South Africa's role in the continent impact Sino-African relations?

D: What we see is that we are a part of various continental arrangements, where we all interact with each other as equals. In that context, we are obviously a member of the African Union; we participate in the regional arrangement of the Southern African Development Community; we are also committed to the implementation of the continental development program, the New Partnership for Africa's Development (NEPAD).

Whenever we interact with China bilaterally, we always have on the agenda, the issues of continental cooperation where China can assist in helping regional integration and implementing NEPAD. The discussion has also been taken to other arenas. For example, at the moment we serve with China in the United Nations Security Council, and we are also lucky enough to be invited to the G8 Summit, along with China, Brazil, Mexico and India as the "plus five" partners. In those forums, G8+5 and UN Security Council, we also have ongoing discussions with China on how to implement the NEPAD program and how China can assist in implementing Africa's agenda, which also covers Africa's security, resolutions of conflicts, governance issues and so on.

Certainly, with the steps China has taken of appointing a special envoy to Africa, sending peacekeepers to Africa, working with us in the Security Council on African issues, we value these things very much in terms of supporting the development of Africa. As I said, we used all these opportunities, bilateral and multilateral, to talk to our Chinese partners on how they can assist the overall development of the continent.

课文词语/Words and Expressions from the Text

Minister plenipotentiary	全权公使
strategic partners	战略伙伴
the Shanghai 2010 World Expo	2010年上海世博会
Industrial and Commercial Bank of China	中国工商银行
higher value-added commodities	高增值产品
agro-processing	农产品加工
mineral beneficiation	矿产品加工和利用
The New Partnership for Africa's Development (NEPAD)	非洲发展新伙伴
The G8 Summit	八国集团首脑会议

第二篇/Passage 2

Towards a Community of Common Destiny and a New Future for Asia
Keynote Speech at the Boao Forum for Asia Annual Conference 2015
Xi Jinping, President of the People's Republic of China
Boao, March 28, 2015

Your Excellencies Heads of State and Government,

Ministers,

Heads of International and Regional Organizations,

Members of the Board of Directors of the Boao Forum for Asia,

Ladies and Gentlemen,

Dear Friends,

Boao today greets us with vast ocean, high sky and warm breeze. In this beautiful season of spring, it is of great significance that so many distinguished guests gather here to discuss the development strategies for Asia and the world.

At the outset, let me extend, on behalf of the Chinese government and people and in my own name, heartfelt welcome to all the distinguished guests attending the Boao Forum for Asia Annual Conference 2015, and my warm congratulations on the opening of the conference.

The theme of this year's conference is "Asia's New Future: Towards a Community of Common Destiny". The timing could not be better in that the theme has not only great immediate relevance but also long-term historical significance. And I am looking to all of you to express yourselves fully and contribute your insightful views to the cause of peace and development of Asia and beyond.

Ladies and Gentlemen,

Dear Friends,

There are certain historic occasions that are likely to remind people of what happened in the past and set people reflecting on them. This year marks the 70th anniversary of the end of the World Anti-Fascist War, the victory of the Chinese People's War of Resistance Against Japanese Aggression and the founding of the United Nations. This year is also the 60th anniversary of the Bandung Conference and will witness the completion of the ASEAN Community. As such, it is an important year to be commemorated as well as a historic juncture to reflect on the past and look to the future.

Over the past 70 years, the world has experienced profound changes as never before, making a difference to the destiny of mankind. With the days of global colonialism and the Cold War long gone, countries are now increasingly interconnected and interdependent. Peace, development and win-win cooperation have become the prevailing trend of our times. The international forces are shifting in a way that is more favorable to maintaining world peace.

Countries are now in a better position to uphold general stability in the world and seek common development.

Over the past 70 years, Asia has also gone through unprecedented changes. After gaining national independence, Asian countries took their destiny in their own hands and strengthened the force for regional and world peace. Asian countries were the first to advocate the Five Principles of Peaceful Co-existence and, together with African countries, put forward the Ten Principles on handling state-to-state relations at the Bandung Conference. Since the end of the Cold War, Asian countries have gradually come up with an Asian way of cooperation in the course of advancing regional cooperation, which features mutual respect, consensus-building and accommodation of each other's comfort levels. All this has contributed to a proper approach to state-to-state relations and to progress in building a new type of international relations.

Over the past 70 years, more and more Asian countries have found development paths that suit their own national conditions and embarked on a fast-track of economic growth. Having emerged from poverty and backwardness, they are on course to achieve development and prosperity. Regional and inter-regional cooperation is flourishing. Connectivity is pursued at a faster pace. As a result, there is a strong momentum in Asia with countries striving to outperform each other. Accounting for one third of the world economy, Asia is one of the most dynamic regions with the most potential and its global strategic importance has been rising.

Over the past 70 years, Asian countries have gradually transcended their differences in ideology and social system. No longer cut off from each other, they are now open and inclusive, with suspicion and estrangement giving way to growing trust and appreciation. The interests of Asian countries have become intertwined, and a community of common destiny has increasingly taken shape. Be it the arduous struggle for national independence, or the difficult periods of the Asian financial crisis and the international financial crisis, or the hard time in the wake of devastating disasters including the Indian Ocean tsunami and earthquake in Wenchuan, China, the people of Asian countries have always come to those in need with a helping hand and worked together to overcome one challenge after another, demonstrating the power of unity in face of difficulties and the spirit of sharing weal and woe. This said, Asia still faces numerous challenges. Some are the old issues left over from history and others are new ones associated with current disputes. Asia is also confronted with various traditional and non-traditional security threats. Hence it remains an uphill battle for Asian countries to grow the economy, improve people's livelihood and eliminate poverty.

A review of the path traversed over the past 70 years shows that what has been accomplished in Asia today is attributable to the persistent efforts of several generations of people in Asian countries and to the hard work of many statesmen and people of great vision. Tomorrow, Singapore will hold a state funeral for Mr. Lee Kuan Yew. Mr. Lee was a strategist and statesman respected across the world for his outstanding contribution to the peace and development of Asia and the exchanges and cooperation between Asia and the world. I want to take this opportunity to pay high tribute to Mr. Lee Kuan Yew and all those who made contribution to Asia's peace and development.

Ladies and Gentlemen,

Dear Friends,

Asia belongs to the world. For Asia to move towards a community of common destiny and embrace a new future, it has to follow the world trend and seek progress and development in tandem with that of the world.

The international situation continues to experience profound and complex changes, with significant development in multipolarization and economic globalization. Cultural diversity and IT application are making constant progress while readjustment is accelerating in international landscape and order. Countries around the world are losing no time in adjusting their development strategies, pursuing transformation and innovation, changing their economic development models, improving economic structures and opening up new horizons for further development. At the same time, however, the world economy is still in a period of profound adjustment, with risks of low growth, low inflation and low demand interwoven with risks of high unemployment, high debt and high level of bubbles. The performance and policies of major economies continue to diverge, and uncertainties in the economic climate remain prominent. Geopolitical factors are more at play and local turmoils keep cropping up. Non-traditional security threats and global challenges including terrorism, cyber security, energy security, food security, climate change and major infectious diseases are on the rise, and the North-South gap is still wide. The noble cause of peace and development remains a long and arduous journey for mankind.

We have only one planet, and countries share one world. To do well, Asia and the world could not do without each other. Facing the fast changing international and regional landscapes, we must see the whole picture, follow the trend of our times and jointly build a regional order that is more favorable to Asia and the world. We should, through efforts towards such a community for Asia, promote a community of common interest for all mankind. I wish to take this opportunity to share with you my thoughts on this vision.

To build a community of common destiny, we need to make sure that all countries respect one another and treat each other as equals. Countries may differ in size, strength or level of development, but they are all equal members of the international community with equal rights to participate in regional and international affairs. On matters that involve us all, we should discuss and look for a solution together. Being a big country means shouldering greater responsibilities for regional and world peace and development, as opposed to seeking greater monopoly over regional and world affairs.

To respect one another and treat each other as equals, countries need to, first and foremost, respect other countries' social systems and development paths of their own choice, respect each other's core interests and major concerns and have objective and rational perception of other countries' growing strength, policies and visions. Efforts should be made to seek common ground while shelving differences, and better still to increase common interests and dissolve differences. The hard-won peace and stability in Asia and the sound momentum for development should be upheld by all. All of us must oppose interference in other countries' internal affairs and reject attempts to destabilize the region out of selfish motives.

To build a community of common destiny, we need to seek win-win cooperation and common development. Our friends in Southeast Asia say that the lotus flowers grow taller as the water rises. Our friends in Africa say that if you want to go fast, walk alone; and if you want to go far, walk together. Our friends in Europe say that a single tree cannot block the chilly wind. And Chinese people say that when big rivers have water, the small ones are filled; and when small rivers have water, the big ones are filled. All these sayings speak to one same truth, that is, only through win-win cooperation can we make big and sustainable achievements that are beneficial to all. The old mindset of zero-sum game should give way to a new approach of win-win and all-win cooperation. The interests of others must be accommodated while pursuing one's own interests, and common development must be promoted while seeking one's own development. The vision of win-win cooperation not only applies to the economic field, but also to the political, security, cultural and many other fields. It not only applies to countries within the region, but also to cooperation with countries from outside the region. We should enhance coordination of macroeconomic policies to prevent negative spill-over effects that may arise from economic policy changes in individual economies. We should actively promote reform of global economic governance, uphold an open world economy, and jointly respond to risks and challenges in the world economy.

China and ASEAN countries will join hands in building an even closer China-ASEAN community of common destiny. The building of an East Asia economic community for ASEAN, China, Japan and ROK will be completed in 2020. We should actively build a free trade cooperation network in Asia and strive to conclude negotiations on an upgraded China-ASEAN FTA and on Regional Comprehensive Economic Partnership (RCEP) in 2015. In advancing economic integration in Asia, we need to stay committed to open regionalism and move forward trans-regional cooperation, including APEC, in a coordinated manner.

We will vigorously promote a system of regional financial cooperation, explore a platform for exchanges and cooperation among Asian financial institutions, and advance complementary and coordinated development between the Asian Infrastructure Investment Bank (AIIB) and such multilateral financial institutions as the Asian Development Bank and the World Bank. We will strengthen practical cooperation in currency stability, investment and financing, and credit rating, make progress in institution building for the Chiang Mai Initiative Multilateralization and build a regional financial security network. We will work towards an energy and resources cooperation mechanism in Asia to ensure energy and resources security.

China proposes that plans be formulated regarding connectivity building in East Asia and Asia at large to advance full integration in infrastructure, policies and institutions and personnel flow. We may increase maritime connectivity, speed up institution building for marine cooperation in Asia, and step up cooperation in marine economy, environmental protection, disaster management and fishery. This way, we could turn the seas of Asia into seas of peace, friendship and cooperation for Asian countries.

To build a community of common destiny, we need to pursue common, comprehensive, cooperative and sustainable security. In today's world, security means much more than before and its implications go well beyond a single region or time frame. All sorts of factors could have a bearing on a country's security. As people of all countries share common destiny and become increasingly interdependent, no country could have its own security ensured without the security of other countries or of the wider world. The Cold War mentality should truly be discarded and new security concepts be nurtured as we explore a path for Asia that ensures security for all, by all and of all.

We believe that countries are all entitled to take an equal part in regional security affairs and all are obliged to work to ensure security for the region. The legitimate security concerns of each country need to be respected and addressed. At the same time, in handling security issues in Asia, it is important to bear in mind both the history and reality of Asia, take a multi-pronged and holistic approach, improve coordinated regional security governance, and safeguard security in both the traditional and non-traditional realms. It is important to conduct dialogue and cooperation to enhance security at national and regional levels, and to increase cooperation as the way to safeguard peace and security. It is important to resolve disputes through peaceful means, and oppose the willful use or threat of force. Security should be given equal emphasis as development, and sustainable development surely provides a way to sustainable security. Countries in Asia need to step up cooperation with countries and organizations outside the region and all parties are welcome to play a positive and constructive role in upholding development and security in Asia.

To build a community of common destiny, we need to ensure inclusiveness and mutual learning among civilizations. History, over the past millennia, has witnessed ancient civilizations appear and thrive along the Yellow and Yangtze Rivers, the Indus, the Ganges, the Euphrates, and the Tigris River as well as in Southeast Asia, each adding its own splendour to the progress of human civilization. Today, Asia has proudly maintained its distinct diversity and still nurtures all the civilizations, ethnic groups and religions in this big Asian family.

Mencius, the great philosopher in ancient China, said, "Things are born to be different." Civilizations are only unique, and no one is superior to the other. There need to be more exchange and dialogue among civilizations and development models, so that each could draw on the strength of the other and all could thrive and prosper by way of mutual learning and common development. Let us promote inter-civilization exchanges to build bridges of friendship for our people, drive human development and safeguard peace of the world.

China proposes that a conference of dialogue among Asian civilizations be held to provide a platform upon which to enhance interactions among the youth, people's groups, local communities and the media and to form a network of think-tank cooperation, so as to add to Asian people's rich cultural life and contribute to more vibrant regional cooperation and development.

Ladies and Gentlemen,

Dear Friends,

Right now, the Chinese people are working in unison under the strategic plans to complete the building of a moderately prosperous society in all respects, and to comprehensively deepen reform, advance law-based governance, and enforce strict Party conduct. Our objective is to realize the "two centenary" goals for China's development and for realizing the Chinese dream of great national rejuvenation. I wish to use this opportunity to reaffirm China's commitment to the path of peaceful development, and to promoting cooperation and common development in the Asia-Pacific. China will be firm in its determination and resolve and all its policies will be designed to achieve such a purpose.

Now, the Chinese economy has entered a state of new normal. It is shifting gear from high speed to medium-to-high speed growth, from an extensive model that emphasized scale and speed to a more intensive one emphasizing quality and efficiency, and from being driven by investment in production factors to being driven by innovation. China's economy grew by 7.4% in 2014, with 7% increase in labor productivity and 4.8% decrease in energy intensity. The share of domestic consumption in GDP rose, the services sector expanded at a faster pace, and the economy's efficiency and quality continued to improve. When looking at China's economy, one should not focus on growth rate only. As the economy continues to grow in size, around 7% growth would be quite impressive, and the momentum it generates would be larger than growth at double digits in previous years. It is fair to say that the Chinese economy is highly resilient and has much potential, which gives us enough room to leverage a host of policy tools. Having said that, China will continue to be responsive to the new trend and take initiatives to shape the new normal in our favor. We will focus on improving quality and efficiency, and give even greater priority to shifting the growth model and adjusting the structure of development. We will make more solid efforts to boost economic development and deepen reform and opening-up. We will take more initiatives to unleash the creativity and ingenuity of the people, be more effective in safeguarding equity and social justice, raise people's living standards and make sure that China's economic and social development are both sound and stable.

This new normal of the Chinese economy will continue to bring more opportunities of trade, growth, investment and cooperation for other countries in Asia and beyond. In the coming five years, China will import more than US$10 trillion of goods, Chinese investment abroad will exceed US$500 billion, and more than 500 million outbound visits will be made by Chinese tourists. China will stick to its basic state policy of opening up, improve its investment climate, and protect the lawful rights and interests of investors. I believe that together, the people of Asian countries could drive this train of Asia's development to take Asia to an even brighter future.

What China needs most is a harmonious and stable domestic environment and a peaceful and tranquil international environment. Turbulence or war runs against the fundamental interests of the Chinese people. The Chinese nation loves peace and has, since ancient times, held high such philosophies that "harmony is the most valuable", "peace and harmony should prevail" and "all men under heaven are brothers". China has suffered from turbulence and war for more than a century since modern times, and the Chinese people would never want to inflict the same tragedy on other countries or peoples. History has taught us that no country who tried to achieve its goal with force ever succeeded. China will be steadfast in pursuing the independent foreign policy of peace, the path of peaceful development, the win-win strategy of opening-up, and the approach of upholding justice while pursuing shared interests. China will work to promote a new type of international relations of win-win cooperation and will always remain a staunch force for world peace and common development.

Close neighbors are better than distant relatives. This is a simple truth that the Chinese people got to know in ancient times. That explains China's firm commitment to building friendship and partnership with its neighbors to foster an amicable, secure and prosperous neighborhood. Under the principle of amity, sincerity, mutual benefit and inclusiveness, China is working actively to deepen win-win cooperation and connectivity with its neighbors to bring them even more benefit with its own development. China has signed treaties of good-neighborliness, friendship and cooperation with eight of its neighbors and is holding discussion to sign a same treaty with ASEAN. China stands ready to sigh such a treaty with all its neighbors to provide strong support for the development of bilateral relations as well as prosperity and stability in the region.

In 2013, during my visit to Kazakhstan and Indonesia, I put forward the initiatives of building a Silk Road economic belt and a 21st century maritime Silk Road. The "Belt and Road" initiative, meeting the development needs of China, countries along the routes and the region at large, will serve the common interests of relevant parties and answer the call of our time for regional and global cooperation.

In promoting this initiative, China will follow the principle of wide consultation, joint contribution and shared benefits. The programs of development will be open and inclusive, not exclusive. They will be a real chorus comprising all countries along the routes, not a solo for

China itself. To develop the Belt and Road is not to replace existing mechanisms or initiatives for regional cooperation. Much to the contrary, we will build on the existing basis to help countries align their development strategies and form complementarity. Currently, more than 60 countries along the routes and international organizations have shown interest in taking part in the development of the Belt and the Road. The "Belt and Road" and the AIIB are both open initiatives. We welcome all countries along the routes and in Asia, as well as our friends and partners around the world, to take an active part in these endeavors.

The "Belt and Road" initiative is not meant as rhetoric. It represents real work that could be seen and felt to bring real benefits to countries in the region. Thanks to the concerted efforts of relevant parties, the vision and action paper of the initiative has been developed. Substantive progress has been made in the establishment of the AIIB. The Silk Road Fund has been launched, and constructions of a number of infrastructure connectivity projects are moving forward. These early harvests have truly pointed to the broad prospects the "Belt and Road" initiative will bring.

Ladies and Gentlemen,

Dear Friends,

The cause of peace and development of mankind is as lofty as it is challenging. The journey ahead will not be smooth sailing, and success may not come easily. No matter how long and difficult the journey may be, those who work together and never give up will eventually prevail. I believe that as long as we keep to our goals and make hard efforts, we will together bring about a community of common destiny and usher in a new future for Asia.

I wish the Annual Conference a complete success.

Thank you very much.

(*Beijing Review*, April 9, 2015)

课文词语/Words and Expressions from the Text

the Chinese People's War of Resistance Against Japanese Aggression	抗日战争
the Bandung Conference	万隆会议
win-win cooperation	合作共赢
zero-sum game	零和游戏
regional Comprehensive Economic Partnership (RCEP)	地区金融合作体系
two centenary	两个一百年
belt and road	一带一路
close neighbors are better than distance relatives	远亲不如近邻

二、口译实践/Interpretation Practice

句子口译/Sentence Interpretation

(一)英译汉/E-C

Interpret the following sentences into Chinese.

 10-1.mp3

1. Development, security and human rights are the three pillars of our common vision of the future.

2. A peaceful world requires collective measures for the prevention of war, international cooperation to solve economic and social problems and respect for human rights.

3. Whatever our differences are, in our interdependent world, we stand or fall together. Whether our challenge is peacemaking, nation-building, democratization, or responding to natural or man-made disasters, we've seen that even the strongest among us can not succeed alone.

4. The World Summit made breakthroughs in adopting strategies to fight poverty and diseases, creating new machinery to win the peace in war-torn countries, and pledging collective action to prevent genocide. It made real progress in terrorism, human rights, democracy, peace-keeping and humanitarian response.

5. A healthy, effective United Nations is vital. If properly utilized, it can be a unique marriage of power and principle in the service of all the world's peoples. That's why the UN reform process matters and must continue. No matter how frustrating things are, there is no escaping fact that the challenges of our time must be met by collective action.

(二)汉译英/C-E

Interpret the following sentences into English.

 10-2.mp3

1. 通过和平的方式解决国际争端是联合国宪章的重要原则之一，这有利于世界的和平与稳定。

2. 我们的世界处于转型时期，朝着多极化发展。和平与发展是世界各国人民的共同愿望，但仍然面临着严峻的挑战。

3. 为了促进世界的和平、繁荣与稳定，联合国应进行必要、合理的改革，以确保其高效率地运作，并能更好地代表国际社会。

4. 中华民族历来爱好和平，自古就崇尚"以和为贵"、"协和万邦"、"四海之内皆兄弟也"等思想。

5. 在这里，我愿重申：中国将坚定不移地高举和平、发展、合作的旗帜，走和平发展的道路。中国将始终不渝地把自身的发展与人类共同进步联系在一起。

对话口译/Dialogue Interpretation

Interpret the following dialogues alternatively into English and Chinese.

10-3.mp3

A: Thank you so much for your hospitality. This is my first visit to Shanghai, and we've been so impressed with the incredible growth in the city and the great warmth of the people who have received us.

B: 上海是一座见证了过去30年间中国与美国外交关系发展的城市。1972年，上海公报在上海这座城市宣布，这已经为两国之间外交关系的正常化奠定了坚实基础。

A: Well, obviously both countries have benefited greatly from the progress that we've made over the last three decades. I know that many U.S. businesses are now located here in Shanghai and they consider it really the center for the region, commercially and financially. And it is very impressive to travel through the city and to see what extraordinary progress has been made.

B: 上海市民非常高兴，因为上海是您中国之行的第一站。

A: Well. Thank you.

B: 在众多驻上海的美国公司当中，最有名的制造企业之一是通用汽车。通用汽车在上海的业务很好。截至今年10月底，他们的销售额比去年同期增长了40%以上。我认为他们在上海这里的出色业绩肯定会推动他们在美国的业务。

A: Absolutely. I think they can learn from their operations here in terms of increasing sales back in the United States.

段落口译/Short Passage Interpretation

(一)英译汉/E-C

Interpret the following short passages into Chinese.

10-4.mp3

In the age of globalization, we should regard international cooperation as part of our national interest. The United Nations and the way we approach collective security must be adapted to changing circumstances. At this summit, we have an opportunity to take decisions that may shape international cooperation for many years to come. We come here because we know challenges facing us in the era of globalization can not be met in isolation. Poverty must be eradicated, resources of our planet used sustainably, human rights respected, equality between men and women strengthened, AIDS and other diseases prevented, terrorism stopped and disarmament and nuclear non-proliferation secured. We need to find collective solution to these problems based on the rule of law.

(二)汉译英/C-E

Interpret the following short passage into English.

10-5.mp3

维护国际和平与安全,是广大成员国通过《联合国宪章》赋予安理会的神圣职责。一年来,安理会继续致力于解决各类地区热点,在防止大规模杀伤性武器扩散,维持地区稳定,帮助冲突后国家重建和平等方面做出了积极的努力。一个高效、负责的安理会符合各方共同利益。安理会在履行其自身职责的同时,将不断采取措施改进工作,增强工作透明度。

篇章口译/Passage Interpretation

Passage 1

相关词语/Related Words and Expressions

ASEM (Asia–Europe Meeting)	亚欧会议
SMEs (Small and Medium Enterprises)	中小企业
Drive the Future with Innovation	创新引领未来
Promote Development Through Cooperation	合作促进发展
tangible benefits	切实的利益
reflecting diverse development	体现多元发展
revitalizing regional economy	实现地区振兴
highly complementary to each other	互补性强
trade facilitation	贸易便利化
intellectual property rights (IPRs)	知识产权
transfer of industries and services around the globe	国际产业和服务转移
removal of tariff and non-tariff barriers	消除关税和非关税壁垒
optimizing resource allocation	优化资源配置
be of positive significance	具有积极意义
industrial clusters	产业集群
innovative capability	创新能力
sustainable development	可持续发展
entrepreneurship	创业精神
narrowing the gap between the rich and the poor	缩小贫富差距
financing guarantee	融资担保

market exploration	市场开拓
outsourcing of products and services	产品和服务外包
facilitate SMEs' access to business opportunities	便利中小企业获得商机
China International Small and Medium Enterprises Fair	中国国际中小企业博览会
biennially	每两年一次

Interpret the following passages into Chinese.

10-6.mp3

Beijing Declaration on Strengthening Cooperation Among ASEM Members on Small and Medium Enterprises (AMEs) Beijing, China (excerpted)

The First ASEM SMEs Ministerial Meeting was held in Beijing on October 30 to 31, 2007. SMEs Ministers and their representatives from 45 ASEM members gathered under the theme "Drive the Future with Innovation, Promote Development Through Cooperation" and conducted extensive and in-depth discussions on issues of common interests regarding SMEs such as technological innovation, business development services, and cooperation and development, and achieved the following outcomes.

Main Consensus

1. Promote the development of SMEs to build a harmonious world. SMEs play an important role in economic and social development. Ministers recognized that the development of SMEs can bring tangible benefits to the economic growth of ASEM members. All members should make every effort to promote the development of SMEs, and to bring into play their roles in creating employment opportunities, reflecting diverse development, revitalizing regional economy, reducing poverty and enhancing the well-being of the people.

2. Reinforce economic and trade cooperation to promote economic prosperity in Asia and Europe. Ministers noted that Asia is the most dynamic region in the world and Europe is the largest developed economy. Asian SMEs and European SMEs are highly complementary to each other in terms of product, technology, labor and market with huge potential of cooperation. It is of great necessity to further improve trade and investment climate, enhance exchanges among ASEM members, establish effective cooperation mechanisms for SMEs, and promote cooperation in multiple fields, notably trade facilitation, services, transfer of technology, intellectual property rights (IPRs), corporate social responsibility and accountability, with a view to narrowing the gap of development among members and promoting common economic prosperity in Asia and Europe.

3. Improve industrial structure, facilitate open markets, and promote fair competition to assist SMEs to address challenges of globalization. Ministers recognized that the deepening

economic globalization and accelerating transfer of industries and services around the globe bring new opportunities and challenges to the development of Asian and European SMEs. Ministers highlighted the importance of opening up markets, fair competition, and removal of tariff and non-tariff barriers to the economic and trade cooperation among SMEs of ASEM members. To strengthen industrial cooperation between Asia and Europe is of positive significance to optimizing resource allocation and enhancing regional competitiveness. Ministers noted that industrial clusters characterized by congregated SMEs have become the source of regional economic vitality and diversity. To enable clusters to play a positive role in specialized division of work, industrial cooperation, optimization and upgrading is of great significance to regional economic development.

4. Enhance innovative capability to achieve sustainable development. Ministers stressed that innovation is a vital driving force for economic and social development, and SMEs are potentially the greatest innovators. ASEM members need to take positive measures to improve the environment for SMEs innovation, attach importance to the protection of IPRs including proper enforcement and promotion of IPRs, enhance the ability to provide services for SMEs in their IPR creation, protection and application, and support the innovation activities of SMEs. In particular, members need to encourage SMEs to strengthen research and development and international cooperation in energy and environment technologies, promote the use of new renewable energies, facilitate SMEs' access to energy-saving and environment-friendly technologies, so as to promote sustainable development.

5. Increase employment opportunities to attain general social affluence. Ministers acknowledged that increasing employment opportunities, encouraging entrepreneurship and creating an enabling environment for entrepreneurs are essential to narrowing the gap between the rich and the poor and enabling all to benefit from economic growth. ASEM members are therefore encouraged to give more support to entrepreneurship, and employment opportunities as well as vocational training, and to simplify procedures for starting business.

6. Complete business development services to improve the environment for enterprises' development. Ministers considered it necessary to continue building the service system for SMEs, provide them with convenient and efficient services and meet their diverse needs for services. Ministers encouraged ASEM members to take measures to improve business development services for SMEs in microfinance, financing guarantee, market exploration, human resources, outsourcing and information consultation, and to further improve the environment for enterprises' development. Ministers encouraged financial institutions of ASEM members to extend credit facilities to SMEs in rural and underdeveloped areas.

7. Ministers suggested that technology exchanges, consultations and cooperation be carried out among ASEM SMEs in the field of resource conservation and environmental protection, and that ASEM SMEs be encouraged to jointly cope with impacts and challenges of climate, energy

and environment by developing technologies and mitigating impacts.

8. Ministers encouraged SMEs to pay attention to environmental protection in their production and business activities, fulfill their social responsibilities, improve working conditions and protect employees' rights.

9. Ministers encouraged Asian and European SMEs to engage themselves in development and cooperation related to technology, investment, and economic and trade exchanges, and supported exchanges and cooperation on personnel training, IPR protection, and IT technology application among service agencies for SMEs in ASEM members.

10. Ministers suggested that ASEM members learn and share best policy initiatives and practice concerning SMEs' innovation and development, make more extensive use of IT technologies and the Internet, develop e-commerce and facilitate SMEs' access to business opportunities.

11. Ministers stressed that exchanges on financing policies for SMEs be strengthened, innovation of financial products and services be promoted, investment mechanism for starting business be improved, and diverse financing services be provided to SMEs.

12. Ministers agreed to promote the development of SMEs industrial clusters, expand trade, investment and technology cooperation among industrial clusters in Asia and Europe, and to advance regional economic development with local characteristics.

13. Ministers appreciated China's decision to provide, during the annual "China International Small and Medium Enterprises Fair" in each September, a free "Hall for ASEM SMEs Cooperation and Exchange" or members to hold exhibitions and conduct exchanges, and a website (www.asem-sme.net) to facilitate members' participation in the fair as well as daily communication.

14. Ministers agreed that ASEM SMEs Ministerial Meeting be held biennially prior to the ASEM Summit and hosted alternatively by Asian and European members so as to build it into regular and sustainable mechanism for policy exchange and dialogue.

15. Ministers agreed to set up a Senior Officials' Meeting Mechanism for ASEM SMEs Cooperation and hold the Senior Officials' Meeting biennially prior to the Ministerial Meeting, with rotation between Asian and European members. Government officials from each member will be designated to participate in the Senior Officials' Meeting and take responsibilities of dail liaison of SMEs cooperation as well as coordination and communication for the preparation of the Ministerial Meeting.

16. Ministers noted that the second ASEM SMEs Ministerial Meeting will be held in Europe in 2009.

Passage 2

相关词语/Related Words and Expressions

Hong Kong Special Administrative Regions	香港特别行政区
Macau Special Administrative Regions	澳门特别行政区
the South-North Water Diversion Project	南水北调
thumbs up	点赞
the National Memorial Day for Victims of the Nanjing Massacre	
南京大屠杀死难者国家公祭日	
an arrow that has been released makes no turning back	
开弓没有回头箭	
a moderately prosperous society	小康社会
two wings of a bird	鸟之两翼

🎵 10-7.mp3

国家主席习近平发表二〇一五年新年贺词

新华社北京12月31日电。新年前夕，国家主席习近平通过中国国际广播电台、中央人民广播电台、中央电视台，发表了2015年新年贺词。全文如下：

时间过得真快，2014年就要过去了，2015年正在向我们走来。在这辞旧迎新的时刻，我向全国各族人民，向香港特别行政区同胞和澳门特别行政区同胞，向台湾同胞和海外侨胞，向世界各国和各地区的朋友们，致以新年的祝福！

2014年是令人难忘的。这一年，我们锐意推进改革，啃下了不少硬骨头，出台了一系列重大改革举措，许多改革举措同老百姓的利益密切相关。我们适应经济发展新常态，积极推动经济社会发展，人民生活有了新的改善。12月12日，南水北调中线一期工程正式通水，沿线40多万人移民搬迁，为这个工程做出了无私奉献，我们要向他们表示敬意，希望他们在新的家园生活幸福。这一年，我们着力正风肃纪，重点反对形式主义、官僚主义、享乐主义和奢靡之风，情况有了很大改观。我们加大反腐败斗争力度，以零容忍的态度严惩腐败分子，显示了反腐惩恶的坚定决心。这一年，我们加强同世界各国的合作交往，主办了北京亚太经合组织领导人非正式会议，我国领导人多次出访，外国领导人也大量来访，这些活动让世界更好地认识了中国。

为了做好这些工作，我们的各级干部也是蛮拼的。当然，没有人民支持，这些工作是难以做好的，我要为我们伟大的人民点赞。

这一年，我们通过立法确定了中国人民抗日战争胜利纪念日、烈士纪念日、南京大屠杀死难者国家公祭日，举行了隆重活动。对一切为国家、为民族、为和平付出宝贵生命的人们，不管时代怎样变化，我们都要永远铭记他们的牺牲和奉献。

这一年，我们也经历了一些令人悲伤的时刻。马航MH370航班失踪，150多名同胞下落不明，我们没有忘记他们，我们一定要持续努力、想方设法找到他们。这一年，我国发生了一些重大自然灾害和安全事故，不少同胞不幸离开了我们，云南鲁甸地震就造成了600多人遇难，我们怀念他们，祝愿他们的亲人们都安好。

新年的钟声即将敲响。我们要继续努力，把人民的期待变成我们的行动，把人民的希望变成生活的现实。我们要继续全面深化改革，开弓没有回头箭，改革关头勇者胜。我们要全面推进依法治国，用法治保障人民权益、维护社会公平正义、促进国家发展。我们要让全面深化改革、全面推进依法治国如鸟之两翼、车之双轮，推动全面建成小康社会的目标如期实现。

我国人民生活总体越来越好，但我们时刻都要想着那些生活中还有难处的群众。我们要满腔热情做好民生工作，特别是要做好扶贫开发和基本生活保障工作，让农村贫困人口、城市困难群众等所有需要帮助的人们都能生活得到保障、心灵充满温暖。

我们要继续全面推进从严治党，毫不动摇转变作风，高举反腐的利剑，扎牢制度的笼子，在中国共产党领导的社会主义国家里，腐败分子发现一个就要查处一个，有腐必惩，有贪必肃。

我们正在从事的事业是伟大的，坚忍不拔才能胜利，半途而废必将一事无成。我们的蓝图是宏伟的，我们的奋斗必将是艰巨的。全党全国各族人民要团结一心，集思广益用好机遇，众志成城应对挑战，立行立改破解难题，奋发有为进行创新，让国家发展和人民生活一年比一年好。

中国人民关注自己国家的前途，也关注世界的前途。非洲发生了埃博拉疫情，我们给予帮助；马尔代夫首都遭遇断水，我们给予支援，许许多多这样的行动展示了中国人民同各国人民同呼吸、共命运的情怀。当前世界仍很不安宁。我们呼唤和平，我真诚希望，世界各国人民共同努力，让所有的人民免于饥寒的煎熬，让所有的家庭免于战火的威胁，让所有的孩子都能在和平的阳光下茁壮成长。

谢谢大家。

参考译文/Reference Version

句子口译/Sentence Interpretation

(一)英译汉/E-C

1. 发展、安全和人权是我们未来的三大目标。

2. 一个和平的世界需要采取共同的措施来防止战争，加强国际合作来解决经济与社会的问题，以及尊重人权。

3. 无论我们之间存在何种差异，在我们这个相互依赖的世界，我们要么一起获胜，要么一起失败。我们面对的挑战无论是维持和平、建设家园、争取民主，还是应对自然灾害或人为的灾难，我们明白即便是我们中最强大的国家也不能独自面对所有这些挑战。

4. 世界领袖高峰会议在以下方面有了突破：采取策略抗击贫困和疾病，建立新的机制为饱受战争的国家赢得和平，承诺采取共同行动防止种族屠杀。峰会在打击恐怖主义、维护人权、推进民主、维护和平及人道主义援助方面取得了真正的进展。

5. 一个健康、有效的联合国是至关重要的。如果合理利用，联合国可以是权利和准则独特的结合，服务于世界各国人民。那也就是为什么联合国的改革进程是很重要的，而且须继续进行。无论形势有多么艰难，无法逃脱的事实是我们必须采取共同的行动来迎接我们这个时代的挑战。

(二)汉译英/C-E

1. Peaceful settlement of international disputes is one of the important principles of the UN Charter and is conducive to world peace and stability.

2. Our world is in transition, moving toward multipolarity. Peace and development are the common aspirations of the world people and still face great challenges.

3. In order to promote world peace, prosperity and stability, the UN must undergo necessary and rational reform to ensure its efficient operation and to best represent international community.

4. The Chinese nation loves peace and has, since ancient times, held high such philosophies that "harmony is the most valuable", "peace and harmony should prevail" and "all men under heaven are brothers".

5. I wish to reiterate here that China will continue to hold high the banner of peace, development and cooperation, unswervingly follow the road of peaceful development. We will, and always, integrated our development with the common progress of mankind.

对话口译/Dialogue Interpretation

A: 非常感谢您的热情款待。这是我第一次访问上海，我们已经被这座城市令人难以置信的发展和接待人员的热情所深深打动。

B: Shanghai is a city that witnessed the progress of the diplomatic relations between China and the United States over the past three decades. In 1972, Shanghai was a city where the *Shanghai Communique* was announced, and this has already made a solid foundation for the normalization of diplomatic ties between the two countries.

A: 嗯，显然两国都已经大大受益于我们在过去30年所取得的进展。我知道，许多美国企业现在都驻扎在上海，无论是从商业还是金融角度来说，他们认为它是该区域真正的中心。穿行于这座城市，其非凡进展令人印象非常深刻。

B: The Shanghai citizens are very pleased because Shanghai is the first stop of your China visit.

A: 嗯，谢谢您。

B: For many U.S. companies here in Shanghai one of the most famous manufacturing companies is General Motor. The business of GM in Shanghai is pretty good. By the end of October this year their sales has increased by more than 40 percent over the same period of last year. I think that the fantastic performance here in Shanghai is definitely a boost to their business in the United States.

A: 当然。我认为他们可以从这里的运营中学习如何增加在美国的销售。

段落口译/Short Passage Interpretation

(一)英译汉/E-C

在全球化时代，我们应该将国际合作视为国家利益的一部分。联合国以及我们对待共同安全的方式应适应不断变化的形势。在本次峰会上，我们有机会作出一些决定，这些决定将对未来许多年的国际合作起着决定的作用。我们聚集一起，因为我们知道我们无法独自应对全球化时代我们所面临的挑战。我们要消除贫困，持续利用地球上的资源，尊重人权，加强男女平等，防止艾滋病和其他疾病，阻止恐怖主义和确保裁军及核不扩散。我们需要在法制的基础上，通过合作找到解决这些问题的共同方法。

(二)汉译英/C-E

The UN Security Council is endowed by the UN members through the UN Charter with the lofty job, which is to keep international peace and security. In the past one year, the UN Security Council has continued to commit itself to resolving various regional hotspot issues and has made positive contributions to preventing proliferation of weapons of mass destruction, easing tensions, maintaining regional stability, helping post-conflict countries rebuild peace. A Security Council with high efficiency and strong responsibility meets with the collective interests of all the members. The UN Security Council will continue to take measures to improve its work and strengthen its transparency when making its commitments.

篇章口译/Passage Interpretation

Passage 1

加强亚欧会议成员间中小企业合作的北京宣言

中国　北京　（节选）

首届亚欧会议中小企业部长级会议于 2007 年 10 月 30—31 日在北京召开。45 个亚欧会议成员的中小企业部长和代表出席会议。部长们围绕"创新引领未来，合作促进发展"主题，就普遍关注的中小企业技术创新、服务体系、合作与发展等议题进行了广泛深入的讨论，并取得以下成果。

主要共识

1. 发展中小企业，携手构建和谐世界。中小企业在经济和社会发展中扮演着重要角色。部长们认为，发展中小企业可为亚欧会议成员的经济发展带来切实的利益。各成员应尽最大努力促进中小企业发展，发挥其在创造社会就业机会、体现多元发展、实现地区振兴、减少社会贫困、增进人民福祉方面的作用。

2. 加强经贸合作，共促亚欧经济繁荣。部长们认为，亚洲是世界上最具活力的地区，欧洲是世界上最大的发达经济体，亚欧中小企业在产品、技术、劳动力和市场等方面的互补性强，合作潜力巨大，有必要进一步改善贸易和投资环境，加强亚欧各成员间的交流，建立有效的中小企业合作机制，推进多领域特别是在贸易便利化、服务业、技术转让、知识产权、企业社会责任等方面的合作，缩小成员间发展差距，促进亚欧经济的共同繁荣。

3. 优化产业结构，促进市场开放和公平竞争，应对全球化的挑战。部长们认识到，经济全球化的日益加深和国际产业与服务转移的不断加速，为亚欧中小企业的发展带来了新的机遇与挑战。部长们强调了开放市场、公平竞争，消除关税壁垒和非关税壁垒对于推动亚欧会议成员中小企业经贸合作的重要性。加强亚欧产业合作对优化资源配置、提高区域竞争力具有积极的意义。部长们注意到，以中小企业集聚为特征的产业集群已成为地区经济活力和多样性所在，发挥集群在专业化分工、产业协作和优化升级等方面的积极作用，对推动地区经济发展具有重要意义。

4. 提高创新能力，实现可持续的发展。部长们强调，创新是经济和社会发展的不竭动力，中小企业是最具创新潜力的群体。亚欧各成员要积极改善中小企业的创新环境，重视知识产权的保护和执法，增强对中小企业知识产权创造、保护和应用等方面的服务能力。加大对中小企业创新活动的支持，特别鼓励中小企业加强能源、环境技术方面的研发和国际合作，推广使用新型和可再生能源，使中小企业更易获得和采用节能和环保技术，促进可持续发展。

5. 增加就业机会，促进社会普遍富裕。部长们认为，扩大就业机会，激发创业精神，形成有利于企业家成长的环境，对缩小贫富差距，使经济增长带来的好处惠及所有民众至关重要。鼓励亚欧会议各成员加大对创业、职业培训的扶持，简化创业程序。

6. 健全社会服务，改善企业发展环境。部长们认为，有必要进一步推进中小企业服务体系的建设，为中小企业提供便捷、高效的服务，满足企业多样化的服务需求。部长们鼓励亚欧会议各成员采取措施完善中小企业小额贷款、融资担保、市场开拓、人力资源、产品和服务外包、信息咨询等方面的社会服务，继续改善企业经营环境，鼓励各类金融机构为农村及落后地区的小企业提供融资便利。

7. 部长们建议在亚欧中小企业中开展"节约资源，保护环境"方面的技术交流、咨询和合作，鼓励中小企业共同应对气候、能源、环境带来的影响和挑战，积极贡献技术，消除影响。

8. 部长们鼓励中小企业在其生产和经营活动中关注环境保护，履行社会责任，改善工作环境，维护职工利益。

9. 部长们鼓励亚欧中小企业在技术、投资、经贸往来等方面的发展和合作，支持亚欧会议成员中小企业服务机构在人力资源培训、知识产权保护、信息化等方面的交流与合作。

10. 部长们建议，亚欧会议成员应相互学习和分享促进中小企业创新与发展的成功实践和最佳案例，更广泛地开发和利用现代信息技术和网络，发展电子商务，便利中小企业获得商机。

11. 部长们强调要加强亚欧中小企业融资政策交流，推进金融产品和服务的创新，完善创业投资机制，为中小企业融资提供多种服务。

12. 部长们同意，促进中小企业产业集群的形成和发展，扩大亚欧产业集群间贸易、投资和技术合作，推进特色区域经济的发展。

13. 部长们赞赏，为便利亚欧中小企业经贸合作和开拓市场，中国政府在每年9月举办"中国国际中小企业博览会"期间，专设"亚欧中小企业合作交流馆"为各成员提供免费展位，并建立亚欧会议中小企业部长级会议网站(www.asem-sme.net)，为各成员参会、参展及沟通和联络提供便利。

14. 部长们一致同意，每两年在亚欧峰会召开前召开一次亚欧会议中小企业部长级会议，形成由亚洲和欧洲成员轮流主办的、定期可持续的政策交流对话机制。

15. 部长们同意建立亚欧会议中小企业合作高官会议机制，每两年举办一次，在部长级会议之前召开，由各成员指派政府官员参加，负责为部长级会议相关工作的协调、日常联系，做好前期准备。

16. 部长们明确第二届亚欧会议中小企业部长级会议将于2009年由欧洲成员举办。

Passage 2

Chinese President Xi Jinping's 2015 New Year Message

Time flies. 2014 is coming to an end and 2015 is approaching. At this turn of the year, I wish to extend my best wishes to people of all ethnic groups in China, to our compatriots in the Hong Kong and Macau Special Administrative Regions, to our compatriots in Taiwan and overseas Chinese, as well as to friends in other countries and regions in the world.

2014 is unforgettable. During the past year, we have pushed forward reform with strong determination, cracked many hard nuts, and introduced a string of major reform measures, many of which are closely related to the interests of the general public. We have adapted to the new normal of economic growth, actively promoted economic and social development, and brought about further improvement in people's lives. On December 12, the first phase of the central route of the South-North Water Diversion Project went into operation. More than 400,000 people along the route have been relocated. We pay tribute to them for their selfless contribution, and wish them a happy life in their new homes. In the past year, we have endeavored to improve our work style and strengthen party and government discipline, with efforts focusing on fighting against formalism, bureaucracy, hedonism and extravagance. The situation has greatly improved. We have stepped up the fight against corruption and punished corrupt officials with a zero-tolerance attitude, which demonstrates our commitment to fighting against corruption and other evil forces. In the past year, we have enhanced our cooperation and exchanges with countries around the world. We hosted the APEC Economic Leaders' Meeting in Beijing. Our leaders have visited many countries and received many foreign leaders. These exchanges of visits have helped the world understand China better.

Officials at various levels have spared no efforts to perform their duty. Of course, those achievements would not have been possible without the support of the people. I would like to give a "thumbs up" to our great people.

During the past year, we have established the Victory Day of the Chinese People's War of Resistance against Japanese Aggression, the Martyrs' Day and the National Memorial Day for Victims of the Nanjing Massacre through legislation. These new memorial days included many solemn events. Despite the change of times, we would always remember the sacrifice and contribution of those who gave their lives for the Chinese nation and for peace.

During the past year, we have also experienced some sad moments. Malaysia Airlines MH370 went missing. The whereabouts of more than 150 of our fellow countrymen remain unknown. We have not forgotten them. We will continue to make all possible efforts to find them. During the past year, our country has also suffered from a number of major natural disasters and work safety accidents, in which some compatriots lost their lives. The Ludian earthquake in Yunnan Province claimed more than 600 lives. Our hearts are with them and we wish their families well.

The New Year bell is about to ring. We will continue our efforts to act upon people's expectations and turn their aspirations into reality. We will continue to deepen reform in an all-round way. An arrow that has been released makes no turning back. At this critical moment of our reform process, only those who brave hardships would prevail. We must advance the rule of law in an all-round way, and use the rule of law to guarantee people's rights and interests, uphold social equity and justice, and promote national development. For the goal of building a moderately prosperous society in an all-round way to be completed in due course, comprehensively deepening reform and strengthening the rule of law must go forward hand in hand, like the two wings of a bird or the two wheels of a car.

The living standards of the Chinese people are constantly improving, but we should always keep in mind those who are still living in hardships. We will work with passion to improve their well-being, with efforts focusing on poverty alleviation and guaranteeing basic living conditions. We will provide assistance to all those in need of help, including poverty-stricken farmers and urban residents with difficulties, so that their basic living conditions are guaranteed and their hearts are filled with warmth.

We will continue to comprehensively strengthen party discipline, and unswervingly improve our work style. We will always resort to anti-corruption as a sharp weapon, and consolidate mechanism-building as a cage to contain powers. In this socialist country led by the Communist Party of China, any corrupt official who is exposed must be dealt with. All those involved in corruption and embezzlement must be prosecuted and punished.

We are now pursuing a lofty mission. Only perseverance will lead to victory, while giving up halfway will lead us nowhere. Our blueprint is ambitious, but our task is arduous. All party members and people of all ethnic groups in the country must stand united. We must pool our wisdom to seize opportunities, work together to embrace challenges, tackle problems with quick action, and carry on innovation with determination, in order to make China a better country year by year and constantly improve people's living standards.

The Chinese people care greatly about the country's future and the future of the world. When Ebola emerged in Africa, we offered our help. When a water shortage occurred in the capital of the Maldives, we provided assistance. There are numerous examples like these which demonstrate the spirit of common destiny of the Chinese people and all humanity. The world is not yet a tranquil place. We long for peace and we sincerely hope that people of all countries can work together to ensure that all humanity will be free from the suffering of hunger and all families free from the threat of wars, and that all children can grow up in the sunshine of peace.

Thank you all!

第十一章 经济和贸易口译
Interpretation of Trade and Economy

一、热身阅读材料/Warming-up Reading Material

第一篇/Passage 1

US Rounds on UK over China Deal

The White House accused the UK on Thursday of a "constant accommodation" of China after the British government decided to join a new China-led financial institution that could become a rival to the World Bank.

The rare rebuke of one of the US's closest allies comes as Britain prepares to announce it will become a founding member of the $50bn Asian Infrastructure Investment Bank, making it the first G7 country to join an institution launched by China last October.

The reprimand is a rare breach in the "special relationship" that has been a backbone of western policy for decades. It also underlines US concerns over China's efforts to establish a new generation of international development banks that could challenge Washington-based global institutions. The US has been lobbying other allies not to join the AIIB.

Relations between Washington and David Cameron's government have been strained over recent weeks, with senior US officials criticising Britain over falling defence spending, which could soon fall below the Nato target of 2 per cent of gross domestic product.

A senior administration official told the *Financial Times* that the British decision was taken after "virtually no consultation with the US" and at a time when the G7 had been discussing how to approach the new bank.

"We are wary about a trend toward constant accommodation of China, which is not the best way to engage a rising power," the US official said.

While Beijing has long been suspicious about US influence over the World Bank and IMF, China also believes that the US and Japan have too much control over the Manila-based Asian Development Bank. In addition to the AIIB, China is the driving force behind the creation last year of the BRICS Development Bank and is promoting a $40bn Silk Road Fund to finance economic integration with Central Asia.

The Obama administration has said it is not opposed to the AIIB, but US officials fear it could become an instrument of Chinese foreign policy if Beijing ends up having veto power over the bank's decisions.

The UK Treasury said George Osborne, chancellor of the exchequer, had discussed his intention to become a founding member of the new bank with Jack Lew, his US counterpart. Mr Osborne was aware his decision would not be popular with Washington.

Mr Osborne was unrepentant, arguing that Britain should be in at the start of the new bank, ensuring that it operates in a transparent way. He believes it fills an important gap in providing finance for infrastructure for Asia.

"Joining the AIIB at the founding stage will create an unrivalled opportunity for the UK and Asia to invest and grow together," Mr Osborne said. He expects other western countries, which have been making positive noises privately about the new bank, to become involved.

Beijing launched the AIIB in October with the backing of 20 other countries, but Japan, South Korea and Australia — America's main allies in the region — did not become founding members. There has been a strong debate with the Australian cabinet about whether to join, after US pressure to stay on the sidelines.

A decision by the major economies to join now would give up leverage they might have over the AIIB as it was being set up, the US official said: "Large economies can have more influence by staying on the outside and trying to shape the standards it adopts than by getting on the inside at a time when they can have no confidence that China will not retain veto powers."

Mr Osborne's decision reflects London's desire to pursue commercial relations with China aggressively, even at the expense of antagonising Washington.

When Mr Osborne visited Beijing in 2013 he said he wanted to "change Britain's attitude to China"; last October the chancellor hailed the British government's sovereign renminbi bond issue, the first by a western government. It has been keen to establish the City of London as a platform for overseas business in the Chinese currency as it starts to play a bigger role in the global economy.

Last week, the House of Commons foreign affairs committee said the British government should press China harder to introduce political reforms in Hong Kong. The committee also said it was "profoundly disappointed" at the "mild" response of the government when its members were prevented from visiting Hong Kong in November during the protests.

课文词语/Words and Expressions from the Text

Asian Infrastructure Investment Bank (AIIB)	亚洲基础设施投资银行(简称亚投行)
World Bank (WB)	世界银行
Gross domestic product (GDP)	国内生产总值
International Monetary Fund (IMF)	国际货币基金组织
Asian Development Bank	亚洲开发银行
BRIC	金砖四国
Silk Road Fund	丝绸之路基金

第二篇/Passage 2

Apple in China: Big Country, Big Company

Could Apple outgrow China? Some executives and investors talk as if, as a market, China were inexhaustible. If you could cut through the red tape and get the distribution, you could sell as many cars, pills, insurance policies, widgets or sprockets as you could churn out. So suggesting that any company could be too big for China sounds a bit like John Lennon's 1966 assertion that The Beatles were bigger than Jesus.

Apple has not saturated China yet, obviously: Its Chinese sales grew 55 per cent in the quarter reported yesterday, to $16bn. A big number, but it comes to something on the order of 20m iPhones. That's only one iPhone for every 60 people (come on, guys!). That Apple had $31bn in sales in the US is suggestive of how big China can be.

It is not, however, as if everyone else in China is waiting in a very long line at the Apple Store in Beijing. Barclays estimates that half the population has a smartphone, and that 390m smartphones were sold in China last year. GDP per capita is about $7,000 (an average iPhone 6 is a shade under $700). Apple is not going to have the penetration in China it has in the US anytime soon.

And the competition is vicious. The local contenders Xiaomi, Lenovo, and Huawei are all focused on lower priced phones, but are pushing higher.

But it may be a mistake to think too much about growth when assessing Apple's prospects. The key concept, instead, might be recurring revenue.

Apple's most striking financial feature is its ability to maintain prices. Consumer electronics prices are almost universally deflationary. But by adding features and marketing intelligently, it has kept iPhone prices high. The average iPhone sold for in the last quarter — seven years after its launch — was $687, the highest ever.

Analysts at Canalys estimate that Apple's iPhones outsold all other brands in China in the three months to December for the first time — a remarkable recovery from sales that had ranked in seventh place in the previous quarter. That may not last. But as long as Apple is dominating the top end of the Chinese market, and those customers become hooked on its suite of apps and services, the model is working. Apple's growth last quarter — in China and elsewhere — will not be sustained. But with the pricing to support 40 per cent gross margins, that may not matter much to the stock.

课文词语/Words and Expressions from the Text

the red tape   繁文缛节

The Beatles	披头士
the Apple Store	苹果专卖店
smartphone	智能手机
Xiaomi	小米
Lenovo	联想
Huawei	华为
recurring revenue	经常性收入
suite of apps and services	应用和服务套餐

二、口译实践/Interpretation Practice

句子口译/Sentence Interpretation

(一)英译汉/E-C

Interpret the following sentences into Chinese.

11-1.mp3

1. It was extremely gracious of you to have invited me to the reception, and I enjoyed it very much.

2. Now please allow me to propose a toast to our successful cooperation and to our long-standing friendship. Cheers!

3. The Covpress plant in Shandong Province, when operational in March, will have the capacity to produce £1.5bn worth of pressings a year, more than 10 times the size of the UK operation.

4. An Indian court has launched an inquiry into allegations Xiaomi disobeyed an order restricting its phone sales as part of a patent case with implications for the Chinese smartphone maker's expansion plans.

5. Beijing launched the AIIB in October with the backing of 20 other countries, but Japan, South Korea and Australia — America's main allies in the region — did not become founding members. There has been a strong debate with the Australian cabinet about whether to join, after US pressure to stay on the sidelines.

(二)汉译英/C-E

Interpret the following sentences into English.

11-2.mp3

1. 为什么呢？美国它今天说你对我出口太多，进口太少，造成了我的外贸收支不平衡，明天又说另外一套，你，对我外贸也是造成了不平衡。
2. 墨西哥本来在汽车贸易上它的限制非常严格，进口一台汽车的话要出口2.7部墨西哥的车，那是非常严格的。
3. 美国外贸进出口的统计办法是用的产品原产地原则。也就是说，这个产品生产在哪个国家里头，然后出口到美国去，就算这个国家对美国的出口，而不管这家工厂是属于谁的，赚的钱给谁，不去管这个问题。
4. 国际经济竞争激烈，许多发展中国家的经济环境进一步恶化，南北差距不断扩大。因此，联合国应满足发展中国家社会经济发展的需求，以达到和平与发展的总体目标。
5. 中国经济要行稳致远，必须全面深化改革。用好政府和市场这"两只手"，形成"双引擎"。一方面要使市场在资源配置中起决定性作用，培育打造新引擎；另一方面要更好发挥政府作用，改造升级传统引擎。

对话口译/Dialogue Interpretation

Interpret the following dialogues alternatively into English and Chinese.

11-3.mp3

A: 谢谢你陪我参观了贵公司，贵公司给我留下了非常深刻的印象，特别是你们全新的质量控制方法。

B: I'm glad to see that you're satisfied with our quality control. As you saw, we make an overall test on every set of LCD at the assembly line, instead of doing sampling test.

A: 我早就从美国的生意伙伴那里得知你们的质量控制办法了，现在我真是佩服得五体投地了。

B: It is safe to say that no one can match us on quality and price.

A: 绝对没错！你能把产品的详细资料给我一些吗？

B: I'll give you the brochures for our products. You will see the specifications of the models and their corresponding prices.

A: 你们所有的报价到年底一直有效吗？

B: Yes, I guarantee that.

A: 你们是否会给些数量或其他方面的折扣？

B: It depends on the order.

A: 支付条件呢？

B: By letter of credit.

A: 你们提供什么样的售后服务？

B: We offer three-year free of charge guarantee and life maintenance service. We have special maintenance services in most large cities across Russia.

A: 那就太好了，非常感谢！

B: You are welcome.

段落口译/Short Passage Interpretation

(一)英译汉/E-C

Interpret the following short passage into Chinese.

11-4.mp3

Obviously, we are in some important senses apart of Europe, but in other important senses we are not. We are not in the Eurozone and we are perceived by China as being a very different animal, obviously, from the United States and also from Continental Europe, and that is to our advantage. The nature of our political economy and the nature of our business system has evolved in a very different way from that of France, and particularly from that of Germany. We have gone down a different path and the possibility for engaging with this country in wider issues of mutual benefit and of common interest from the whole world puts United Kingdom in an interesting position. We are by far the most open of all the high-income countries. If we have time, perhaps we can talk a bit more later about the degree of our openness. Just today, GE has bought Wood, which is one of the most important manufactures in its niche in oilfield services sector. Just every day there is a story of this kind, which is not a good or a bad thing, but it differentiates us sharply from Germany and to some degree from France.

(二)汉译英/C-E

Interpret the following short passage into English.

11-5.mp3

共建"一带一路"致力于亚欧非大陆及附近海洋的互联互通，建立和加强沿线各国互联互通伙伴关系，构建全方位、多层次、复合型的互联互通网络，实现沿线各国多元、自主、平衡、可持续的发展。"一带一路"的互联互通项目将推动沿线各国发展战略的对接与耦合，发掘区域内市场的潜力，促进投资和消费，创造需求和就业，增进沿线各国人民的人文交流与文明互鉴，让各国人民相逢相知、互信互敬，共享和谐、安宁、富裕的生活。

篇章口译/Passage Interpretation

Passage 1

相关词语/Related Words and Expressions

Shangdong Yongtai   山东永泰

Covpress	英国考普莱公司
West Midlands	英国西米德兰兹公司
The Society of Motor Manufacturers and Traders	英国汽车制造贸易协会
Shanghai Automotive	上海汽车工业
Lifan	力帆
Volvo	沃尔沃
Geely	吉利
Manganese Bronze	英国锰铜控股公司
Jaguar Land Rover	捷豹路虎

Interpret the following passage into Chinese.

11-6.mp3

China Fuels Revival for Motor Suppliers

A Chinese company yesterday opened one of the world's biggest motor press shops for large car parts — with the help of 40 engineers from Coventry.

Shandong Yongtai in northern China, a privately owned industrial group, is using the skills and know how of Covpress, a 100-year-old West Midlands precision metal pressing company it acquired in 2013.

The link has already transformed the fortunes of the UK company, resulting in increased investment and a near-50 per cent rise in its workforce. Turnover is up 70 per cent in the two years since the takeover.

The Covpress plant in Shandong Province, when operational in March, will have the capacity to produce £1.5bn worth of pressings a year, more than 10 times the size of the UK operation.

Kit Halliday, joint chief executive and 30 per cent shareholder in the Coventry company, says the group can now supply the global operations of all the big car manufacturers.

"If Yongtai only wanted to supply Chinese car makers they could have done that without buying us. But we open doors for them," he says.

The collaboration is just the latest example of growing Chinese interest in the UK motor sector.

Centres while Geely, owner of the Volvo brand, manufactures the famous black London taxi, having bought Manganese Bronze in 2013.

The UK car market is enjoying record sales, with exports accounting for 85 per cent of the vehicles produced. However, the lack of suitable local suppliers has meant manufacturers import about 60 per cent of components by value, compared with 30 per cent in Germany.

Global manufacturers say they would like to increase the level of parts purchasing done in the UK.

The Society of Motor Manufacturers and Traders in November estimated there were £5bn worth of new business opportunities for UK supply chain companies, if they were ready to make the required investments.

Currently, around £11bn is spent with UK suppliers by global car manufacturers — but a report in 2012 by KPMG, the professional services firm, suggested this figure could double by 2016.

But UK supply chain companies are typically family-owned, risk-averse and much smaller than their German counterparts, with an average of 30 employees compared with 180 in Germany.

Recent decades have also seen a hollowing out, with press shops closing and the loss of key capabilities.

John Leech, a partner with KPMG and author of the report on the UK motor supply chain, says component makers have to internationalise to service.

Mr Leech says much of the impetus is coming from companies such as Jaguar Land Rover, which has large operations in the UK but which is now also making cars under a joint venture in China for the local market. "The choice for companies like JLR is to find a local Chinese supplier or persuade their UK suppliers to follow them to China," says Mr Leech.

Sertec, a components supplier in Birmingham, has a small contract tool making operation in China and is understood to be considering setting up a manufacturing operation to supply JLR.

"Local content rules means we have to be there," says Grant Adams, Sertec chief executive.

Delcam, which makes design software for motor toolmakers, went worldwide a long time ago, as the sourcing of component parts became more globalised.

"For us, where cars are made doesn't have that much impact. We can supply companies making cars or car parts whether they're in China, the UK, America, Brazil or Mexico. We basically follow the manufacturers around the world," says Peter Dickin, marketing director.

Passage 2

相关词语/Related Words and Expressions

Creating Value Through Innovation	推动创新，创造价值
an inexhaustible engine driving economic and social development 经济社会发展的不熄引擎	
targeted tax reduction	定向减税
target reduction of required bank reserve ratio	定向降准
express delivery	物流快递
golden key	金钥匙
science and technology innovation	科技创新
great vision that makes a country prosper is but the result of collective wisdom	

大智兴邦，不过集众思

Interpret the following short passage into English.

11-7.mp3

紧紧依靠改革创新 增强经济发展新动力
——在第八届夏季达沃斯论坛上的致辞（节选）
李克强
(2014年9月10日)

尊敬的施瓦布先生，
尊敬的各国元首和政府首脑，
尊敬的各位来宾，
女士们，先生们，朋友们：

很高兴和大家相聚中国天津，共同出席第八届夏季达沃斯论坛。我谨代表中国政府对论坛召开表示热烈祝贺！对各位远道而来的嘉宾表示诚挚欢迎！

本届论坛以"推动创新，创造价值"为主题，具有很强的现实意义。创新是人类社会的永恒话题，也是经济社会发展的不熄引擎。世界经济稳定复苏要靠创新，中国经济提质增效升级也要靠创新。近几年，中国经济之所以能够保持持续发展，向着健康方向前进，主要动力还是来自于改革创新。

今年以来，世界经济形势错综复杂，发达国家经济复苏艰难曲折，新兴市场国家经济增速放缓，中国经济下行压力加大。我们坚持稳中求进的工作总基调，保持定力，主动作为，不搞强刺激，没有放松银根，而是强力推进改革，大力调整结构，着力改善民生，保持了经济平稳运行。上半年，中国经济增长7.4%，居民消费价格涨幅为2.3%。在经济增速放缓的情况下，1~8月，31个大中城市调查失业率保持在5%左右，城镇新增就业970多万人，与去年同期相比多增了10多万人。

经济下行压力加大，但就业不降反增，主要是改革发了力。本届政府成立以来，我们大力推进行政审批制度改革，各部门已取消和下放了600多项行政审批事项，今年又在全国推行商事制度等改革，企业准入的门槛低了，"紧箍咒"松了，极大地调动了全社会创业兴业的热情。1~8月，新登记注册市场主体800多万户，其中3~8月工商登记制度改革后新登记注册企业同比增长61%，出现"井喷式"增长，带动1000万人以上就业。我们不仅推进商事制度改革，而且推进投融资、税收、流通等体制改革，进一步打开了服务业等新兴产业发展的闸门，对扩大就业起到重要的"推进器"、"容纳器"作用。

中国经济的积极变化，不仅表现在就业增加和居民收入增长上，也体现在结构优化上。简政放权加上"定向减税"、"定向降准"等财税金融措施，有力地支持了服务业、"三农"、小微企业、民营企业和新兴业态的发展。上半年，物流快递、电子商务等新产业、新商业模式迅速成长；新登记注册服务业企业增幅达70%以上，第三产业增速和比重继续超过第二产业，在国民经济中处于领先地位；民间投资占固定资产投资比重同比提高1.4个百分点；高技术产业和装备制造业增长均快于工业整体增长。

结构调整深入推进，提高了经济增长质量。我们以改革创新为动力，一手抓压减过剩产能，尤其是淘汰落后产能，一手抓培育新的增长点。上半年，高耗能、高排放行业投资和生产增速明显放慢。单位GDP能耗同比下降4.2%，碳排放强度下降5%左右，是多年来降幅最大的。

女士们，先生们！

中国还是一个发展中国家，必须始终坚持以经济建设为中心。发展是硬道理，是解决一切问题的根本。经济发展方式不转变不行，经济发展不适度也不行。当然，我们所说的发展，是就业和收入增加的发展，是质量效益提高和节能环保的发展，也就是符合经济规律、社会规律和自然规律的科学发展。

当前，世界经济不稳定不确定因素依然较多，中国经济正处于深层次矛盾凸显和"三期叠加"的阶段，到了爬坡过坎的关键时候。下半年和今后一段时间，我们将进一步加快经济发展方式的转变，以结构性改革促进结构性调整，用好创新这把"金钥匙"，着力推进体制创新和科技创新，使中国经济保持中高速增长、迈向中高端水平，创造价值，打造中国经济升级版。

加快体制机制创新步伐。中国经济每一回破茧成蝶，靠的都是创新。创新不单是技术创新，更包括体制机制创新、管理创新、模式创新。中国30多年来改革开放本身就是规模宏大的创新行动，今后创新发展的巨大潜能依然蕴藏在体制改革之中。试想，13亿人口中有8、9亿的劳动者，如果他们都投入创业和创新创造，这将是巨大的力量。关键是要进一步解放思想，进一步解放和发展社会创造力，进一步激发企业和市场活力，破除一切束缚发展的体制机制障碍，让每个有创业意愿的人都拥有自主创业的空间，让创新创造的血液在全社会自由流动，让自我发展的精神在群众中蔚然成风。借改革创新的"东风"，在中国960万平方公里土地上掀起一个"大众创业"、"草根创业"的新浪潮，中国人民勤劳智慧的"自然禀赋"就会充分发挥，中国经济持续发展的"发动机"就会更新换代升级。

加大科技创新力度。中国经济虽然已居世界前列，但许多产业仍处在世界的中低端，传统的粗放式增长路径已经行不通了，必须更多地依靠科技进步调整结构。这是一种战略性、结构性、创新性调整。我们将坚持有扶有控、有保有压，培育壮大新产品、新业态，促进服务业、高技术产业、新兴产业加快发展；积极化解产能过剩矛盾，加快传统产业改造步伐，淘汰落后产能，提升中国产品和服务业在全球价值链中的位置，使创新真正能创造出更高的价值；加强人力资本投入，提高劳动者素质，提升产业技术、质量和品牌水平。特别是要通过加快改革，解除对个体、对企业创新的种种束缚，中国有各类专业技术人员和各类技能劳动者近两亿人。如果这么多人哪怕是大部分人都能发挥出他们的聪明才智，形成"万众创新"、"人人创新"的新态势，体力加脑力，制造加创造，开发出先进技术乃至所谓颠覆性技术，中国发展就一定能够创造更多价值，上新台阶。

女士们，先生们！

人类已进入经济全球化深入发展的时代，各国利益相互依存，彼此命运休戚与共，世界离不开中国，中国也离不开世界。中国实现"两个一百年"奋斗目标和中华民族伟大复兴"中国梦"，将会给世界带来发展机遇和巨大市场。各国间不应再是你输我赢、"零和博弈",而应该是双赢多赢、互利共赢,唯此世界才能繁荣进步。中国将坚定不移走和平发展道路,我们是国际体系的积极参与者、建设者和贡献者。我们致力于维护和平稳定的大环境,主张遵循国际关系基本准则,以和平方式、政治手段、通过对话解决地区冲突与热点问题。我们愿与亚洲邻国不断深化合作,妥善处理分歧,维护稳定安全大局,维护和平的秩序。我们倡导开放公平的全球统一大市场,支持多边自贸安排和双边自贸区建设"两个轮子一起转",努力形成"面向全球的高标准自贸区网络",反对各种形式的保护主义,更不赞成打贸易战。我们坚持实行更加积极主动的开放战略,完善开放型经济体系,重视稳定出口,也积极扩大进口,加快服务业、沿边和中西部地区开放,保持外资政策稳定,而且会更加开放。我们将不断完善和规范营商环境,继续吸引外国企业来华投资兴业,同时学习国外先进的技术、成熟管理经验和优秀的文化成果,兼容并蓄、消化吸收。中国永远做一个开放的大国、学习的大国、包容的大国,从中国国情出发,努力建设成为一个创新的大国。

"大智兴邦,不过集众思。"也就是说,智慧来自于大众。我刚才强调的大众创业、万众创新将会迸发出灿烂的火花。我们比任何时候都需要改革创新,更需要分享改革创新成果。这用中国的成语说,就是众人拾柴火焰高。希望与会各位畅所欲言,共同探索改革创新和开放发展之路,共同谋划创造价值与互利共赢之策,为中国经济社会发展、为世界繁荣进步做出应有的努力与贡献。

预祝本届夏季达沃斯论坛圆满成功!愿各位嘉宾在华工作顺利、身体健康!

谢谢大家!

参考译文/Reference Version

句子口译/Sentence Interpretation

(一)英译汉/E-C

1. 非常感谢您能邀请我参加这次招待会,我的确过得很愉快。
2. 现在,请举杯,为我们的成功合作和双方长期的友谊,干杯!
3. 考普莱位于中国山东的工厂3月份投产之后,每年可生产价值15亿英镑的冲压件,是其英国工厂的10倍多。
4. 印度一家法庭对有关小米没有遵守限制其手机销售的命令的指控展开了调查,该项命令是一宗专利案的一部分,对这家中国智能手机制造商的扩张计划具有潜在影响。
5. 去年10月,北京方面在其他20个国家的支持下发起了亚投行,但是美国在亚洲的主要盟友日本、韩国和澳大利亚并未成为创始成员国。在美国施压澳大利亚保持观望后,该国内阁就是否加入亚投行展开了激烈辩论。

(二)汉译英/C-E

1. Why? Beacuse at some point, the United States will accuse one country of exporting too

much and importing too little, and therefore causing its trade imbalance; at another point, it may accuse another country of causing its trade imbalance.

2. Mexico once had a very strict control over the trade of automabiles. For each car imported, 2.7 cars need to be exported.

3. The foreign trade statistics of the United States are based on the place of origin. That means that if the product is produced in one country and exported to the US, that'll be counted as the export of this country, regardless of who owns the factory or whom the profit goes to.

4. Competition in international economy is becoming increasingly fiercer and the economic situations in many developing nations are further worsening. The gap between the North and the South continues to widen. Therefore, the UN must meet the needs for economic and social development in developing nations in order to achieve the overall.

5. To ensure long-term and steady growth of the Chinese economy, we need to comprehensively deepen reforms. We need to properly use both the hand of the government and the hand of the market, and rely on both the traditional and new engines of growth. We will let the market play a decisive role in resource allocation to foster a new engine of growth. At the same time, we will give better scope to the role of the government to transform and upgrade the traditional engine of growth.

对话口译/Dialogue Interpretation

A: It's very kind of you to show me round your company. It's impressive, especially your new way of quality control.

B: 很高兴您对我们新的质量控制方法感到满意。您在装配线也看到了，我们对每一台液晶显示器都要进行全面测试，而不仅仅是抽样检测。

A: I heard a lot from my business friends in the United States about your quality control. Now I'm completely convinced.

B: 可以说，我们生产的液晶显示器在价格和质量上都是很有优势的。

A: Sure, can you give me the details of your LCD?

B: 我会把产品的宣传册给你的，上面标明了不同的型号和相应的价格。

A: Are the prices quoted firm to the end of the year?

B: 是的，这点我可以保证。

A: Do you grant any quantity or other discounts?

B: 这个要取决于订单的大小了。

A: What about the terms of payment?

B: 以信用证的形式支付。

A: What kind of after-sales service do you provide?

B: 我们提供三年的免费保修和终身维修服务。在俄罗斯各大主要城市，基本上都有我们专门的维修点。

A: That is terrific. Thank you very much.
B: 不客气。

段落口译/Short Passage Interpretation

(一)英译汉/E-C

显然,从很多重要的方面来说,我们是欧洲的一部分,但是从另外一些重要方面来说,我们又不是。我们不在欧元区,被中国视为明显不同于美国以及欧洲大陆的异类,但是这对我们是有利的。我们的政治经济和企业制度的演进过程跟法国不同,与德国的更是大相径庭。我们走了一条很不一样的路,因此能与我们开展更广泛的互利合作以及符合全世界共同利益的合作,英国都有其独特的优势。迄今为止,我们绝对是高收入国家中最开放的一个。如果有时间,我过会儿或许可以多谈谈英国的开放程度。就在今天,美国通用电器收购了伍德,伍德在油田服务行业是最重要的制造商之一。像这样的事情每天都在发生,没有好坏之分,却将我们与德国,以及某种程度上与法国相比的优势清晰地体现了出来。

(二)汉译英/C-E

The Belt and Road Initiative aims to promote the connectivity of Asian, European and African continents and their adjacent seas, establish and strengthen partnerships among the countries along the Belt and Road, set up all-dimensional, multitiered and composite connectivity networks, and realize diversified, independent, balanced and sustainable development in these countries. The connectivity projects of the Initiative will help align and coordinate the development strategies of the countries along the Belt and Road, tap market potential in this region, promote investment and consumption, create demands and job opportunities, enhance people-to-people and cultural exchanges, and mutual learning among the peoples of the relevant countries, and enable them to understand, trust and respect each other and live in harmony, peace and prosperity.

篇章口译/Passage Interpretation

Passage 1

英国汽车制造商引领供应商进入中国

在来自英国考文垂的40名工程师帮助下,一家中国公司昨日开启了世界最大的冲压生产线之一,生产大型汽车部件。

私有制造企业山东永泰将利用英国考普莱公司的技术和专业知识,后者是它在2013年收购的一家位于英国西米德兰兹的精密金属冲压公司,已有百年历史。

这场联姻已经改变了考普莱的命运,带来了新的投资,雇员人数增加了近50%。在被收购后的两年时间里,该公司营业额已增加70%。

考普莱位于中国山东的工厂3月份投产之后,每年可生产价值15亿英镑的冲压件,是其英国工厂的10倍多。

联名首席执行官、持有考普莱30%股份的大股东基特·哈利迪表示，该公司如今可以为所有大型汽车制造商的全球生产线供应产品。

他说："如果永泰只想供应中国汽车制造商，他们不用收购我们就能做到。但我们为他们带来了新的机会。"

双方的合作正是中方对英国汽车业兴趣日益浓厚的最新例证。

沃尔沃品牌的所有者吉利在2013年收购英国锰铜控股公司之后，生产著名的黑色伦敦出租车。

英国汽车市场销量正处于创纪录水平，生产的85%车辆用于出口。然而，缺乏合适的本土供应商意味着，制造商所用零件的进口率为60%左右（以价值计），而德国的这个数字为30%。

跨国汽车制造商表示，他们愿意增加在英国本土采购零部件的比重。

英国汽车制造贸易协会去年11月估计，如果愿意进行必要的投资，英国供应链企业能获得价值50亿英镑的新商业机会。

目前，跨国汽车制造从英国供应商那里采购金额在110亿英镑左右，但专业服务公司毕马威2012年的一份报告显示，这个数字到2016年可能翻番。

但英国供应链企业往往是家族企业，它们厌恶风险，规模也远远小于德国同行，平均雇员人数为30人，而德国的这个数字为180人。

近几十年来，英国供应链还出现了"空心化"，许多冲压厂倒闭，一些关键的产能丧失。

毕马威合伙人、上述有关英国汽车供应链的报告的作者约翰·李奇表示，零部件制造商必须走向国际才能生存下去。

李奇表示，很大一部分推动力来自捷豹路虎这样的企业，它们在英国有规模很大的生产线，但现在也在中国通过合资企业为中国本土市场生产汽车。李奇说："像捷豹路虎这样的企业面临的选择是，寻找一家中国本土供应商，或者说服他们的英国供应商跟随他们进军中国。"

伯明翰零部件供应商Sertec在中国有一间不大的合同工具制造厂，据悉正考虑设立制造生产线，供应捷豹路虎。

Sertec首席执行官格兰特·亚当斯表示："零部件采购本地化率的规定，意味着我们必须在当地设厂。"

随着零部件采购变得更加国际化，面向汽车工具制造的软件开发商Delcam早已走向全球。

Delcam营销总监彼得·迪金说："汽车在哪里制造对我们的影响并没有那么大。无论汽车制造企业或零部件企业在中国、英国、美国、巴西还是墨西哥，我们都能做它们的供应商。基本上制造商去哪里，我们就跟去哪里。"

Passage 2

Creating New Dynamism Through Reform and Innovation

Address at the Eighth Summer Davos Forum (Excerpted)

By Premier Li Keqiang

10 September 2014

Dear Professor Klaus Schwab,
Your Excellencies Heads of State and Government,
Distinguished Guests, Ladies and Gentlemen,
Dear Friends,

It gives me great pleasure to meet you here in Tianjin at the eighth Annual Meeting of the New Champions, or the Summer Davos Forum. On behalf of the Chinese government, I wish to extend warm congratulations on the opening of the Forum and a cordial welcome to all of you who have come from afar.

The theme for this year's Forum, namely "Creating Value Through Innovation", is a most relevant one. Innovation is an eternal topic of the human society and an inexhaustible engine driving economic and social development. Innovation is vital to the steady recovery of the world economy. Innovation is also essential to upgrading the Chinese economy and improving its performance. And it is thanks to reform and innovation that the Chinese economy has in recent years maintained steady and sound growth.

The global economic environment has remained an intricate one since the beginning of this year. The road to recovery in developed countries has remained bumpy. Growth in emerging market economies has slowed down, and the Chinese economy faces greater downward pressure. Facing this challenging environment, we have continued to follow the general principle of making progress while maintaining stability. We have stayed the course and pursued a proactive approach. Instead of adopting strong economic stimulus or easing monetary policy, we have vigorously promoted reform and economic readjustment, and made efforts to improve people's lives. As a result, we have maintained steady economic performance. In the first half of the year, the Chinese economy registered a 7.4 percent growth, and CPI rise was kept at 2.3 percent. Despite economic slowdown, between January and August, the surveyed unemployment rate was kept at around 5 percent in 31 big and medium-sized cities. More than 9.7 million urban jobs were created, which is over one hundred thousand more compared with the same period last year.

Despite growing downward pressure on the economy, more jobs were created, thanks to new steps of reform taken. Since the beginning of this government, we have advanced the reform of the administrative review and approval system. Government departments have removed or delegated to lower levels administrative approval on over 600 items, and this year, the business registration reform, among others, has been carried out nationwide. This has lowered the threshold for starting businesses and removed restrictions on them, thus giving a great boost to business development in the whole country. Between January and August, the amount of newly registered market entities was more than 8 million, and from March to August, with the business registration reform, the number of newly registered businesses grew by 61 percent over the previous year, all pointing to a massive upsurge which has generated more than 10 million jobs. In addition to reforming the business registration system, we have also introduced reforms to investment financing, taxation and logistics systems, and further opened the gate for the development of the service sector and other emerging industries. All these measures have been vital in fostering and increasing job opportunities.

The positive changes in China's economy are not only reflected in the increase of jobs and residents' incomes, but also in the structural upgrading. We have streamlined administration, delegated powers to the lower levels, and adopted fiscal, taxation and financial measures such as targeted tax reduction and targeted reduction of required bank reserve ratio. All these measures have spurred the growth of the service sector, agriculture, rural area and the welfare of farmers, as well as small and micro-businesses, private businesses and emerging industries. In the first half of the year, new businesses and new business models such as logistics, express delivery and e-commerce all developed fast. The number of newly registered service businesses surged by more than 70 percent. The tertiary industry continued to outperform the secondary industry in terms of growth rate and share of GDP, and is a leading sector of the economy. The share of private investment in fixed asset investment increased by 1.4 percentage points year on year. High-tech industries and equipment manufacturing grew faster than the industrial average.

Deepening structural readjustment has improved the quality of economic growth. On the basis of carrying out reform and innovation, we have reduced overcapacity, eliminating outdated capacity in particular, and fostered new growth areas. In the first half of the year, the growth of investment and production of industries with high energy consumption and emissions noticeably slowed down. The per unit GDP energy consumption dropped by 4.2 percent year on year, and carbon intensity was cut by about 5 percent, the largest drop in many years.

Ladies and Gentlemen,

China is still a developing country. We must give top priority to economic development. Only development will deliver progress. Ultimately, it is only development that will resolve all the problems in China. We cannot advance without changing the growth model, nor can we advance without adequate development. Of course, the development we pursue should be one that promotes employment, increases incomes, improves economic performance and boosts energy conservation and environmental protection. It should be scientific development, namely, sound and balanced development that is in keeping with the laws governing economic activities, social development and nature.

Currently, there are many destabilizing and uncertain factors in the global economy, and

China's economic development also faces an array of overlapping and deep-seated problems. It is in a critical stage where its path upward is particularly steep. In the latter half of the year and beyond, we will further accelerate the transformation of the development model, push forward structural readjustment through structural reform, make good use of the "golden key" of innovation and promote institutional innovation as well as innovation in science and technology. By doing so, we will be able to maintain a medium-high growth rate, move toward medium-high level of development, create more value and upgrade the Chinese economy.

We will accelerate the pace of institutional innovation. Innovation has been the ultimate cause of the leapfrog development of the Chinese economy. China's innovation involves not only technology but more of institution, management and growth models. China's reform and opening-up for the past three decades and more has in itself been a huge innovation drive, and the huge, untapped potential of innovation and development in the future still lies in institutional reform. Just imagine how big a force it could be when the 800 or 900 million laborers among the 1.3 billion population are engaged in entrepreneurship, innovation and creation. I believe the key to realizing that is to further liberate our mind, further liberate and develop the creativity of society, further energize businesses and the market, and remove all institutional obstacles to development so that everyone interested in starting a business is given more space for entrepreneurship and the blood of innovation could flow unhampered in a society where everyone is full of the spirit of self-development. When reform and innovation fuels the massive wave of entrepreneurship by the people and at the grassroots level on the land of the 9.6 million square kilometers of China, the enormous power of the diligent and resourceful Chinese people will be fully unlocked and the engine driving China's sustained economic development will constantly regenerate itself and remain powerful.

We will step up science and technology innovation. The Chinese economy is among the largest in the world, but in many sectors China still ranks fairly low and its traditional, extensive way of seeking growth has been proved unsustainable. Readjusting the structure must be driven, more than ever, by science and technology progress, and that requires strategic, structural, and innovative readjustment. We will support and provide guarantee to certain sectors and curb and scale back some others, cultivate and promote new products and new businesses and speed up the development of service, high technology and emerging sectors. At the same time, we will phase out overcapacity, accelerate the transformation of traditional sectors and eliminate outdated capacity so that Chinese products and China's service sector can move up the global value chain and more value could be created through innovation. We must invest more in human capital and increase the ranks of high-caliber workers. We will improve the technological sophistication, quality and brand awareness of Chinese industries. In particular, we need to step up reforms to remove restraints on innovation by individuals and companies. When the talent of all, or at least most of the nearly 200 million professionals and skilled workers is brought to the full, a new pattern of innovation by the people and innovation by all, supported by the massive physical and mental power of the people and the strength of China's manufacturing and creative capability, will be fostered. This, coupled with the development of advanced and even revolutionary technologies, will create more value and move China's development to a higher level.

Ladies and Gentlemen,

We now live in an era defined by deepening economic globalization, with countries increasingly depending on one another in interests and sharing their destinies closely. The world needs China, and China needs the world. China's endeavor to realize the two centenary goals (namely, to complete the building of a moderately prosperous society in all respects when the Communist Party of China celebrates its centenary in 2021, and to turn China into a modern socialist country that is prosperous, strong, democratic, culturally advanced and harmonious when the People's Republic of China celebrates its centenary in 2049) and the Chinese dream of the great renewal of the Chinese nation will present great development opportunities and a huge market to the world. Instead of "I win, you lose" or a "zero-sum game", we need win-win or all-win, which ensures mutual benefit. Only in this way could the world prosper and advance forward. China is resolute in following the path of peaceful development. China is a defender and builder of the existing international system and is dedicated to maintaining an overall environment of peace and stability. We call for observance of the basic norms governing international relations and believe that regional conflicts and hotspot issues should be solved peacefully and politically through dialogue. We stand ready to deepen cooperation with our Asian neighbors, properly handle differences as there may be, maintain the overall interest of stability and security and uphold the order of peace. We advocate the building of an open, fair and integrated global market and support the establishment of both multilateral free trade arrangements and bilateral free trade agreements, in order to build a high-standard free trade agreement network that is globally oriented. We oppose protectionism in all its forms and do not favor fighting trade wars. We will continue to pursue a more proactive strategy of opening-up and improve the open economic system. We will focus on stabilizing export and actively expanding import. We will move faster to bring greater openness in the service sector, as well as China's areas bordering other countries and its vast central and western regions. We will follow a stable and more open policy on foreign capital. We will continue to improve and standardize the business environment, in order to attract more foreign businesses and investment and draw upon and adopt the advanced technologies, mature managerial expertise and fine cultural achievements of other countries. China will always be a major country committed to learning from others and to being open and inclusive. Acting on the basis of its actual conditions, China will strive to become a major country driven by innovation.

As the saying goes, great vision that makes a country prosper is but the result of collective wisdom. In other words, wisdom comes from the people. In the same line, the massive entrepreneurship and innovation by all, as I emphasized earlier, will generate enormous power.

Today more than any other time, we need reform and innovation and the sharing of the result of reform and innovation. To use a Chinese idiom, the fire will burn higher when everyone adds wood to it. I hope that all our distinguished participants will speak up your minds, jointly explore ways for reform, innovation and open development, share your views on how to create value and achieve mutual benefit, and do what you can to help China's economic development and world prosperity and progress.

Let me conclude by wishing this Summer Davos a complete success, and I wish all of you work better in China and very good health!

Thank you.

第三部分　全国翻译专业资格(水平)考试
China Accreditation Test for Translators and Interpreters (CATTI)

一、三级口译考试简介

全国翻译专业资格(水平)考试是在翻译专业实行的面向社会、国内最具权威的翻译专业资格(水平)认证，考试分为四个等级，即资深翻译和一、二、三级口、笔译考试。考试合格由人力资源和社会保障部颁发《中华人民共和国翻译专业资格(水平)证书》，在全国范围内有效。实行全国考试后，各地各部门不再进行相应语种、相应级别的翻译专业技术职务评审工作。2003 年 12 月首先在北京、上海、广州等城市推出英语二、三级的口、笔译考试，并在 2004 年推向全国。

根据全国翻译专业资格(水平)考试大纲，英语口译三级考试设"口译综合能力"测试和"口译实务"测试两个模块，考试的目的是测试应试者的口译实践能力是否达到准专业口译译员水平。考试的基本要求是应试者需掌握 5,000 个以上的英语词汇，初步了解中国和英语国家的文化背景知识并能胜任一般场合的交替传译。其中"口译综合能力"测试检验应试者的听力理解及信息处理的基本能力。"口译实务"测试检验应试者的听力理解、记忆、信息处理及语言表达能力，这一模块要求应试者发音正确，吐字清楚，语速适中，能够运用口译技巧传递原话信息并且无明显漏译、错译和语法错误。

有关英语口译三级——口译综合能力测试的题目说明如表 3.1 所示。

表 3.1　英语口译三级——口译综合能力

序号	题型		题量	记分	时间(分钟)
1	听力理解	判断	20 题	20	10
		篇章理解	15 题	30	10
		填空	20 题	20	10
		听力综述	听约 500 单词的英文文章后写一篇 150 单词的英语综述	30	30
总　计				100	60

各题型详细说明如下。

1. "口译综合能力"考试的第一部分的"判断"题有 A、B 两小部分。

在 A 部分，应试者听一段 200~250 个英语单词的英语段落，试卷上有 10 个短句，要求根据所听内容，判断短句的正或误(True/False)。录音只放一遍，每题 1 分。

在 B 部分，应试者将听到 10 个短句，试卷上有 10 个问题，每个问题下有 a、b、c、d 四个选项，要求根据所听短句和所提问题，选择与短句内容最相适合的选项。录音只放一遍，每题 1 分。

2. "口译综合能力"考试的第二部分为"篇章理解"。应试者听 3 篇录音材料，每篇约 200 个英语单词。每篇材料后面有 5 个问题，每个问题后有 4 个选项，问题和选项均出现在试卷上。要求根据录音材料内容和问题，选择最适合的选项。录音放一遍。3 篇材料共有 15 个问题，每题 2 分。

3. "口译综合能力"考试的第三部分为"填空"。应试者听一段 250 个词左右的英语段落，试卷上出现同一段落，但是其中有 20 个空格，要求根据所听内容，每个空格填 1 个词。录音放一遍，每空 1 分。

4. "口译综合能力"考试的第四部分为"听力综述"。应试者听一段长约 500 个英语词的文章，要求写一篇 150 至 200 个词的英语综述。

有关英语口译三级——口译实务测试的题目说明如表 3.2 所示。

表 3.2 英语口译三级——口译实务

序 号	题 型	题 量	记 分	时间(分钟)
1	英汉互译(对话)	150~200 词	20	10
2	英汉交替传译	约 300 单词的英语讲话 1 篇	40	10
3	汉英交替传译	约 200 字的汉语讲话 1 篇	40	10
总 计			100	30

各题型简要说明：

"口译实务"考试主要考查交替传译能力，应试者在讲话人讲完一句、一个意群、一段甚至整篇后译出目标语言。何时开始口译，录音材料中会给予提示。录音只放一遍。

二、"口译综合能力"备考

下面将以英语三级口译综合能力试题为例，从试题、答案和解析三方面进行介绍①。

(一)试题

Part Ⅰ

A. Listen to the following passage and then decide whether the statements below are true or false. After hearing a short passage, tick the circle for "True" on the answer sheet if

---

① 听力文字稿附在试题后。

you think the statement is true, or tick the circle for "False" if it is false. There are 10 statements in this part of the test, with 1 point each. You will hear the passage only once. At the end of the recording, you will have 2 minutes to finish this part.

1. The black people did not vote in America in 1941.
   ○ True
   ○ False

2. When Henry turned twenty-one, he drove to the courthouse to vote.
   ○ True
   ○ False

3. The registrar had decided not to enter the black people's names in the voting book.
   ○ True
   ○ False

4. In order to register, people had to understand the Constitution of the United States.
   ○ True
   ○ False

5. According to the passage, only literate people could vote.
   ○ True
   ○ False

6. Henry was the first black person to vote in his county.
   ○ True
   ○ False

7. Henry's father and five other black people were also registered to vote that night.
   ○ True
   ○ False

8. The next day the clerk refused to register the people Henry brought in because they were not able to read.
   ○ True
   ○ False

9. Not all the white people coming to register could read.
   ○ True
   ○ False

10. Henry finally managed to get all the black people in his county registered.
    ○ True
    ○ False

B. Listen to the following short statements and then choose one of the answers that best fits the meaning of each statement by ticking the corresponding circle. There are 10 questions in this part of the test, 1 point for each question. You will hear the statement only once.

11. What does the speaker mean?

    a. He usually starts working without breakfast.

    b. He likes to eat a lot for breakfast.

    c. He doesn't eat a lot for breakfast.

    d. He prefers something else in the morning to a big breakfast.

12. What is the speaker's problem?

    a. He knows nothing about engineering.

    b. He wants to postpone the presentation.

    c. He never spoke to high school students before.

    d. He is not yet ready for the presentation.

13. Why will the speaker make the call?

    a. Because he will let the other person know about the assignment.

    b. Because he needs to talk to somebody.

    c. Because he can't talk about the assignment now.

    d. Because he wants to know about the assignment.

14. Which of the following statements is true about Sara?

    a. She rarely makes mistakes.

    b. She makes known what she thinks.

    c. She has many original ideas.

    d. She doesn't like to express her opinions.

15. What did Dave do?

    a. He lost his temper for no reason at all.

    b. He left without saying a word.

    c. He suddenly slipped and fell.

    d. He suddenly fainted.

16. According to the speaker, why did he fail to catch the point?

    a. Because he was away for a while.

    b. Because he simply couldn't understand.

    c. Because he was thinking about something else.

    d. Because he fell asleep.

17. What will the speaker probably do?

    a. He will refuse to work overtime.

    b. He will quit this job.

    c. He will probably say yes to his boss and work overtime.

    d. He will have to give up his studies.

18. Which of the following is true about the picture?

    a. It doesn't cost much.

b. It would not be good enough for "my" room.

c. It costs about 30 dollars.

d. It is very famous.

19. What does the speaker think of Kevin's haircut?

a. He doesn't like Kevin's haircut.

b. Kevin often gets strange haircuts.

c. He wants a haircut like Kevin's.

d. Kevin's haircut looks good.

20. What does the speaker say about the international festival?

a. It won't be held.

b. It will be delayed.

c. The proposal is groundless.

d. It will definitely be held outdoors.

Part II

Listen to the following passages and then choose the best answer to each question by ticking the corresponding circle. You may need to scribble a few notes in order to answer the questions satisfactorily. There are 3 passages in this part, each with 5 questions. And each question carries 2 points. You will hear the passages only once. At the end of each passage, you will have 2 minutes to finish the questions.

Passage One

21. What is this talk mainly about?

a. How historical events affected an art movement.

b. How artists can influence economic conditions.

c. Why a certain art movement failed to become popular.

d. How valuable paintings were lost during wartime.

22. What does the speaker say about the artists in the United States during the Great Depression?

a. Many artists lost faith in the value of art.

b. Many artists were forced to take jobs in other fields.

c. Many artists moved away from large cities.

d. Many artists in the United States moved to other countries.

23. What kind of scene might be shown in a typical regionalist painting?

a. People working in a large factory.

b. People walking on crowded city streets.

c. An everyday activity in a small town.

d. A well-known historical event.

24. Why did regionalism become so popular in the U.S. during the Great Depression?

   a. Because the paintings sold very well.

   b. Because it helped strengthen people's faith in their country.

   c. Because people liked to live in the country at that time.

   d. Because it helped recover the economy.

25. According to the speaker, what happened in the U.S. in the 1940s around the time of the Second World War that affected the popularity of the regionalist art?

   a. The population of small towns increased rapidly.

   b. Art critics in cities began to take notice of regionalism.

   c. Some regionalist painters began a new art movement.

   d. Society became more internationally focused.

Passage Two

26. According to the passage, how many universities in the United States took part in the study?

   a. Four.

   b. Three.

   c. Five.

   d. Six.

27. Why does a lack of sleep cause people to gain weight?

   a. Because people burn fewer calories when they are awake.

   b. Because people feel hungry when they lack sleep.

   c. Because their hormones stay unchanged.

   d. Because people don't exercise when they don't have enough sleep.

28. According to the passage, what is NOT true about the first study?

   a. More than 1,000 people took part in the study.

   b. People who slept less had higher blood levels of ghrelin.

   c. People who slept more had higher blood levers of leptin.

   d. The amount of exercise can influence the result of the study.

29. What is the best amount of sleep for weight control?

   a. 8 hours a night.

   b. 7.7 hours a night.

   c. 7 hours a night.

   d. 9 hours a night.

30. Two groups of people are compared in the third study. They are people _____.

   a. with less than 5 hours of sleep a night and with 7 to 9 hours of sleep

   b. who slept 4 hours a night and who slept 4 hours for 2 nights

c. with less than 4 hours of sleep a night and with 7 to 9 hours of sleep

d. with less than 5 hours of sleep a night and with 8 hours of sleep

Passage Three

31. How much was the net income at Sony Ericsson in 2004?

a. 55 million euros.

b. 43million euros.

c. 45million euros.

d. 44million euros.

32. To whom did Sony Ericsson lose its position as the world's fifth-biggest handset maker?

a. Nokia.

b. Motorola.

c. LG Electronics.

d. An Asian manufacturer.

33. Which of the following contributed to the growth of Sony Ericsson's global market share?

a. Competition from Asian manufacturers.

b. Strong sales in Western Europe.

c. Rise of mobile phone shipments.

d. Pressure from Nokia.

34. Where is Sony Ericsson based?

a. In London.

b. In Paris.

c. In Tokyo.

d. In New York City.

35. What is the average selling price of Sony Ericsson's phones in the 4th quarter of 2004?

a. 157 euros.

b. 165 euros.

c. 140 euros.

d. 160 euros.

Part III

Parts of the following text are missing. While listening to the tape, complete the passage by filling in each blank space with an appropriate word or words. There are 20 blanks, each carrying 1 point. You will hear the passage only once. At the end of the recording, you will have 3 minutes to finish this part.

Kofi Annan says helping survivors of last week's earthquake and _____(1)_____ in the Indian Ocean is _____(2)_____. The United Nations secretary-general says countries that have offered aid must _____(3)_____ and provide it. The offers add up to around _____(4)_____ dollars. United Nations officials say _____(5)_____ of that is needed during the next six months.

The concern about offers of international aid is _____(6)_____. For example, the earthquake in Bam, Iran, in _____(7)_____ of 2003 killed more than _____(8)_____ people. Countries and groups offered hundreds of millions of dollars _____(9)_____. The United Nations says it has _____(10)_____ only about _____(11)_____ dollars in aid received so far. Governments and organizations that offered help _____(12)_____ that, however.

On _____(13)_____ Mr. Annan met with world leaders in Jakarta, Indonesia to discuss aid for _____(14)_____. The leaders discussed and _____(15)_____ the idea of _____(16)_____ owed by affected nations. But the leaders did not say they would do so. Some said that _____(17)_____ to survivors would be more helpful.

Representatives of _____(18)_____ countries and international organizations attended the meeting in Jakarta. Officials say they will cooperate to develop _____(19)_____ for the Indian Ocean and the _____(20)_____.

Part IV

Listen to the following passage. Write a short English summary of around 150 words of what you have heard. This part of the test carries 30 points. You will hear the passage only once. At the end of the recording, you will have 25 minutes to finish this part. You may need to scribble a few notes in order to write your summary satisfactorily.

_____
_____
_____
_____
_____
_____
_____

(二)参考答案

Part I

A (10 points, 1 point per question)

1. False   2. False   3. True   4. True   5. True
6. False   7. True   8. False   9. True   10. False

B (10 points, 1 point per question)

11～15 b d a b a   16～20 d c a d a

Part Ⅱ

(30 points, 2 points per question)

21～25 a c c b d   26～30 a b d b c   31～35 a c b a d

Part Ⅲ

(20 points, 1 point per blank)

1. killer waves
2. a race against time
3. hurry
4. four billion
5. one-fourth
6. based on history
7. December
8. twenty-six thousand
9. worth of assistance
10. confirmed
11. seventeen million
12. dispute
13. Thursday
14. victims of the tsunami
15. welcomed
16. suspending some debt
17. making direct payments
18. twenty-six
19. a tsunami warning system
20. South China Sea

Part Ⅳ

(30 points)

全篇共有 5 个主要点和 12 个次要点：黑斜体的句子为 5 个主要点；波浪线标出的句子为 12 个次要点。

Snow is a subject of great interest to weather experts. Experts sometimes have difficulty estimating where, when or how much snow will fall.(1) One reason is that heavy amounts of snow fall in surprisingly small areas. Another reason is that a small change in temperature can mean the difference between snow and rain.

Snow falls in extreme northern and southern areas of the world throughout the year. However, the heaviest snowfalls have been reported in the mountains of other areas during winter. (2)These areas include the Alps in Italy and Switzerland, the coastal mountains of western Canada, and the Sierra Nevada and Rocky Mountains in the United States. In warmer climates, snow is known to fall in areas over four thousand nine hundred meters above sea level.

Snow can be beautiful to look at, but it can also be dangerous.

Snow is responsible for the deaths of hundreds of people in the United States every year. Many people die in traffic accidents on roads that are covered with snow or ice.(3) Others die from being out in the cold or from heart attacks caused by extreme physical activity.(4)

A few years ago, a major storm caused serious problems in the eastern United States. (5)It struck the Southeast in January nineteen ninety-six, before moving up the East Coast. The storm was blamed for more than one hundred deaths.(6) It forced nine states to declare emergency measures.(7)

Virginia and West Virginia were hit hardest. In some areas there, snowfall amounts were more than one meter high. Several states limited driving to emergency vehicles. Most major airports were closed for at least a day or two.

A week later, two other storms brought additional snow to the East Coast. In the New York City area, the added weight of the snow forced the tops of some buildings to break down. Many travelers were forced to walk long distances through deep snow to get to train stations.

People may not be able to avoid living in areas where it snows often. ***However, they can avoid becoming victims of winter snowstorms.***

People should stay in their homes until the storm has passed.(8) While removing large amounts of snow, they should stop and rest often. Difficult physical activity during snow removal can cause a heart attack. It is always a good idea to keep a lot of necessary supplies in the home even before winter begins. (9)These supplies include food, medicine, clean water, and extra power supplies.

Some drivers have become trapped in their vehicles during a snowstorm.(10) If this happens, people should remain in or near their car unless they see some kind of help. (11)They should get out and clear space around the vehicle to prevent the possibility of carbon monoxide gas poisoning.

People should tie a bright-colored object to the top of their car to increase the chance of rescue. Inside the car, they should open a window a little for fresh air and turn on the engine for ten or fifteen minutes every hour for heat.

People living in areas with winter storms should carry emergency supplies in their vehicles.(12)These include food, emergency medical supplies, and extra clothing to stay warm and dry. People in these areas should always be prepared for winter emergencies.

(三)综合解析

Part Ⅰ

【解题技巧】

"口译综合能力"考试中的判断题分两部分：段落和单句，测试考生能否听清并理解句子，然后根据选项作出判断。

在答题时应注意以下几个要点。

(1) 迅速预览题干，了解句子大意。

(2) 听写结合，双管齐下。听的同时应快速记下关键词，在记笔记时要有效、专注地听，获取全文信息。

(3) 段落判断题不仅是对某一句或某一短语的理解，而是对段落的整体理解。所以在对细节信息进行捕捉时也要把握段落的整体意义。单句判断题在很大程度上考查对句中关键词语的正确认识，包括各种短语和成语，以及同一意义的其他表达方式，在答题过程中要多加留意。

A

【文章大意】

这是一篇关于黑人争取选举权的短文。一个叫亨利的年轻人，在他 21 岁以后，从法律上拥有了选举权。但是在 1941 年亨利生活的戴维逊郡，黑人还是不能参与选举。于是在他过了 21 岁后，他和他的父亲及其他 5 个人来到选举登记员家。选举登记员本来决定不把黑人加入选举名单，但亨利符合条件，所以只好同意将其加入选举名单。因此亨利成为这个郡第一个登记注册选举权的黑人。不仅如此，亨利还帮他的父亲以及同去的 5 个人都争取到了选举权。第二天，亨利带了更多的人到郡政府，通过据理力争也使这些人都登记注册了选举权。

【分析】

1. False——细节信息题

根据原文"When Henry turned twenty-one, he was legally allowed to vote, but in Davidson County in 1941, blacks could not vote."原文说 1941 年在戴维逊郡，黑人不能参与选举，而题干中的地点是美国与原文不符，所以题干表述是错误的。

2. False——细节信息题

根据原文"One night, after he had turned twenty-one, Henry put his father and five other people in his father's Model A Ford and drove to the house of the voting registrar."原文说亨利开车来到选举登记员家，而题干说亨利驾车到了法院，与原文的细节不符，所以题干表述是错误的。

3. True——理解推断题

根据原文"The registrar was prepared for this. He said the literacy regulation required that Henry be able to read the Constitution of the United States. He placed a copy on the table. Henry picked it up and read it. The registrar looked at Henry and realized he had no choice."大意为：登记员对此早有准备，他说亨利必须能读懂美国的宪法才能注册选举权。当登记员把一本美国宪法复印本放在桌上，亨利拿起就读。登记员看着亨利，意识到他已别无选择。据此可以推断登记员本来是决定不把黑人加入选举名单的，但亨利符合条件，所以他不得不给亨利登记。所以题干表述是正确的。

4. True——语法题(虚拟语气)

根据原文"He said the literacy regulation required that Henry be able to read the Constitution of the United States."译文为：他(登记员)说亨利必须能够读懂美国的宪法。此句是 require 引导的宾语从句，是虚拟语气，表示是应具备的能力，所以题干表述是正确的。

5. True——理解推断题

根据原文的多处信息，如"He said the literacy regulation required that Henry be able to read the Constitution of the United States.""'I believe you ought to register these folks. They're able to read. Not all of your folks coming in here can read.'"据此可以推断出，只有会读写的人才能取得选举权，所以题干的表述是正确的。

6. False——细节信息题

根据原文"He was the first black to register in the county",表明亨利是这个郡第一个登记注册选举权的黑人,而题干表述的是亨利是第一个投票的人,与原文表述不符,所以题干表述是错误的。

7. True——固定搭配题

根据原文"He was the first black to register in the county. The second was his father, because Henry would not leave until his father's name, and the names of the five others, were put in the book",可知亨利是第一个登记注册选举权的黑人。第二句话中有个固定搭配很重要:not...until,意思是"直到……才"。第二句话的译文为:第二个登记选举权的人是他的父亲,因为直到他父亲的名字,还有其他 5 个人的名字被登记在册,他才会离开。据此可知亨利的父亲和同去的 5 个人都注册了选举权,所以题干表述是正确的。

8. False——理解推断题

根据原文"The next day Henry brought more people to the courthouse, where he faced a different clerk who refused to register the people. Henry told him, 'I believe you ought to register these folks. They're able to read. Not all of your folks coming in here can read.'"译文为:第二天亨利带着更多的人到郡政府,这儿的登记员拒绝为这些人注册。亨利坚持说,"我认为你应当为这些人注册登记,他们都能够读懂宪法。而且不是所有到这儿来的白人都可以读懂宪法。"根据上下文可以推断出,如果来的人会读写的话,登记员是不能拒绝的,所以题干表述是错误的。

9. True——细节信息题

根据原文"Not all of your folks coming in here can read",可知不是所有到这儿来的白人都可以读懂宪法。本题关键是"your folks"指的是白人,即和登记员他们一类的人。据此推断题干表述是正确的。

10. False——理解推断题

根据原文"Henry got the people registered",可知亨利使这些人都登记注册了。这些人指亨利带去注册的人,而题干表述的是他们整个郡的黑人,显然题干表述扩大了原文所指的范围,所以题干表述是错误的。

B

11. b——固定搭配

根据原文"There is nothing I like better to get me started in the morning than a big breakfast."关键在于理解特殊比较结构"nothing better than",否定词 + 比较级 = 最高级。意思是:没有什么比这更好,用于强调某事物非常好。该句译文为:没有什么比早上吃一顿丰盛的早餐,更能让我有良好开端的。a 选项为"他通常不吃早餐就开始工作";b 选项为"他喜欢丰盛的早餐";c 选项为"他早餐吃得不多";d 选项为"他早上喜欢吃别的胜于吃一顿丰盛的早餐"。所以选 b。

12. d——理解推断

根据原文"I am speaking to a group of high school students about engineering this afternoon. But I have no idea how I am going to simplify some of the concepts for them."译文为：今天下午我要为一群高中生讲解工程学，但是我不知道怎样为他们简化一些概念。据此可以推断作者对于怎样讲演还没有把握。a 选项为"他对于工程学一无所知"；b 选项为"他想推迟作报告"；c 选项为"他以前从未为高中生做过讲演"；d 选项为"他没有准备好作报告"。只有选项 d 与原文传达的意思最贴近，所以选 d。

13. a——因果关系

根据原文"I don't remember the assignment off hand, but I've got it written down at home. How about if I call you tonight?"译文为：我现在不记得作业，但是我在家里做了记录。我晚上打电话给你如何？题干问打电话的原因，据此可以推断是为了告诉别人作业是什么。a 选项为"因为他想让其他人知道作业是什么"；b 选项为"因为他得跟某人谈谈"；c 选项为"因为他现在还不能谈论有关作业的事"；d 选项为"因为他想知道有关作业的事"。所以选 a。

14. b——是非判断

根据原文"You know Sara. If she has an opinion, everyone has got to know it."译文为：你是了解莎拉的，一旦她有了个主意，所有人就都会知道的。a 选项为"她很少犯错误"；b 选项为"她让别人知道她的想法"；c 选项为"她有很多新点子"；d 选项为"她不喜欢表达自己的观点"。选项 b 换用固定搭配 make sth. known 来表达原意，这是听力理解题出题时的惯常做法，所以选 b。

15. a——同义替换

根据原文"What's wrong with Dave today? He snapped for no reason."译文为：戴夫今天怎么了？他没有理由地大发脾气。本题关键是理解 snap 的词义，snap 在本句指"突然发怒、脾气暴躁"。a 选项用"lose his temper"代替了原句中的"snap"，"lose his temper"意思是"发脾气"。b、c、d 选项的意思与原文意思差之千里，所以选 a。

16. d——固定搭配

根据原文"I didn't catch that point. I must have dozed off for a minute."意思是：我没听清这一点，我可能中间打瞌睡了。本题关键是理解固定搭配 doze off，意思是"打瞌睡"，所以选 d。

17. c——理解推断

根据原文"My boss keeps asking me to work overtime but I always say no because I don't want to jeopardize my studies. But I'm starting to waver."译文为：老板一再要求我加班，我一直拒绝因为我不想影响学业，但现在我开始犹豫了。据此可以推断，作者一直以来的态度开始动摇。a 选项为"他会拒绝老板加班的要求"；b 选项为"他将辞去这份工作"；c 选项为"他大概要服从老板的安排，同意加班工作"；d 选项为"他将不得不放弃他的学业"。所以选 c。

18. a——是非判断

根据原文"This painting would go great with my room, but they want 30 dollars for it and it's probably mostly for the frame."译文为：这幅画和我的房间很相配。但是他们要价是30美元，这个价钱大概主要是画框的要价。据此可以推断这幅画本身并不值钱，所以选a。

19. d——理解推断

根据原文"Kevin's new haircut really complements his beard."译文为：凯文的新发型和他的胡须很相称，互为补充。本句关键是理解complement的词义，complement意思是："补充、使更完美"，据此可以推断凯文的新发型看起来还不错，所以选d。

20. a——固定搭配

根据原文"Do you remember that proposal for an international festival next spring? I don't think there is any chance it'll ever get off the ground."译文为：你还记得明年春天举行国际节的那个提议吗？我认为这项提议没有一点付诸实施的可能性。本题关键是理解两个固定搭配"there isn't any chance"，意思是"没有任何机会"；get off the ground 意思是"(使某事物)顺利开始"。a项为"国际节不会举行"，与原文意思最贴近，所以选a。

Part II

【解题技巧】

"口译综合能力"考试中的"篇章理解"部分听力材料为3篇，每篇附有5个问题。就内容来说，作为篇章理解题的材料题材一般比较广泛，一般是大家比较熟悉的题材，包括政治、经济、外交、科技、环境、商务、广告、教育、就业、旅游、英美文化等。

在答题时应注意以下几个要点。

(1) 篇章听力理解的题目顺序一般是随内容的自然发展而出的，因此在听录音前把各题的选项浏览一下，可大致猜出会是什么样的问题，从答题选项中寻找答题线索，对做题很有好处。

(2) 篇章理解题有一部分问题会集中于某些特殊的句子结构，比如一些常用成语、动词短语等。这时，考的不仅仅是听力，还有词汇和句法知识。因此，造成考生做错题的不是听不清录音材料，而是不理解这些特殊结构和词汇，所以平常要注意这方面的积累。

(3) 如果选项中有数字或日期出现，就应该对录音中的相关内容予以特别关注。如果同一题中的选项其中有两项是意义截然相反的，那么很可能其中一项是正确答案。

Passage One

【文章大意】

这是一篇关于艺术运动的听力材料。短文首句就引出主题：艺术运动的流行、普及受到社会条件的影响，而社会条件本身又常常受到历史事件的影响。接着描述了20世纪初期大萧条时期美国所发生的艺术运动，即地方主义。讲述了地方主义特色的绘画展示的风景，地方主义艺术在大萧条时期在美国流行的原因以及20世纪40年代第二次世界大战(以下简称"二战")前后，美国呈现的越来越多的国际精神影响到地方主义艺术特色的流行。

【分析】

21. a——主旨归纳题

题干：这篇讲话主要是关于什么的？文章的首句常常是主题句。根据原文"One important thing about art movements is that their popularity can be affected by social conditions, which are themselves often affected by historical events."译文为：关于艺术运动的一件重要的事情是它的流行普及受到社会条件的影响，而社会条件本身又常常受到历史事件的影响。所以选 a。

22．c——要点理解题

题干：作者怎样描述在大萧条时期美国的艺术家？根据"many artists who had been living in big cities were forced by the economic crisis to leave those big cities and move back to their small towns in rural America."译文为：许多原先居住在大城市的艺术家迫于经济危机的压力，离开了大城市，返回到美国乡间的小城镇。a 选项为"许多艺术家对艺术价值失去了信念"；b 选项为"许多艺术家被迫在其他领域找工作"；c 选项"许多艺术家搬离了大城市"；d 选项为"美国的许多艺术家搬到了其他国家"。所以选 c。

23．c——要点理解题

题干：典型的地方主义特色的绘画会展示什么样的风景？根据原文"They created things from everyday life in small towns or farming areas."译文为：他们的作品来源于小城镇或农业区的日常生活。所以选 c。

24．b——因果关系题

题干：为什么地方主义艺术在大萧条时期的美国如此流行？根据原文"And this style became very popular, in part because of the economic conditions of the time…So the movement helped strengthen people's faith in their country, faith that had weakened as the result of the Depression."译文为：这种风格变得很流行，一定程度上是由于当时的经济状况，所以该运动巩固了人们的信念，那些由于大萧条而削弱的信念。所以选 b。

25．d——细节信息题

题干：根据作者所言，在 20 世纪 40 年代"二战"前后，在美国什么影响到地方主义艺术特色的流行？根据原文"But in the 1940's, …American society began to take on a much more international spirit, and Regionalism, … lost a lot of popularity."，译文为：但是在 20 世纪 40 年代……美国社会逐渐呈现更多的国际精神，……地方主义特色流行程度失去了很多。所以选 d。

Passage Two

【文章大意】

这是一篇关于睡眠与体重关系的说明文。美国有四所大学参与了该项研究。他们得出的结论是缺乏睡眠会导致人们变胖。原因是：缺乏睡眠会导致荷尔蒙的变化，这种变化会增加饥饿感。研究人员做了三次研究，第一次研究人员根据对 1,000 多人的调查，发现睡眠较少的人胃饥饿素(ghrelin)的血压高，其荷尔蒙瘦素(leptin)低于正常人15%。第二次研究发现控制体重所需的最佳睡眠量为每晚 7.7 个小时。在第三次研究中发现，每晚睡眠少于 4 个小时的人与每晚睡眠 9 个小时的人相比，睡眠较少的人为了生存，身体会储存更多的脂肪。

【分析】

26. a——要点归纳题

题干：根据文章，美国有几所大学参与了该项研究？原文提到的大学有：Stanford University, University of Wisconsin, University of Chicago, Columbia University。所以选 a。

27. b——因果关系题

题干：为什么缺乏睡眠会导致人们变胖？根据原文"Researchers say a lack of sleep can produce hormonal changes that increase feelings of hunger"，译文为：研究人员说缺乏睡眠会导致荷尔蒙的变化，这种变化会增强饥饿感。a 选项为"因为在清醒的时候燃烧的卡路里较少"；b 选项"因为人们缺乏睡眠时会感到饥饿"；c 选项为"因为他们的荷尔蒙没有改变"；d 选项为"因为人们睡眠不足时不运动"。所以选 b。

28. d——是非判断题

题干：根据文章，关于第一次研究，哪个说法不正确？a 选项为"超过 1,000 人参与了该研究。"；根据原文"researchers…examined information on more than one thousand people."研究人员调查了超过 1,000 人的信息，所以该选项是正确的。b 选项为"睡眠较少的人 ghrelin 的血压高"；根据原文"Some people slept less … They had fifteen percent higher blood levels of a hormone called ghrelin…"，译文为：睡眠较少的人他们的一种荷尔蒙 ghrelin 的血压高出 15%。所以选项是正确的。c 选项为"睡眠较多的人 leptin 的血压高"；根据原文"…people slept less … they had fifteen percent less of the hormone leptin."译文为：睡眠较少的荷尔蒙 leptin 低于正常人 15%。由此可以推断睡眠多的人该项指标高，所以该选项正确。d 选项为"运动量能够影响研究的结果"，根据原文"The results were not affected by how much people exercised."译文为：结果并不受人们运动量的影响。所以选 d。

29. b——数字信息题

题干：控制体重需要的最佳睡眠量是多少？根据原文"Researchers found that the best amount of sleep for weight control is seven-point-seven hours a night."译文为：研究人员发现控制体重所需要的最佳睡眠量为每晚 7.7 个小时。所以选 b。

30. c——细节信息题

题干：在第三次研究中，两组人做了对比，这两组人分别是哪些人？根据原文"They found that people who got less than four hours of sleep a night…This was compared to people with seven to nine hours of sleep."译文为：他们发现每晚睡眠少于 4 个小时的人……，和睡眠 7~9 小时的人做了对比。所以选 c。

Passage Three

【文章大意】

这是一篇关于索尼爱立信手机全球市场份额变化情况的介绍。短文首先介绍了 2004 年索尼爱立信的净收入。接着阐述了索尼爱立信失去手机世界产量第五的原因以及 2004 年第四季度平均销售价格的变化情况。最后阐述了索尼爱立信全球市场份额增长的原因，指出是由于西欧的强劲销售导致的。

【分析】

31．a——数字信息题

题干：2004 年索尼爱立信的净收入为多少？根据原文"In 2004, net income at Sony Ericsson, the world's sixth-biggest mobile phone maker, rose to 55 million euros from 43 million euros a year earlier."译文为：2004 年索尼爱立信作为世界第六大手机生产商，其净收入从一年前的 43,000,000 欧元上升到 55,000,000 欧元。所以选 a。

32．c——细节信息题

题干：索尼爱立信失去了手机生产世界第五的位置，这个位置被谁替代了？根据原文，"Sony Ericsson, which lost its position as the world's fifth-biggest handset maker to LG Electronics in the third quarter."译文为：索尼爱立信在第三季度失去了世界产量第五的位置，这个位置被 LG 电子替代了。所以选 c。

33．b——细节信息题

题干：下列哪些原因促成了索尼爱立信全球市场份额增长？根据原文"Sony Ericsson's third-quarter global market share grew to 6.4 percent from 5.3 percent a year earlier, spurred by strong sales in Western Europe"，译文为：索尼爱立信第三季度全球市场份额从一年前的 5.3%增长至 6.4%，这是由于西欧的强劲销售导致的。所以选 b。

34．a——地点信息题

题干：索尼爱立信的总部在哪儿？根据原文"The company, based in London"，译文为：公司总部位于伦敦。所以选 a。

35．d——数字信息题

题干：2004 年第四季度索尼爱立信手机的平均销售价格是多少？根据原文"In 2004, the average selling price of Sony Ericsson's phones rose to 160 euros from 157 euros in the 4th quarter."译文为：2004 年第四季度索尼爱立信手机的平均销售价格从 157 欧元上升到 160 欧元。所以选 d。

Part Ⅲ

【解题技巧】

"口译综合能力"考试中的"填空"部分属主观性试题，要求应试者在全面理解所听内容的基础上，准确地填写出试题中要求填写的部分。这部分是对应试者听的能力、拼写能力、记笔记能力和书面表达能力的综合测试。

在答题时应注意以下几个要点。

(1) 在录音开始前，预览文章，对段落的大意有所了解；同时利用词汇在段落中出现的频率根据上下文推测词汇的运用。

(2) 听写结合。听的同时应快速记下关键信息，而在做笔记时要有效、专注地去听，获取全文信息。

(3) 提高笔记的效率。比如使用缩略语、字母较多的单词只写该词的前几个字母。等录音结束后，再根据这些记号，依靠记忆把答案写出来。还要注意有选择地做笔记，应重点记下句子的中心词。

【文章大意】

联合国秘书长科菲·安南强调帮助印度洋海啸和地震的幸存者是一场和时间的比赛，他呼吁承诺捐助的国家要迅速行动。

进行国际援助是有历史依据的。例如，2003年发生在伊朗的地震夺去了26,000人的生命。国际社会和团体已经答应提供价值数亿美元的资助，但是联合国确认到目前为止只收到17,000,000美元的捐资。国际社会对此有争论。

安南在雅加达和各国领导人会面讨论对海啸受难者的援助事宜。各国领导讨论并同意暂缓受灾国的一些债务，但是也表示直接的捐助将更有帮助。官员们称将合作建立印度洋和中国南海的海啸预警机制。

【分析】

1. killer waves

此处考查的是名词短语结构，要注意中心词和修饰词的关系，关键是中心词 waves，killer waves 的意思是"海啸"。

2. a race against time

此处考查的是名词短语结构，要注意中心词和修饰语的关系，关键是中心词 race，a race against time 的意思是"和时间的比赛"。

3. hurry

此处考查情态动词后的动词，应用动词原形。

4. four billion

此处考查数字信息，注意拼写形式。

5. one-fourth

此处考查数字信息，注意拼写形式。

6. based on history

此处是谓语动词的一部分，是被动语态结构，意思是：建立在历史的基础上。

7. December

此处考查的是专有名词，应注意单词拼写的大写情况。

8. twenty-six thousand

此处考查数字信息，注意拼写形式。

9. worth of assistance

此处考查的是形容词短语结构，要注意中心词和修饰词的关系，关键是中心词 worth of，worth of assistance 意思是"相当于……价值的援助"。

10. confirmed

此处考查的是谓语动词，应注意动词时态。此处是现在完成时态，应填动词的过去分词形式。confirmed 的意思是"确认、证实"。

11. seventeen million

此处考查数字信息，注意拼写形式。

12. dispute

此处考查的是谓语动词，应注意动词时态。本句话中是对事实的陈述，所以用一般现在时态。dispute 的意思是"争论、辩论"。

13. Thursday

此处考查的是专有名词，应注意单词拼写的大写情况。

14. victims of the tsunami

此处考查的是名词短语结构，要注意中心词和修饰词的关系，关键是中心词 victims，victims of the tsunami 的意思是"海啸受害者"。

15. welcomed

此处考查的是谓语动词，应注意动词时态。本句中与所填词并列的谓语动词 discussed 用的是一般过去时态，所以应填动词的一般过去式。

16. suspending some debt

此处考查的是动词短语，应注意动词时态。介词后如果是动词应接动名词。suspending some debt 的意思是"暂缓部分债务"。

17. making direct payments

此处考查的是动词短语，应注意动词时态。本句中宾语从句的主语是动词短语，动词应用动名词。making direct payments 的意思是"直接支付"。

18. twenty-six

此处考查数字信息，注意拼写形式。

19. a tsunami warning system

此处考查的是名词短语结构，要注意中心词和修饰词的关系，关键是中心词 system，a tsunami warning system 的意思是"一种海啸预警机制"。

20. South China Sea

此处考查的是专有名词，应注意单词拼写的大写情况。

Part Ⅳ

【解题技巧】

"口译综合能力"考试中的"听力综合"部分是一篇 500 词左右的文章，要求听完后写一篇 150 词左右的英语综述。要做好听力综述的前提是应试者必须具备听懂英语篇章、把握整篇文章大意的能力。其次，作为"听力综述"题的英语材料往往是事先准备的演讲或是新闻稿，所以整个篇章一般来说应该是结构完整、承接清晰、有脉络可寻的。

在答题时应注意以下几个要点。

(1) 在写综述时，应特别注意文章的开头段落和结尾段落。在每个段落中，要特别注意主题句，即开头句和结尾句。

(2) 要抓住文章的逻辑发展关系，了解文章的结构，并注意连词的使用。

(3) 要做好听力综述题，考生的英语写作能力至关重要。应试者要尽力避免语法、用词搭配、修辞等方面的各种错误；句子完整，避免破句，注意通顺简洁；字数控制在 150 字左右的范围内。

【文章大意】

雪是气象专家们很感兴趣的一个话题。在世界的最北部和最南部终年都在下雪。而据报道最大的降雪发生在冬季的山区。雪很美丽但是也很危险，每年在美国发生的雪灾会导致数百人死亡。几年前美国东部的一场暴风雪带来了严重的后果，导致 100 多人死亡，使得 9 个州宣布紧急避险。

人们可以避免成为暴风雪的受害者。在暴风雪期间人们应该待在家中，并准备充足的日常供给；困在风雪中的司机应尽量呆在车里或车附近；住在冬季有暴风雪地区的人们应在家用车中储备紧急供应品。

【分析】

一、高分表述

高分表述指能写出段落中的主题句即段落中的开头句或是结尾句。本文的高分表述包括：

1. Snow is a subject of great interest to weather experts.

2. Snow falls in extreme northern and southern areas of the world throughout the year.

3. Snow can be beautiful to look at, but it can also be dangerous.

4. Snow is responsible for the deaths of hundreds of people in the United States every year.

5. However, they can avoid becoming victims of winter snowstorms.

二、细节表述

细节表述指能写出段落中除主题句外的句子，能对主题句起进一步补充说明的作用。

1. Experts sometimes have difficulty estimating where, when or how much snow will fall.

2. However, the heaviest snowfalls have been reported in the mountains of other areas during winter.

3. Many people die in traffic accidents on roads that are covered with snow or ice.

4. Others die from being out in the cold or from heart attacks caused by extreme physical activity.

5. A few years ago, a major storm caused serious problems in eastern United States.

6. The storm was blamed for more than one hundred deaths.

7. It forced nine states to declare emergency measures.

8. People should stay in their homes until the storm has passed.

9. It is always a good idea to keep a lot of necessary supplies in the home even before winter begins.

10. Some drivers have become trapped in their vehicles during a snowstorm.

11. If this happens, people should remain in or near their car unless they see some kind of help.

12. People living in areas with winter storms should carry emergency supplies in their vehicles.

(四)听力材料

Part I

A. Listen to the following passage and then decide whether the statements below are true or false. After hearing a short passage, tick the circle of "True" on the answer sheet if you think the statement is true, or tick the circle for "False" if it is false. There are 10 statements in this part of the test, with 1 point each. You will hear the passage only once. At the end of the recording, you will have 2 minutes to finish this part.

When Henry turned twenty-one, he was legally allowed to vote, but in Davidson County in 1941, blacks could not vote. One night, after he had turned twenty-one, Henry put his father and five other people in his father's Model A Ford and drove to the house of the voting registrar. He said they were there to put their names in the voting book. The registrar was prepared for this. He said the literacy regulation required that Henry be able to read the Constitution of the United States. He placed a copy on the table. Henry picked it up and read it. The registrar looked at Henry and realized he had no choice. He entered Henry's name in the book. He was the first black to register in the county. The second was his father, because Henry would not leave until his father's name, and the name of the five others, were put in the book. That was not enough. The next day Henry brought more people to the courthouse, where he faced a different clerk who refused to register the people. Henry told him, "I believe you ought to register these folks. They're able to read. Not all of your folks coming in here can read." For the first time the county government encountered a man who would not budge from his belief in his rights. Henry got the people registered.

B. Listen to the following short statements and then choose one of the answers that best fits the meaning of each statement by ticking the corresponding circle. There are 10 questions in this part of the test, 1 point for each question. You will hear the statement only once.

11. There is nothing I like better to get me started in the morning than a big breakfast.

12. I am speaking to a group of high school students about engineering this afternoon. But I have no idea how I am going to simplify some of the concepts for them.

13. I don't remember the assignment off hand, but I've got it written down at home. How about if I call you tonight?

14. You know Sara. If she has an opinion, everyone has got to know it.

15. What's wrong with Dave today? He snapped for no reason.

16. I didn't catch that point. I must have dozed off for a minute.

17. My boss keeps asking me to work overtime but I always say no because I don't want to jeopardize my studies. But I'm starting to waver.

18. This painting would go great with my room, but they want 30 dollars for it and it's probably mostly for the frame.

19. Kevin's new haircut really complements his beard.

20. Do you remember that proposal for an international festival next spring? I don't think there is any chance it'll ever get off the ground.

Part II

Listen to the following passages and then choose the best answer to each question by ticking the corresponding circle. You may need to scribble a few notes in order to answer the questions satisfactorily. There are 3 passages in this part, each with 5 questions. And each question carries 2 points. You will hear the passages only once. At the end of each passage, you will have 2 minutes to finish the questions.

Passage One

One important thing about art movements is that their popularity can be affected by social conditions, which are themselves often affected by historical events. As an example, look at what happened in the United States early in the 20th century, around the time of the Great Depression. The art movement known as the Regionalism had begun in the United States even before the Depression occurred. But it really flourished in the 1930's, during the Depression years. Why? Well, many artists who had been living in big cities were forced by the economic crisis to leave those big cities and move back to their small towns in rural America. Some of these artists came to truly embrace the life in small towns and to eject city life in so-called "sophisticated society". These artists, or more specifically, certain painters, really built the regionalist movement. They created things from everyday life in small towns or farming areas. And they depicted the really big glorified or romanticized country life, showing it as stable, wholesome, and embodying important American traditions. And this style became very popular, in part because of the economic conditions of the time. You see, the Depression had caused many Americans to begin to doubt their society. But regionalist artists painted scenes that glorified American values, scenes that many Americans could easily identify with. So the movement helped strengthen people's faith in their country, faith that had weakened as the result of the Depression. But in the 1940's, before and after the Second World War, American society began to take on a much more international spirit, and Regionalism, with its focus on small town life, lost a lot of popularity.

Passage Two

There are new findings that people with inadequate sleep are likely to gain weight. Researchers say a lack of sleep can produce hormonal changes that increase feelings of hunger.

In one study, researchers from Stanford University in California and the University of Wisconsin examined information on more than one thousand people. The people had taken part in a long-term study of sleep disorders.

Some people slept less than five hours a night. They had fifteen percent higher blood levels of a hormone called ghrelin than people who slept eight hours. And they had fifteen percent less of the hormone leptin. Experts say ghrelin helps make people feel hungry; leptin makes you feel full.

The results were not affected by how much people exercised. People who are awake longer have more time to burn energy. But the researchers say loss of sleep may increase hunger especially for high-calorie foods, so people gain weight.

Researchers found that the best amount of sleep for weight control is seven-point-seven hours a night.

Researchers at the University of Chicago did a smaller study. They found that people who slept just four hours a night for two nights had an eighteen percent reduction in leptin. And they had a twenty-eight percent increase in ghrelin. The young men in that study also appeared to want more sweet and starchy foods.

Researchers from Columbia University in New York did a third study. They found that people who got less than four hours of sleep a night were seventy-three percent more likely to be overweight. This was compared to people with seven to nine hours of sleep. The researchers say that for survival, the body may be designed to store more fat during times with less sleep.

Passage Three

Sony Ericsson Mobile Communications, the cellphone joint venture owned by the Sony Corporation and the Swedish telecommunications equipment maker Ericsson, reported a 28 percent gain in fourth-quarter profit Tuesday as mobile phone shipments rose more than 50 percent.

In 2004, net income at Sony Ericsson, the world's sixth-biggest mobile phone maker, rose to 55 million euros from 43 million euros a year earlier. Earnings included a tax charge of 45 million euros. Sales jumped to 2 billion euros from 1.44 billion euros a year before.

The company, based in London, became profitable for the first time last year as its handsets featuring cameras became popular. At the same time, competitions from Asian manufacturers and price cuts by Nokia have put pressure on Sony Ericsson, which lost its position as the world's fifth-biggest handset maker to LG Electronics in the third quarter.

The company shipped 12.6 million phones in the quarter, 56 percent more than a year earlier. Pretax profit rose to 140 million euros from 46 million euros a year earlier; the latest results were just short of 165 million euros.

In 2004, the average selling price of Sony Ericsson's phones rose to 160 euros from 157 euros in the 4th quarter. The comparative price was calculated by Bloomberg by dividing revenue by the number of phones shipped.

Sony Ericsson's third-quarter global market share grew to 6.4 percent from 5.3 percent a year earlier, spurred by strong sales in Western Europe, according to the latest figures from the research firm Gartner. LG's market share grew to 6.7 percent from 5.3 percent.

Part III

Parts of the following text are missing. While listening to the tape, complete the passage by filling in each blank space with an appropriate word or words. There are 20 blanks, each carrying 1 point. You will hear the passage only once. At the end of the recording, you will have 3 minutes to finish this part.

Kofi Annan says helping survivors of last week's earthquake and <u>killer waves</u> in the Indian Ocean is <u>a race against time</u>. The United Nations secretary-general says countries that have offered aid must <u>hurry</u> and provide it. The offers add up to around <u>four billion</u> dollars. United Nations officials say <u>one-fourth</u> of that is needed during the next six months.

The concern about offers of international aid is <u>based on history</u>. For example, the earthquake in Bam, Iran, in <u>December</u> of 2003 killed more than <u>twenty-six thousand</u> people. Countries and groups offered hundreds of millions of dollars <u>worth of assistance</u>. The United Nations says it has <u>confirmed</u> only about <u>seventeen million</u> dollars in aid received so far. Governments and organizations that offered help <u>dispute</u> that, however.

On <u>Thursday</u> Mr. Annan met with world leaders in Jakarta, Indonesia to discuss aid for <u>victims of the tsunami</u>. The leaders discussed and <u>welcomed</u> the idea of <u>suspending some debt</u> owed by affected nations. But the leaders did not say they would do so. Some said that <u>making direct payments</u> to survivors would be more helpful.

Representatives of <u>twenty-six</u> countries and international organizations attended the meeting in Jakarta. Officials say they will cooperate to develop <u>a tsunami warning system</u> for the Indian Ocean and the <u>South China Sea</u>.

Part IV

Listen to the following passage. Write a short English summary of around 150 words of what you have heard. This part of the test carries 30 points. You will hear the passage only once. At the end of the recording, you will have 25 minutes to finish this part. You may need to scribble a few notes in order to write your summary satisfactorily.

Snow is a subject of great interest to weather experts. Experts sometimes have difficulty estimating where, when or how much snow will fall. One reason is that heavy amounts of snow fall in surprisingly small areas. Another reason is that a small change in temperature can mean the difference between snow and rain.

Snow falls in extreme northern and southern areas of the world throughout the year. However, the heaviest snowfalls have been reported in the mountains of other areas during winter. These areas include the Alps in Italy and Switzerland, the coastal mountains of western Canada, and the Sierra Nevada and Rocky Mountains in the United States. In warmer climates, snow is known to fall in areas over four thousand nine hundred meters above sea level.

Snow can be beautiful to look at, but it can also be dangerous.

Snow is responsible for the deaths of hundreds of people in the United States every year. Many people die in traffic accidents on roads that are covered with snow or ice. Others die from being out in the cold or from heart attacks caused by extreme physical activity.

A few years ago, a major storm caused serious problems in the eastern United States. It struck the Southeast in January 1996, before moving up the East Coast. The storm was blamed for more than one hundred deaths. It forced nine states to declare emergency measures.

Virginia and West Virginia were hit hardest. In some areas, snowfall amounts were more than one meter high. Several states limited driving to emergency vehicles. Most major airports were closed for at least a day or two.

A week later, two other storms brought additional snow to the East Coast. In the New York City area, the added weight of the snow forced the tops of some buildings to collapse. Many travelers were forced to walk long distances through deep snow to get to train stations.

People may not be able to avoid living in areas where it snows often. However, they can avoid becoming victims of winter snowstorms.

People should stay in their homes until the storm has passed. While removing large amounts of snow, they should stop and rest often. Difficult physical activity during snow removal can cause a heart attack. It is always a good idea to keep a lot of necessary supplies in the home even before winter begins. These supplies include food, medicine, clean water, and extra power supplies.

Some drivers have become trapped in their vehicles during a snowstorm. If this happens, people should remain in or near their car unless they see some kind of help. They should get out and clear space around the vehicle to prevent the possibility of carbon monoxide gas poisoning.

People should tie a bright-colored object to the top of their car to increase the chance of rescue. Inside the car, they should open a window a little for fresh air and turn on the engine for ten or fifteen minutes every hour for heat.

People living in areas with winter storms should carry emergency supplies in their vehicles. They should include food, emergency medical supplies, and extra clothing to stay warm and dry. People in these areas should always be prepared for winter emergencies.

三、"口译实务"备考

——英语三级"口译实务"试题（录音材料）

Part I

Listen to the following dialogue and interpret it as required. After you hear a sentence

or a short passage in Chinese, interpret into English by speaking to the microphone. And after you hear an English sentence or a short passage, interpret it into Chinese. Start interpreting at the signal and stop it at the signal. You may take notes while you are listening. You will hear the dialogue only once. Now let's begin.

下面是一段关于麦当劳快餐店的对话。

Mike：Let's go and get something to eat. I am starving.

李：我也有点饿。正好，前面有家麦当劳。

Mike：There is always a McDonald's up ahead. Everywhere you turn there is another blasted McDonald's. They are just too convenient. I am just plain sick of seeing the "Golden Arches" everywhere I turn. Do you know that there are over 8,000 McDonald's restaurants in the U.S. alone and over 11,000 franchises worldwide? By the year 2020, everyone will eat at McDonald's every day.

李：反正我爱吃汉堡包。现在全世界好像没有几个地方没有麦当劳，卖出的汉堡包都超过 1,000 亿个了。仅中国这几年就建了几百家，小孩都到那儿过生日。当然，也不是每种产品都好吃，可起码都很标准，不管什么时候去吃，汉堡包都是一个样儿。

Mike：Whatever you say. I just don't think their food is all that great. By the way, do you know that their spokesman, Ronald McDonald, is now recognized by 96% of all American children? They are the largest minimum-wage employers in America and own more real estate than any other company on earth. What is more, they say that one of every seven American millionaires got their start at McDonald's.

李：别说了，我都要饿死了。

Mike：But I just lost my appetite.

Part II

Interpret the following passage from English into Chinese. Start interpreting at the signal and stop it at the signal. You may take notes while you are listening. You will hear the passage only once. Now let's begin.

下面是一段关于亚洲价值与繁荣的讲话。

Ladies and Gentlemen,

What values should we pursue for the prosperity of Asia in the new century? I believe that the three values of freedom, diversity and openness are the driving forces behind peace and development in Asia.

First, it goes without saying that freedom refers to democracy and human rights politically, Economically, it means the development of a market economy.

Political freedom and economic freedom are reinforcing each other in the process of their development. With some twists and turns, Asia as a whole has been taking significant steps towards freedom over the last half century.

Transition to a democratic political system has been inevitable, as economic development has created the conditions for the emergence of a middle class and civil society. I believe that the historic trends that are apparent in Asia should be a source of pride for us all.

Second, development in Asia has occurred against a background of tremendous diversity, where each country has its own distinctive history and social and cultural values. Naturally, we thus see differences in the processes and speed of development.

While respecting diversity, however, it is important for us to promote our common interests and our shared goals, recognizing positive influences of each other despite differences among countries.

In other words, we must leave behind parochial nationalism and dogmatism, promote mutually beneficial cooperation based on equality in order to enjoy common prosperity. This should be our guiding principle.

Third, our cooperation must not be of an inward-looking, closed nature, but one characterized by openness to the world outside Asia.

In a world economy where globalization is advancing and economic integration, such as in Europe and Americas, is proceeding, cooperation both within Asia and between Asia and other regions must be pursued. This cooperation must be based on the principles of openness and transparency.

I believe Asia should set an example for the world by seeking regional cooperation that surpasses national and ethnic distinction.

So, as we pursue prosperity in a free, diverse and open Asia, what are the specific challenges that we face? I'd like to discuss three challenges. They are reform, cooperation and conveying Asia's voice to the world.

Part III

Interpret the following passage from Chinese into English. Start interpreting at the signal and stop it at the signal. You may take notes while you are listening. You will hear the passage only once. Now let's begin.

下面你将听到一段有关新加坡情况的介绍。

新加坡是一座美丽的花园城市，也是一个充满活力的国家。新加坡政治稳定，民族和睦，经济发展，并在国际和地区舞台上发挥着独特的作用。

凭借坚实的经济基础和健全的金融体制，新加坡有效地抵御了亚洲金融危机的冲击，使经济很快回到了持续发展的轨道。我们对此深表钦佩。

金融危机是挑战，同时也是机遇。我相信，在贵国政府的卓越领导下，通过全体人民的不懈努力，新加坡定能在未来的岁月里取得新的更大的发展。

参考译文及综合解析

Part I

【参考译文】

迈克：赶紧找点东西吃，我饿坏了。

Li：I'm also quite hungry. Hey. There is a McDonald's up ahead.

迈克：只要你向前走，总能碰上麦当劳；不管你向哪看，总能看见一家该死的麦当劳。它们简直太方便了。无处不在的"金色双拱形"真叫人厌烦。你知不知道仅美国就有8,000多家麦当劳餐馆，全世界的连锁店超过了11,000家。到2020年，每个人每天都要光顾麦当劳。

Li: I like the burgers anyway. Few places in the world are McDonald's-free. They have sold more than 100 billion burgers worldwide. In China alone, several hundred McDonald's restaurants have been set up in recent years, and many children prefer to have their birthdayparties there. Of course, not all their food is good, but at least they are consistent. One burger is completely like the other no matter when you go.

迈克：随你怎么说，我反正认为那里的食物不怎么样。还有，你知不知道美国96%的孩子都认识麦当劳的标志——麦克唐纳大叔？麦当劳是美国最大的给出的工资最低的雇主，却拥有比地球上任何公司都多的房地产。更有甚者，据说美国每7个百万富翁中就有1个是从麦当劳起家的。

Li：Give me a break, will you? I am starving.

迈克：可我已经没有胃口了。

【难句解析】

1. Everywhere you turn there is another blasted McDonald's.

此句是一个口语化的句子，结构简单。翻译时可采用顺译法，并对句子部分结构进行转化，使译文符合中文的表达习惯。句中blasted是口语中常用词，意思是"该死的"。参考译文：不管你向哪看，总能看见一家该死的麦当劳。

2. 现在全世界好像没有几个地方没有麦当劳，卖出的汉堡包都超过1000亿个了。

此句是由两个并列短语组成，翻译时可采用拆译法，把两个并列成分拆分成独立的句子，使理解更容易。

参考译文：Few places in the world are McDonald's-free. They have sold more than 100 billion burgers worldwide.

3. 当然，也不是每种产品都好吃，可起码都很标准，不管什么时候去吃，汉堡包都是一个样儿。

此句中文动词较多，如：好吃、去吃、是。翻译时可采用拆译法，把原句中大量的短语结构拆成两个单独的句子，使理解更容易，还可将原句中大量的动词转化为符合英文表达习惯的介词短语，并增译句子所需要的实词和主语。

参考译文：Of course, not all their food is good, but at least they are consistent. One burger is completely like the other no matter when you go.

4. They are the largest minimum-wage employers in America and own more real estate than any other company on earth.

此句是由 there be 句型和连词 and 连接的两个并列结构组成，但并列成分实际上构成对比转折关系。翻译时可采用顺译法，用连词表示转折关系，使译文清楚。参考译文：麦当劳是美国最大的给出的工资最低的雇主，却拥有比地球上任何公司都多的房地产。

Part II

【参考译文】

女士们、先生们：

为了新世纪亚洲的繁荣，我们应该追求一些什么样的价值观呢？我认为，自由、多样化和开放是促进亚洲和平与发展的三大价值观。

首先，毋庸置疑的是，自由在政治上是指民主和人权，在经济上是指发展市场经济。

政治自由和经济自由的发展是相辅相成的。在过去的半个世纪中尽管经历了种种曲折，亚洲作为一个整体在走向自由方面迈出了很大的步伐。

在经济发展为中产阶级和市民社会的形成创造条件时，向民主政治制度的过渡已势不可挡。我相信，亚洲显现的这一历史潮流是我们大家都引以为自豪的。

第二，亚洲发展具有多样化的背景，每一个国家都有自己独特的历史和社会文化价值，所以他们的发展进程和速度是不同的。

然而，在尊重多样化的同时，尽管各国之间存在差异，我们应认识到相互之间的积极影响，重要的是要促进我们的共同利益，向共同目标迈进。

也就是说，我们必须摒弃狭隘的民族主义和教条主义，在平等的基础上推动互利合作，从而达到共同繁荣。这应该成为我们的指导原则。

第三，我们的合作不应是内向型和封闭式的，而应是面向亚洲以外的世界。

当今，在全球化以及在欧洲和美洲的经济一体化进程中，我们必须推进亚洲国家之间的合作以及亚洲与其他地区的合作。这种合作必须在公开和透明的原则下进行。

我认为，亚洲应该在寻求跨国家和跨民族的区域合作方面为世界树立一个榜样。

当我们为一个自由、多样化和开放的亚洲的繁荣而努力的时候，我们要面对什么样的挑战呢？它们来自三个方面，那就是改革、合作和向世界传达亚洲的声音。

【难句解析】

1. I believe that the three values of freedom, diversity and openness are the driving forces behind peace and development in Asia.

此句包含一个宾语从句，宾语从句的主干是：(主语)three values + (谓语)are + (表语)driving force。宾语从句中还含有一个较长的介词短语。翻译时可采用转化法，把介词短语转化成名词短语，使译文符合中文表达方式。参考译文：我认为，自由、多样化和开放是促进亚洲和平与发展的三大价值观。

2. With some twists and turns, Asia as a whole has been taking significant steps towards freedom over the last half century.

此句的主干是：(主语)Asia + (谓语)take + (宾语)steps。句子主干前后是两个介词短语。翻译时可采用转化法和变序法，把介词短语转化成动词短语，并调整句子顺序，使译文更符合中文表达习惯。参考译文：在过去的半个世纪中尽管经历了种种曲折，但亚洲作为一个整体在走向自由方面已迈出了很大的步伐。

3. Transition to a democratic political system has been inevitable, as economic development has created the conditions for the emergence of a middle class and civil society.

此句是 as 引导的时间状语从句。主句的结构为：(主语)transition + (谓语) has been + (表语) inevitable。不定式 to a democratic political system 作后置定语，修饰、限定 transition。从句的结构为：(主语)development + (谓语)has created + (宾语) conditions。翻译时可采用变序法，调整句子顺序，使译文更符合中文表达习惯。参考译文：在经济发展为中产阶级和市民社会的形成创造条件时，向民主政治制度的过渡已势不可挡。

4. While respecting diversity, however, it is important for us to promote our common interests and our shared goals, recognizing positive influences of each other despite differences among countries.

此句的主干是：(主语)it + (谓语)is + (表语)important。句中的现在分词 recognizing 作伴随状语，伴随状语中还含有 despite 引导的表示让步的结构句子，还包括介词短语结构和转折连词 however。翻译时可用变序法和顺译法，改变伴随状语和让步结构的句序，把介词短语转化为动词结构，使译文更符合中文表达习惯。参考译文：然而，在尊重多样化的同时，尽管各国之间存在差异，我们应认识到相互之间的积极影响，重要的是要促进我们的共同利益，向共同目标迈进。

5. In other words, we must leave behind parochial nationalism and dogmatism, promote mutually beneficial cooperation based on equality in order to enjoy common prosperity.

此句的主干是(主语)we + (谓语)must leave…promote，并列动词结构，based on…是过去分词短语作后置定语，修饰 cooperation，in order to 介词短语作目的状语。翻译时可采用变序法和转化法，把后置定语提前，把介词短语转化成动词短语，使译文更符合中文表达习惯。参考译文：也就是说，我们必须摒弃狭隘的民族主义和教条主义，在平等的基础上推动互利合作，从而达到共同繁荣。

6. In a world economy where globalization is advancing and economic integration, such as in Europe and Americas, is proceeding, cooperation both within Asia and between Asia and other regions must be pursued.

此句的主干是(主语)cooperation + (谓语)must be pursued，被动语态结构，句子主干前"In a world economy where…"是地点状语，状语从句的主干是两个并列结构，globalization is advancing + economic integration is proceeding, such as 作插入语。翻译时采用转化法，将被动语态转化为主动语态，并将并列结构和插入语合并，使译文更符合中文表达习惯。参考译文：当今，在全球化以及欧洲和美洲的经济一体化的进程中，我们必须推进亚洲国家之间的合作以及亚洲与其他地区的合作。

Part III

【参考译文】

Singapore is a country full of vitality, as well as a beautiful city. It enjoys political stability, ethnic harmony and economic growth, and is playing a unique role internationally and in the regional arena.

Thanks to its sound economic base and financial system, Singapore has withstood the impact of the Asian financial crisis and rapidly brought its economy back onto the track of sustainable development. We highly admire your success.

Financial crises bring both challenges and opportunities. I believe that under the brilliant leadership of your government and with the unremitting efforts of all your people, Singapore will attain new and even greater achievements in the years to come.

【难句解析】

1. 新加坡是一座美丽的花园城市，也是一个充满活力的国家。

此句主干结构为："新加坡是 + 新加坡也是"两组并列结构。翻译时可采用并列连词将并列的结构连接起来，并根据句意的主次调整句序，使译文符合英文的表达习惯。参考译文：Singapore is a country full of vitality, as well as a beautiful city.

2. 新加坡政治稳定，民族和睦，经济发展，并在国际和地区舞台上发挥着独特的作用。

此句主干结构为：(主语)新加坡 + 四个并列结构。并列结构包含三个名词短语和一个动词短语，由连词"并"连接两部分组成。翻译时可用合并法，把三个名词短语合并，同时采用增译法，把中文中的名词短语转化成符合英文表达的动词结构，使译文更流畅。参考译文：It enjoys political stability, ethnic harmony and economic growth, and is playing a unique role internationally and in the regional arena.

3. 凭借坚实的经济基础和健全的金融体制，新加坡有效地抵御了亚洲金融危机的冲击，使经济很快回到了持续发展的轨道。

此句主干结构为：(主语)新加坡 +(谓语)抵御 +(宾语)冲击。句子主干前后分别是介词短语和目的状语。翻译时可用顺译法和转化法，把目的状语转化为动词短语，使译文符合英文表达习惯。参考译文：Thanks to its sound economic base and financial system, Singapore has withstood the impact of the Asian financial crisis and rapidly brought its economy back onto the track of sustainable development.

4. 金融危机是挑战，同时也是机遇。

此句主干结构为：并列结构"金融危机是……又是……"。翻译时可采用衔接法，用关联词把两个并列成分连接成句。参考译文：Financial crises bring both challenges and opportunities.

5. 我相信，在贵国政府的卓越领导下，通过全体人民的不懈努力，新加坡定能在未来的岁月里取得新的更大的发展。

此句主干结构为：(主语)我 +(谓语)相信 +(宾语从句)。宾语从句的主干为"新加坡 + 取得 + 发展"，同时包含两个介词短语结构"在……领导下"和"通过……"。翻译时可采用顺译法，并用连词衔接两个并列介词短语。参考译文：I believe that under the brilliant leadership of your government and with the unremitting efforts of all your people, Singapore will attain new and even greater achievements in the years to come.

第四部分 时文语林
——实用口译必备词汇

Practical Phrases of C-E Translation in Current Politics, Economy, Law, Education and Culture

一、学位名称/Academic Degrees

博士　doctor; doctorate; Dr
博士后　post-doctorate
地质工程学博士　doctor of science in geological engineering; D.S.Geol.E
地质工程学硕士　master of science in geological engineering; M.S.Geol.E
地质工程学学士　bachelor of science in geological engineering; B.S.Geol.E
电机工程学博士　doctor of science in electrical engineering; DSEE
电机工程学硕士　master of science in electrical engineering; MSEE
法学博士　doctor of law; LD
法学硕士　master of law; LM
工程学博士　doctor of science in engineering; DSE
工程学硕士　master of science in engineering; MSE
工商管理学博士　doctor of business administration; DBA
工商管理学硕士　master of business administration; MBA
化学工程学博士　doctor of chemical engineering; D.CH.E.
化学工程学硕士　master of chemical engineering; M.CH.E.
机械工程学博士　doctor of science in mechanical engineering; DSME
机械工程学硕士　master of science in mechanical engineering; MSME
计算机学博士　doctor of computer science; DCS
计算机学硕士　master of computer science; MCS
教育学博士　doctor of science in education; D.S.Ed.
教育学硕士　master of science in education; M.S.Ed.
理博士　doctor of science; DS
理硕士　master of science; MS

文学博士　doctor of literature or letters; Lit D
文学硕士　master of literature or letters; Lit M
新闻学博士　doctor of science in journalism; DSJ
新闻学硕士　master of science in journalism; MSJ
双学士　dual bachelors
哲学博士　doctor of philosophy; Ph.D.
哲学硕士　master of philosophy; Ph.M.

二、教育、教学机构名称/Educational Institutions

补习学校　continuation school
财经大学　university of finance and economics
残疾学校　cripple school
成人学院　adult school
传播学院　college of communication
大学预备学校　college preparatory school
党校　Communist Party school
地质学院　geological institute
电力学院　institute of electric power
电视大学　TV university
电影学院　cinema college; cinema institute
对外贸易大学　university of foreign trade
法学院　college of law; law school
纺织工学院　institute of textile engineering
分院　branch institute; branch college
佛学院　institute of Buddhist studies
附属学校　attached school
高等师范专科学院　junior teachers' college
大学专科教育　2-to-3-year higher education non-degree
大学文凭　a college diploma
岗位培训　job-specific training

教育要面向现代化，面向世界，面向未来　gear education to the needs of modernization, the world and the future

教育必须为社会主义现代化服务，必须同生产劳动相结合，培养德、智、体全面发展的建设者和接班人　Education must serve the needs of socialist modernization, be integrated with productive labor, and train builders and successors who are well developed morally, intellectually and physically

教书育人   to impart knowledge and educate/cultivate one's students
教员休息室   staff room; common room; teachers' lounge
教学大纲   POI; teaching program; syllabus
学分制   credit system
在职培训   on-the-job/in-service training
工业学校   engineering school
工业大学   poly-technological university
公立学校   public school; provided school
国际关系学院   institute of international relations
国际商学院   institute of international commerce
国际政治学院   institute of international politics
海军军官学校   naval school
海军学院   naval academy
海运学院   mercantile marine institute
函授学校   correspondence school
航天大学   aerospace university
护士学校   nurses' training school; school of nursing
化工学院   college/institute of chemical engineering
寄宿学校   boarding school
继续教育学院   college of further education
技工学校   technical school
教务处   office of the dean of studies
教育学院   educational college
进修学院   college of continuing education
科研处   office of scientific research
老年大学   college of continuing education for senior citizens
理工大学   university of science and technology
理学院   college of science
联合大学   collegiate university
林学院   forestry institute
陆军军官学校   military academy
盲哑学校   blind & dumb school
美术学院   college of fine arts
农业大学   agricultural university
女子学校   girls' school
气象学校   meteorological school
师范大学   normal university

师范学院　teachers' college
师范专科学校　junior teachers' college
石油学院　petroleum institute
水利电力学院　institute of water conservancy and electric power
私立学校　private school
民办大学　non-governmental university
铁道学院　railway institute
团校　Communist Youth League school
外国语大学　university of foreign languages; foreign studies university; international studies university
外国语学院　institute of foreign languages; foreign language school
外交学院　institute of diplomacy
文理学院　college of arts & science
戏剧学院　drama institute
研究生院　graduate school
药学院　college of pharmacy
医科大学　medical university
艺术学校　art school
音乐学院　conservatory of music
邮电学院　institute of post and telecommunications
幼儿师范专科学校　children normal training school
政法学院　institute of political science and law
职业学校　vocational school
中等技术学校　secondary technical school
重点学校　key school

三、职业名称/Various Positions

(一)社会职业/Social Occupation

办公室职员　office staff
办公室主任　office administrator
正教授　(full) professor
副教授　associate professor
讲师　lecturer; instructor
助教　assistant (teacher)
博士生导师　doctoral advisor
大学校长　president; chancellor

党(团)总支书记　general Party (League) branch secretary
导师　tutor; advisor; supervisor
高级讲师　senior lecturer
后勤处长　director of logistics department
教务长　dean
系主任　dean; chair of department
教研组长(主任)　head of teaching & research group
客座教授　visiting professor
名誉教授　emeritus professor
荣誉教授　honorary professor
实验员　laboratory technician
特级教师　special-grade teacher
图书馆管理员　librarian
退学生　dropout
在职研究生　in-service graduate student
自费生　self-paying, self-paid, self-supporting, self-financed, self-funded student
总务处长　director in charge of general affairs
研究员　research fellow
副研究员　associate research fellow
高级工程师　senior engineer
高级会计师　senior accountant
高级经济师　senior economist
高级农艺师　senior agronomist
化验员　chemical analyst
技师，技术员　technician
检验员　inspector
建筑师　architect
院士　academician
助理工程师　assistant engineer
(主)教练　(chief) coach
编辑　editor
主编　editor in chief
高级编辑；编审　senior editor
翻译　translator; interpreter
节目主持人　anchor
铅球运动员　shot putter
体操运动员　gymnast

跳高运动员　high jumper
跳水运动员　diver
跳远运动员　long jumper
掷标枪运动员　javelin thrower
掷铁饼运动员　discus thrower
举重运动员　weight lifter
跨栏运动员　hurdler
长跑运动员　long-distance racer (runner)
短跑运动员　sprinter
射击运动员　marksman; shooter
X 光医生　X-ray technician
产科医生　obstetrician
儿科医生　pediatrician
耳鼻喉科医生　ENT(ear-nose-throat) doctor
放射科医生　radiologist
妇科医生　gynecologist
主任医师　chief physician
副主任医师　associate chief physician
内科医生　physician; internist
外科医生　surgeon
牙科医生　dentist
眼科医生　oculist; eye doctor
中医医生　doctor of traditional Chinese medicine
大堂经理　lobby manager
电工　electrician
董事长　chairman of the board
法律顾问　legal consultant
房地产评估师　real estate appraiser
公关部经理　public relations manager
海关人员　customs officer
人力资源部经理　human resources manager
审计员　auditor
网络互联工程师　networking integrated engineer
系统程序员　system programmer
销售主管　sales administrator

(二)中国人民解放军军衔/Military Ranks of PLA

1. 陆军/Army

一级上将　senior general

上将　general

中将　lieutenant general

少将　major general

大校　senior colonel

上校　colonel

中校　lieutenant colonel

少校　major

上尉　captain

中尉　first lieutenant

少尉　second lieutenant

军士长　master sergeant

专业军士　technical sergeant

上士　sergeant first class

中士　sergeant

下士　corporal

列兵　troopie

新兵　recruit

2. 空军/Air Force

一级上将　general first grade

上将　air general

中将　air lieutenant general

少将　air major general

大校　air senior colonel

上校　air colonel

中校　air lieutenant colonel

少校　air major

上尉　air captain

中尉　air first lieutenant

少尉　air second lieutenant

军士长　air master sergeant

专业军士　air technical sergeant

上士　air sergeant first class

中士　air sergeant
下士　air corporal
上等兵　airman
列兵　airman recruit

3. 海军/Navy

一级上将　general first grade
上将　admiral
中将　vice admiral
少将　rear admiral
大校　senior captain
上校　captain
中校　commander
少校　lieutenant commander
上尉　lieutenant
中尉　lieutenant junior class
少尉　ensign
军士长　chief petty officer
专业军士　technical petty officer
上士　petty officer first class
中士　petty officer second class
下士　petty officer third class
上等兵　seaman
列兵　seaman recruit

四、常见企业和商店名称/Names of Common Enterprises and Stores

(一)企业名称

鞭炮厂　firecrackers factory
玻璃厂　glass factory
茶厂　tea processing factory
灯泡厂　electric bulb factory
电厂　power plant
电池厂　battery plant
电线厂　electric wire factory
阀门厂　valve plant

豆制品厂　bean products factory
纺织厂　textile mill
钢铁厂　iron and steel plant
高压开关厂　high voltage switch gear factory
锅炉厂　boiler factory
化肥厂　chemical fertilizer plant
酒精厂　alcohol plant
冷冻厂　cold storage plant
制糖厂　sugar refinery
炼铁厂　iron smelting factory
炼油厂　oil refinery
毛纺厂　woolen mill
木材厂　timber mill
酿酒厂　winery; brewery
农药厂　insecticide factory
汽车修理厂　car repair plant
肉类加工厂　meat packing plant
食品厂　bakery and confectionery
水泥厂　cement plant
塑料厂　plastics plant
拖拉机厂　tractor plant
橡胶厂　rubber plant
冶炼厂　metallurgical factory
印刷厂　printing house
造船厂　shipyard
造纸厂　paper mill
制药厂　pharmaceutical factory
自来水厂　water work

(二)商店名称

百货公司　department store
百货商场　general merchandise market
保险公司　insurance company
茶馆　tea house
当铺　pawn broker
电器商店　electrical appliance shop
儿童(妇女)用品商店　children's (women's) goods shop

废品收购站　salvage station
服装店　clothing store
古玩珠宝店　antiques and jewelry shop
股票交易所　stock exchange
寄卖商店　commission shop
家具店　furniture shop
进出口公司　import and export corporation
酒店　wine shop
烤肉店　roast meat shop
腊味店　cured meat shop
冷饮店　cold drinks shop
理发店　bather's shop; barbershop; hairdresser's
美容(按摩)厅　beauty (massage) parlor
日用杂货店　daily-use sundry goods shop
水产店　aquatic products shop
文具店　stationer's shop
五金商店　metal products shop
眼镜店　eyeglasses store
药店　drug store
照相馆　photographic studio; photographer's

五、二十四节气/Twenty-four Solar Terms of China

立春　the Beginning of Spring
雨水　Rain Water
惊蛰　the Walking of Insects
春分　the Spring Equinox
清明　Pure Brightness
谷雨　Grain Rain
立夏　the Beginning of Summer
小满　Grain Full
芒种　Grain in Ear
夏至　the Summer Solstice
小暑　Slight Heat
大暑　Great Heat
立秋　the Beginning of Autumn
处暑　the Limit of Heat

白露　White Dew
秋分　the Autumnal Equinox
寒露　Cold Dew
霜降　Frost's Descent
立冬　the Beginning of Winter
小雪　Slight Snow
大雪　Great Snow
冬至　the Winter Solstice
小寒　Slight Cold
大寒　Great Cold

六、经济用语/Economic Terms

经济新常态　new economic normal
亚洲基础设施投资银行（亚投行）Asian Infrastructure Investment Bank（AIIB）
第一/第二/第三产业　the primary/secondary/tertiary industry (service sector)
国内生产总值/国民生产总值　GDP (Gross Domestic Product)/GNP (Gross National Product)
中国加入世界贸易组织后　after China entered/joined the WTO (World Trade Organization); after China's entry into/accession to the WTO
密集型产业　intensive (knowledge-intensive) industries
经济体制改革　economic restructuring
向市场经济转轨　switch to a market economy
使经济进一步市场化　make the economy more market-oriented
经济发展全球化的趋势　the globalization trend in economic development
促使全球经济一体化　foster integration with the global economy
从粗放型经济转变为集约型经济　shift from extensive economy to intensive economy
优化结构　optimize the structure
恶性循环　vicious cycle
良性循环　beneficent (virtuous) cycle
对国有大中型企业进行公司制改革　to corporatize large and medium-sized state-owned enterprises
股份制　the joint stock system
股份合作制　the joint stock cooperative system
谁控股？　Who holds the controlling shares?
支持强强联合，实现优势互补　support association between strong enterprises so that they can take advantage of each other's strengths

鼓励兼并，规范破产　encourage mergers and standardize bankruptcy procedures
独立核算工业企业　an independent accounting unit (enterprise)
企业孵化器　an enterprise incubator
振兴支柱产业　invigorate pillar industries
外向型经济　an export-oriented economy
计划单列市　city specifically designated in the state plan
涉外经济　foreign-oriented (foreign-related) business
刺激内需　stimulate domestic demand
保持良好的增长势头　maintain the healthy (good) momentum of growth
可持续发展战略　the strategy of sustainable development
防止经济过热　prevent an overheated economy
经济萎缩　an economic depression
遏制通货膨胀　curb (check) the inflation
防止国有资产流失　prevent the loss (devaluation) of State assets
规模经济　economy of scale; scaled economy
减轻就业压力　ease the pressure of unemployment
防止泡沫经济　avoid a bubble economy/false property economy
瓶颈制约　"bottleneck" restriction
政企分开　separate administrative functions from enterprise management
总裁　president
首席执行官　CEO (chief executive officer)
技术更新/改造　technological updating/renovation
发展乡镇企业　expand (village and) township industries; develop rural industry (enterprises)
亏损企业　money-losing (debt-ridden, loss-making, unprofitable) enterprises; enterprises that operate at a loss
扭亏为盈　turn losses into profits
私人企业　private enterprises
外资企业　foreign-invested (foreign-funded, foreign-financed, foreign-owned) enterprises
外商独资企业　wholly (solely) foreign-owned enterprises
中外合作企业　Sino-foreign cooperative businesses
中外合资企业100强　the top 100 Sino-foreign (Chinese-foreign) joint ventures
跨国公司　a transnational corporation; a multinational corporation
有限责任公司　limited liability companies
物价指数　the price index
人均年收入　the annual per-capita income
名牌产品　famous-brand products; brand-name products

拳头产品   competitive products
畅销货   marketable products; products with a good market
紧缺商品   commodities in short supply
紧俏货物   goods in great demand
滞销货；积压商品   unmarketable (unsalable, poor-selling) products; overstocked commodities
有高附加值的高新技术产品   high and new technology products with high added value
长线产品   product in excessive supply
尖端产品   highly sophisticated products
开工不足   (enterprises) running under their production capacity
弹性工资   flexible pay
弹性工作时间制   flextime; flexible time
浮动工资   floating wages; fluctuating wages
售后服务   after-sale service
基础设施工程第一期   the first phase (stage) of the infrastructure project
经济强国(省)   an economically-strong country (province)
经济欠发达(不发达地区)   economically underdeveloped regions
经济失调   economic disproportion; economic ailments; dislocation of the economy
关、停、并、转   be closed down, have their operations suspended, or else be merged with other enterprises or switched to the manufacture of other products

七、金融、贸易用语/Terms in Finance and Trade

货币贬值   devaluation of currency
日元的升值   appreciation of the Japanese yen
外汇储备   foreign exchange reserve
美元与英镑之间的兑换率   the exchange rate between the dollar and the pound
市场疲软   business is bad (slack)
在中国银行开一个活期账户   open a current account with the Bank of China
本金与利息   principal and interest
发行股票、债券   issue shares and bonds
融资   financing; fund-raising
融资渠道   financing channels
增加财政收入   increase State tax revenue (fiscal revenue)
缺少流动资金   a shortage of circulating funds (floating capital)
人民币对美元汇率稳定   the stability of the RMB exchange rate against the USD
与美元联系汇率制   the system of pegging the currency to the U. S. dollar

呆账与坏账　stagnant debts and bad debts; non-performing funds
欧元/欧元区　the Euro / Euroland
依法收税　levy taxes according to law
增值税　the value-added tax (VAT)
出口退税　refunding export taxes; refunding taxes to exporters
保护性关税　protective tariffs
反倾销　anti-dumping
上海证券交易所　the Shanghai Securities Exchange
股市指数　the stock market (exchange) index
期货市场/交易　the futures market/transaction
有价证券投资　portfolio investment
牛市/熊市　a bull/bear market
股票指数突破1300点大关　The stock index broke the 1300-point mark.
当日指数以1120点收盘　The index closed (finished, ended) at 1120 on that day.
该公司的股票已上市　the stocks of the company have been listed (have gone public, have been launched).
拥有至少50%的股份　hold a minimum of 50 percent of the equity
一蹶不振的B股股市　a sluggish B-share market
道琼斯工业平均指数飙升至9850点　The Dow Jones industrial average soared to 9850 points.
纳斯达克指数　The NASDAQ index (National Association of Securities Deal Automated Quotations)
(香港)恒生指数宽幅振荡　The Hang Seng Index fluctuated violently.
日经指数跌至今年最低点　The Nikkei Index fell to a record low for the year.
农村/城市信用合作社　rural (urban) credit cooperative
红筹股　red chip
蓝筹股，绩优股　blue chip
股民，股东　shareholder; stockholder
配股　allotment shares
国库券　State treasury bonds; treasury bills
市场准入　market access
买方/卖方市场　the buyer's/seller's market
报价　quote a price; give a quotation
招商　invite (attract) investment
基础设施和基础工业投资　investment in infrastructure and basic industries
招标/投标/中标　invite tenders (bids)/submit a tender/win (get) the tender
贸易顺差/贸易逆差　trade surplus/trade deficit

双赢 a win-win/two-win/double-win situation
关税壁垒 customs barrier; tariff wall
政府采购 government procurement
三角债 chain debt
保税区 tariff-free zone; bonded area; free trade zone
独家经销代理 exclusive selling agency
5%的回扣 a 5 percent kickback (sales commission)
非法传销 illegal pyramid selling (multi-level marketing)
中介人 an intermediary (organ)
电子商务认证 e-business certificate
分期付款 installment payment
商品条码 bar code
专卖店 exclusive agency; franchised store
租赁、承包、拍卖 leasing, contract or sale by auction

八、政治用语/Political Terms

中国梦 the Chinese Dream
具有中国特色的社会主义 socialism with Chinese characteristics
三个代表 the "Three Represents" theory (The Chinese Communist Party represents the trend of development of advanced productive forces, the orientation of advanced culture, and the fundamental interests of the overwhelming majority of the people in China)
丝绸之路经济带和 21 世纪海上丝绸之路（一带一路） Silk Road Economic Belt and 21st-century Maritimes Silk Road (One Belt And One Road(OBAOR); One Belt One Road (OBOR) ; Belt And Road (BAR))
三农问题 the issue of " agriculture, countryside and farmers"; the issue of three Fs (farming, farm and farmers)
振兴中华 the rejuvenation (revitalization) of the Chinese nation
小康生活 a relatively well-off life; a relatively comfortable life; initial prosperity
人均国民生产总值 the average per-capita GNP
中等发达国家水平 standard of moderately developed countries
物质文明和精神文明 material progress and cultural and ethical (cultural and ideological) progress
舆论监督 supervision by public opinion
反对铺张浪费 oppose (combat) extravagance and waste
南水北调 South-to-North water diversion
西部大开发 the development of western regions in China; the West Development

乱收费、乱集资、乱摊派　arbitrary collection of charges, abuse of fund-raising and unchecked apportionment (arbitrary quotas) are still rampant

纠正行业不正之风　rectify malpractice in various trades

人才流失　brain drain

脱贫致富　cast (shake, throw) off poverty and set out on a road to prosperity

科教兴国战略　the strategy of revitalizing (invigorating) China through science and education

打白条　to issue IOUs; illegitimate promissory notes

按揭贷款　mortgage loan

物业管理　estate management; property management

民族问题　the ethnic minority issue

计划生育　family planning; birth control

跳槽　job-hopping

下海　risk one's fortune in business; plunge into the commercial sea

网民　netizen; net citizen; cyber citizen

虚拟网　the virtual net

宽带接入　broadband (wideband) access

宽带网　broadband networks

网络公司　a Dot com; a dot com

发动黑客袭击　launch hacking attacks

腐败分子　a corruptionist

受贿　to take bribes; bribery; bribe-taking

行贿　to commit bribery

加强廉政建设　to exert ourselves in making the government clean; to strive after a clean (incorrupt) government

廉洁清正　to keep the hands clean

廉政　to be honest and free from corruption in carrying out official affairs; to be an official of incorruptible integrity; incorruption

贪官　grafter (corrupt) official

贪赃枉法　to take bribes and bend the law; to pervert justice for a bribe

政治思想工作　political and ideological work

纠正行业不正之风　to correct shameful practices in government departments, trades and professions

坚持任人唯贤，反对任人唯亲，防止和纠正用人上的不正之风　persist in appointing people on their merits and oppose favoritism, and prevent or rectify unsound practices

九、法律用语/Legal Terms

把某人缉拿归案　to bring sb. to justice
报警/报案　to go to (call) the police
被拘留　to be detained; to become a detainee
被判犯有谋杀罪　to be convicted of murder
被判处6年劳役/劳改　to be sentenced to six years at hard labor
被判罚款10万元　to be sentenced to pay a fine of 100,000 yuan
被判处三年徒刑　to be sentenced to three years' imprisonment
被判处缓期三年　to be sentenced to three years' probation
被判无期徒刑　to receive a life sentence
被判死刑　to be sentenced to death
不服判决而上诉　to lodge an appeal from a decision
裁决一个案件　to adjudicate a case
承担刑事责任　to take the rap
出庭　to appear in court
出庭作证　to take the stand
初审法院　a court of first instance
上诉法院　a court of appeal
最高上诉法院　a court of last resort
触犯法律　to go beyond the law
(对某人)处以重罚　to impose a heavy (high, severe) penalty on somebody
法办　to deal with sb. according to law; to bring sb. to justice
法盲　to be law-ignorant/legally illiterate
法制建设　legal system construction
依法治国　rule of law
法网恢恢，疏而不漏　Justice has long arms.
法律规避　evasion of law
法律咨询　legal consultancy service; legal advice
法律面前，人人平等　All people are equal before the law./ Everybody is equal before the law.
法律援助　law aid
法定程序　legal proceedings
法人　juridical (legal) person; corporation
法人代表　legal representative
法人地位　status of a legal person

法人资格　legal personality; corporate capacity; qualification of a legal person
非法监禁　duress of imprisonment
服刑　to do time; to serve a prison sentence
假释出狱　to be released on parole
民事法庭　civil court
刑事法庭　criminal court
军事法庭　military tribunal; court martial
仲裁法庭　arbitration tribunal; court of arbitration
判决书　court verdict; written judgment
陪审团　jury; panel
审问犯人　to interrogate (pump) a prisoner
私了　to settle a case out of court
公了　to settle a case in court
违法乱纪　to commit violation of law and discipline; to offend the law and the discipline
违法必究　offenders against the law must be brought to justice
捉错了人　to get the wrong pig by the tail
自首　to surrender oneself to the law
原告　the prosecution
被告　the defense；the accused
证人　witness
被告辩护律师　counsel for the defense
原告辩护律师　counsel for the prosecution
黑社会性质的犯罪团伙和流氓恶势力　underground gangsters and hoodlums
黄赌毒　pornography, gambling and drug abuse
黄色出版物　pornographic publications

十、常用汉语成语/Common Chinese Idioms

按图索骥　looking for a steed with the aid of its picture
百发百中　a hundred shots, a hundred bull's-eyes
班门弄斧　showing off one's proficiency with the axe before *Lu Ban* the master carpenter
杯弓蛇影　mistaking the reflection of a bow for a snake/be jittery with imaginary fears
病入膏肓　the disease has attacked the vitals
草木皆兵　every bush and tree looks like an enemy
吹毛求疵　blow apart the hairs upon a fur to discover any defect
打草惊蛇　beating the grass and flushing out the snake
调虎离山　luring the tiger out of the mountains

东施效颦	aping the beauty's frown
负荆请罪	bringing the birch and asking for flogging
功亏一篑	running an enterprise for the lack of one basketful
固步自封	content with staying where one is
含沙射影	spitting sand on a shadow-attacking by insinuation
狐假虎威	basking in reflected glory
囫囵吞枣	gulping down a whole date
画饼充饥	allaying hunger with pictures of cakes
画龙点睛	putting the finishing touch to the picture of a dragon
惊弓之鸟	birds startled by the mere twang of a bowstring
精卫填海	jingwei fills up the sea
井底之蛙	a frog in a well
刻舟求剑	notching the boat to find the sword
空中楼阁	a castle in the air
滥竽充数	passing oneself off as a member of the orchestra
狼狈为奸	a wolf working hand in glove with a jackal
老马识途	an old horse knows the way
梁上君子	a gentleman on the beam, a burglar, a thief
临渴掘井	not digging a well until one is thirsty
满城风雨	a storm enveloping the city
盲人摸象	blind men touching an elephant
门庭若市	a courtyard as crowded as a marketplace
名落孙山	failing to pass an examination
南辕北辙	going south by driving the chariot north
怒发冲冠	so angry that one's hair lifts up one's hat
披荆斩棘	breaking open a way through brambles and thorns
蚍蜉撼树	an ant trying to shake a big tree
破釜沉舟	smashing the cauldrons and sinking the boats
破镜重圆	a broken mirror made whole again
杞人忧天	the man of *qi* who worried that the sky would fall
黔驴技穷	the guizhou donkey has exhausted its tricks
日暮途穷	the day is waning and the road is ending
如火如荼	like a raging fire
如鱼得水	to feel just like a fish in water
入木三分	to enter three-tenths of an inch into the timber
塞翁失马	the old man of frontier lost his horse
三顾茅庐	paying three visits to the cottage

三人成虎	repeat a lie enough times, and it will be believed
丧家之犬	a homeless dog
杀鸡儆猴	killing the chicken to frighten the monkeys
甚嚣尘上	making a great clamor
势如破竹	like splitting bamboo
世外桃源	a heaven of peace and happiness
手不释卷	always with a book in hand
守株待兔	sitting by a stump, waiting for a careless hare
蜀犬吠日	a sichuan dog barks at the sun
束之高阁	putting it on a high shelf
水落石出	when the water ebbs, stones will appear
四面楚歌	songs of chu on all sides
谈虎色变	turn pale at the mention of a tiger
昙花一现	a flower that vanishes as soon as it appears
螳臂当车	a mantis trying to halt a chariot
天花乱坠	as if it were raining flowers
天涯海角	the end of sky and the corner of the sea
同舟共济	crossing a river in the same boat
天衣无缝	divine garments without seams
图穷匕见	when the map is unrolled the dagger is revealed
完璧归赵	returning the jade intact to zhao
亡羊补牢	mending the fold after the sheep have been stolen
望梅止渴	looking at plums to quench the thirst
望洋兴叹	gazing at the ocean and sighing
为虎作伥	helping the tiger to pounce upon its victims
卧薪尝胆	sleeping on brushwood and tasting gall
笑里藏刀	hiding a dagger behind a smile
胸有成竹	having a ready-formed plan
削足适履	cutting one's feet to fit one's shoes
揠苗助长	pulling up seedlings to help them grow
掩耳盗铃	plugging one's ears while stealing a bell
偃旗息鼓	to lower the banners and silence the drums
一鼓作气	rousing the spirits with the first drum roll
一箭双雕	killing two birds with one stone
一鸣惊人	amazing the world with a single feat
一丘之貉	jackals of the same lair
愚公移山	the foolish old man who removed the mountains

鱼目混珠　passing off fish eyes as pearls
余音绕梁　the tune lingers in the house
与虎谋皮　borrowing the skin from a tiger
鹬蚌相争　a snipe and a clam locked in combat
朝三暮四　change one's mind frequently
趾高气扬　stepping high and haughtily
指鹿为马　calling a stag a horse
纸上谈兵　discussing stratagems on paper
自相矛盾　contradicting oneself

十一、常用汉语谚语/Common Chinese Proverbs

　　八字衙门朝南开，有理无钱莫进来　The yamen gate is wide open, yet with only right on your side but no money, don't go inside.
　　兵马未动，粮草先行　Provisions should be arranged before an army is mobilized.
　　不经一事，不长一智　Wisdom comes from experience.
　　不入虎穴，焉得虎子　How can you catch tiger cubs without entering the tiger's lair?
　　差之毫厘，谬以千里　A little error may lead to a large discrepancy.
　　长江后浪催前浪，世上新人赶旧人　Just as the waves of the Yangtze River behind drive on those ahead, so does each new generation replace the old one.
　　常将有日思无日，莫待无时想有时　When rich, think of poverty, but don't think of riches when you are poor.
　　吃一堑，长一智　A fall into the pit, a gain in your wit.
　　打蛇不死，后患无穷　Unless you beat a snake to death, it will cause endless trouble in future.
　　大处着眼，小处着手　Keep the general goal in sight while tackling daily tasks.
　　单丝不成线，独木不成林　A single thread can't make a cord, nor a single tree a forest.
　　当局者迷，旁观者清　The spectators see more of the game than the players.
　　刀不磨要生锈，水不流要发臭　A knife will rust if not sharpened regularly, and water will stagnate if it is not allowed to flow.
　　道高一尺，魔高一丈　The law is strong, but the outlaws are ten times stronger.
　　灯不拨不亮，理不辩不明　An oil lamp becomes brighter after trimming, a truth becomes clearer after being discussed.
　　读书需用意，一字值千金　When reading, don't let a single word escape your attention; One word may be worth a thousand pieces of gold.
　　读万卷书，行万里路　Read ten thousand books and walk ten thousand miles.
　　儿不嫌母丑，狗不嫌家贫　A son never thinks his mother ugly, and a dog never shuns its

owner's home however shabby it is.

儿孙自有儿孙福，莫为儿孙做牛马 The children can take care of themselves when they grow up, so the parents don't have to work too hard for the future of their offspring.

凡人不可貌相，海水不可斗量 As a man cannot be known by his looks, neither can the sea be fathomed by a gourd.

放下屠刀，立地成佛 The butcher who lays down his knife, at once becomes a Buddha.

风无常顺，兵无常胜 A boat can't always sail with the wind; an army can't always win battles.

瓜无滚圆，人无十全 No melon is completely round, and no person is perfect.

花有重开日，人无再少年 Flowers may bloom again, but a person never has the chance to be young again.

画虎画皮难画骨，知人知面不知心 In drawing a tiger, you show its skin, but not its bones; in knowing a man, you may know his face, but not his heart.

火要空心，人要虚心 A fire must have space at its center to burn vigorously; a man must be modest to make progress.

见怪不怪，其怪自败 Face odd things fearlessly and their fearsomeness will disappear.

江山易改，本性难移 Rivers and mountains may be changed, but it is hard to alter even a single person's nature.

近水楼台先得月，向阳花木早逢春 A waterfront pavilion gets the moonlight first; spring comes early to plants exposed to the sun.

近水知鱼性，近山识鸟音 Near to rivers, we recognize fish; near to mountains, we recognize the songs of birds.

近朱者赤，近墨者黑 Near vermilion, one gets stained pink; near ink, one gets stained black.

酒逢知己千杯少，话不投机半句多 If you drink with a bosom friend, a thousand cups are not enough; if you argue with someone, half a sentence is too much.

老当益壮，穷当益坚 Old but vigorous, poor but ambitious.

良药苦口利于病，忠言逆耳利于行 It takes bitter medicine to cure a disease properly, and it takes blunt advice to put us on the right track.

两虎相斗，必有一伤 When two tigers fight, one is sure to lose.

路遥知马力，日久见人心 As distance tests a horse's strength, so does time reveal a person's real character.

麻雀虽小，五脏俱全 Small as it is, the sparrow has all the vital organs.

马好不在鞍，人好不在衫 Don't judge a horse by its saddle, and don't judge a person by his clothes.

明人不用细说，响鼓不用重锤 A person of good sense needs no detailed explanation; a resonant drum needs no heavy beating.

明知山有虎，偏向虎山行 Going deep into the mountains, undeterred by the tigers there.

宁为玉碎，不为瓦全 Better to be a shard of jade than a whole tile.

贫居闹市无人问，富在深山有远亲 If you are poor, even if you live in a crowded city you will be alone. But if you are rich, even if you live in uninhabited mountains the most distant relatives will flock to you.

平生不做亏心事，半夜敲门心不惊 A clear conscience sleeps even through thunder.

平时不烧香，临时抱佛脚 Never burning incense when all is well, but clasping Buddha's feet in an emergency.

千军易得，一将难求 It is easy to find a thousand soldiers, but hard to find a good general.

钱财如粪土，仁义值千金 Riches are as worthless as dust; benevolence and justice are the most valuable things.

前人栽树，后人乘凉 One generation plants the trees under whose shade another generation rests.

强中更有强中手，能人背后有能人 However strong you are, there's always someone stronger.

人过留名，雁过留声 A man leaves his name behind wherever he stays, just as a goose utters its cry wherever it flies.

人老心不老，人穷志不穷 Old but young at heart; poor but with lofty ideals.

人善被人欺，马善被人骑 A weak person is liable to be bullied; a tamed horse is often ridden.

人往高处走，水往低处流 Man seeks the heights, while water seeks the lowlands.

人无千日好，花无百日红 Man cannot be always fortunate, nor can flowers last forever.

人无完人，金无足赤 It is as impossible to find a perfect man as it is to find 100 percent pure gold.

人无远虑，必有近忧 Those who do not plan for the future will find trouble on their doorstep.

人心齐，泰山移 When people are of one mind and heart, they can move Mount Tai.

人有失足，马有失蹄 A man is prone to stumble when walking, and a horse is prone to stumble when galloping.

任凭风浪起，稳坐钓鱼船 Sit tight in the fishing boat despite the rising wind and waves.

若要人不知，除非己莫为 If you don't want people to find out, you'd better not do it.

三个臭皮匠，顶个诸葛亮 Three cobblers with their wits combined equal *Zhuge Liang*, the master mind.

三人一条心，黄土变成金 If people are of one heart, even the yellow earth can become gold.

少壮不努力，老大徒伤悲 A man who does not exert himself in his youth will be sorry he didn't when he grows old.

十年窗下无人问，一举成名天下知 One can study for ten years in obscurity, but as soon as one passes the examination the whole world pays attention.

十年树木，百年树人 It takes ten years to grow a tree, but a hundred years to bring up a generation of good men.

书到用时方恨少 It is when you are using what you have learned from books that you wish you had read more.

天外有天，人外有人 As capable as you are, there is always someone more capable — just as there is another heaven beyond heaven.

天下无难事，只怕有心人 Nothing in the world is difficult for one who sets his mind to it.

天下兴亡，匹夫有责 Everyone is responsible for his country.

天有不测风云，人有旦夕祸福 In nature there are unexpected storms, and in life unpredictable vicissitudes.

万事俱备，只欠东风 Everything is ready except the east wind.

小洞不补，大洞吃苦 A small hole not mended in time will become a big hole much more difficult to mend.

小时偷针，大时偷金 A child who steals a needle will grow up to steal gold.

心正不怕影斜，脚正不怕鞋歪 An upright man is not afraid of an oblique shadow; a straight foot is not afraid of a crooked shoe.

秀才不出门，能知天下事 Without even stepping outside his gate the scholar knows all the wide world's affairs.

养兵千日，用兵一时 Armies are to be maintained in the course of long years, but to be used in the nick of time.

一寸光阴一寸金，寸金难买寸光阴 A speck of time is more precious than an ounce of gold.

一个篱笆三个桩，一个好汉三个帮 Just as a fence needs the support of three stakes, an able fellow needs the help of three other people.

一年之计在于春，一日之计在于晨 The whole year's work depends on good planning in spring, and the whole day's work depends on good planning in the early morning.

一人得道，鸡犬升天 When a man is at court, all his followers are in favor.

一失足成千古恨，再回头是百年身 One single slip brings eternal regret, and looking back, you find that your whole life has passed away.

一言既出，驷马难追 A word, once it is uttered, cannot be overtaken even by swift horses.

一朝被蛇咬，十年怕井绳 A man once bitten by a snake will for ten years shy at a rope.

一着不慎，满盘皆输 One careless move forfeits the whole game.

有借有还，再借不难 Timely return of a loan makes it easier to borrow a second time.

有理走遍天下，无理寸步难行 With justice on your side, you can go anywhere; without it, you can't take a step.

有缘千里来相会，无缘对面不相逢 Fate brings people together no matter how far apart they may be.

与君一席话，胜读十年书 Chatting with you for one night is more profitable than studying for ten years.

远水不救近火，远亲不如近邻 Distant water can't put out a nearby fire, and a distant relative is not as helpful as a close neighbor.

月满则亏，水满则溢 The moon waxes only to wane, and water surges only to overflow.

在家不会迎宾客，出外方知少主人 If a person does not treat guests properly when at home, few will wish to entertain him when he is away from home.

知己知彼，百战百胜 Know the enemy, know yourself, and in every battle you will be victorious.

只许州官放火，不许百姓点灯 The magistrates are free to set fire, while the common people are forbidden even to light lamps.

只要功夫深，铁杵磨成针 If you work hard enough at it, you can grind even an iron rod down to a needle.

种瓜得瓜，种豆得豆 As a man sows, so shall he reap.

十二、常用汉语典故/Common Chinese Allusions

杀鸡焉用牛刀 Why use a pole-axe to kill a chicken?

苛政猛于虎 Tyranny is fiercer than a tiger.

多行不义必自毙 Persisting in evil brings self-destruction.

唇亡齿寒 When the lips are gone, the teeth will be cold.

鞭长莫及 Not even the longest whip can reach everywhere.

尔虞我诈 You fool me and I cheat you.

风马牛不相及 Even the runaway livestock would not reach each other.

顾左右而言他 turning aside and changing the subject

坐山观虎斗 sitting on a hill watching tigers fight

狡兔三窟 a wily hare has three burrows

高枕无忧 shake up the pillow and have a good sleep

作法自毙 hoist with his own petard

奇货可居 a rare commodity suitable for hoarding

逐客令 order for guests to leave

一字千金 one word worth a thousand pieces of gold

燕雀焉知鸿鹄之志 How can a swallow know the aspiration of a swan?

先发制人 gain the initiative by striking first

一败涂地 a defeat that brings everything crashing down

孺子可教 The child is worth instructing.

成也萧何，败也萧何 Raised up by *Xiao He* and Cast down by *Xiao He*.

逐鹿中原 hunting deer in the Central Plains

约法三章 agreeing on a three-point law

鸿门宴 the banquet and sword dance at Hongmen

人为刀俎，我为鱼肉 They are the knife and the chopping block, while we are the fish and the meat.

明修栈道，暗度陈仓 Repairing the road while making a secret detour.

背水一战 fighting with one's back to the river.

养虎遗患 to rear a tiger is to court calamity

运筹帷幄 manipulating victory from the command tent

狡兔死，走狗烹 When the crafty hares have been exterminated, the hunting dogs will be cooked.

金屋藏娇 keeping a beauty in a golden house

门可罗雀 you can catch sparrows on the doorstep

劳而无功 working hard but to no avail

视为畏途 regarded as a dangerous road

越俎代庖 abandoning the sacrificial vessels for the saucepans

得心应手 The hands respond to the heart.

死灰复燃 Dying embers may glow again.

投笔从戎 exchanging the writing brush for the sword

马革裹尸 a horsehide shroud

小巫见大巫 a junior sorcerer in the presence of a great one

举案齐眉 holding the tray up to the eyebrows

万事俱备，只欠东风 All that is needed is an east wind.

鹤立鸡群 Like a crane standing among chickens.

乐不思蜀 So happy that one thinks no more of Shu.

不为五斗米折腰 Won't Kowtow for five *dou* of rice.

洛阳纸贵 Paper is expensive in Luoyang.

朝秦暮楚 Serving Qin in the morning and Chu in the evening.

口若悬河 a waterfall of words

江郎才尽 Mr. Jiang has exhausted his talents.

阮囊羞涩 Mr. Ruan's bag feels ashamed.

司空见惯 a common sight to the Sikong

南柯一梦 southern branch dream

东窗事发 east window plot

刘姥姥进大观园 granny Liu in the Grand View Garden

十三、歇后语/Two-part Allegorical Sayings

八仙过海——各显神通。The eight immortals cross the sea — each displaying his or her special prowess.

半夜里偷桃吃——找软的捏。Stealing peaches at midnight — picking only the soft ones.

茶壶里煮饺子——倒不出来。Boiling dumplings in a teapot — no way to get them out.

城门里扛竹竿——直进直出。Carrying a pole through a city gate — in and out in a straight line.

窗户上的纸——一戳就破。Paper window panes — torn by a touch.

打破沙锅——问到底。Breaking an earthenware pot — cracking down to the bottom (getting to the root of the matter).

大姑娘坐花轿——头一回。A girl sitting in a bridal sedan chair — the very first time.

大热天穿棉袄——不是时候。Wearing a padded coat on a hot day — out of season.

大水冲倒龙王庙——一家人不认一家人。The temple of the Dragon King washed away by a flood — not recognizing one's kinsman.

电线杆当筷子——大材小用。Using telephone poles as chopsticks — putting much material to petty use.

擀面杖吹火——一窍不通。Using a rolling pin to blow a fire — totally impenetrable.

高射炮打蚊子——小题大做。Killing a mosquito with a cannon — making a mountain out of a molehill.

狗拿耗子——多管闲事。A dog catching a mouse — poking one's nose into other people's business.

狗咬吕洞宾——不识好人心。A dog biting *Lv Dongbin* — not being able to recognize a kind-hearted man.

棺材里伸手——死要钱。A hand stretched from a coffin — asking for money even when dead.

和尚打伞——无法(发)无天。A monk holding an umbrella — having neither hair (law) nor sky (providence).

黄鼠狼给鸡拜年——没安好心。The weasel pays a New Year call on the hen — not with good intentions.

鸡蛋里挑骨头——故意找错。Picking bones from eggs — finding fault deliberately.

姜太公钓鱼——愿者上钩。A fish jumping to *Jiang Taigong*'s hookless and baitless line — a willing victim.

孔夫子搬家——净是输(书)。Confucius moves house — nothing but books (always lose).

癞蛤蟆想吃天鹅肉——痴心妄想。A toad craving for swan's flesh — an impractical dream.

老鼠掉进书箱里——咬文嚼字。A mouse in a bookcase — chewing up the pages.

老王卖瓜——自卖自夸。*Lao Wang* selling melons — praising his own wares.

聋子的耳朵——摆设。A deaf man's ears — just for show.

猫哭老鼠——假慈悲。A cat crying over a mouse's misfortune — sham mercy.

门缝里瞅人——把人看扁了。Gazing at someone from behind a slightly opened door.

泥菩萨过河——自身难保。A clay Buddha crossing a stream — hardly able to save itself.

骑驴看唱本——走着瞧。Reading a book on donkey back — reading while riding (wait and see).

千里送鹅毛——礼轻情义重。Travel a thousand miles to bestow a goose feather — a small gift may be a token of profound friendship.

秋后的蚂蚱——蹦跶不了几天。A grasshopper at the end of autumn — its jumping days are numbered.

热锅上的蚂蚁——团团转。A swarm of ants on a hot oven — milling around in a panic.

肉包子打狗——有去无回。A meat bun thrown at a dog — by no means retrievable.

十五只吊桶打水——七上八下。Fifteen buckets to draw water from a well — seven up and eight down (all at sixes and sevens).

铁公鸡——一毛不拔。An iron rooster — not a feather can be pulled out.

秃子头上的虱子——明摆着。A louse on a bald head — too obvious.

外甥打灯笼——照旧(舅)。The nephew holds a lantern for his uncle — things stay unchanged.

瞎子点灯——白费蜡。A blind man lighting a candle — wasting wax.

秀才遇见兵——有理说不清。A scholar meeting a warrior — unable to vindicate oneself against an unreasonable opponent.

哑巴吃黄连——有苦说不出。A dumb person tasting bitter herbs — unable to express bitter feelings.

张飞穿针——粗中有细。*Zhang Fei* threading a needle — subtle in one's rough ways.

竹篮子打水——一场空。Drawing water with a bamboo basket — achieving nothing.

十四、《四书》语录/Quotations of *Four Books*

子曰："学而时习之，不亦说乎？有朋自远方来，不亦乐乎？人不知而不愠，不亦君子乎？"

Confucius said, "Is it not a pleasure to learn and practise from time to time what is learned? Is it not a delightful to have friends coming from affair? Is it not gentlemanly to have no resentment when one is not properly understood?"

曾子曰："吾日三省吾身：为人谋而不忠乎？与朋友交而不信乎？传不习乎？"

Zengzi said, "I examine myself three times daily: Have I been faithful in doing things for others? Have I been trustworthy in contacts with friends? Have I reviewed and practised what my teacher has taught me?"

有子曰："礼之用，和为贵。"

Youzi said, "The most valuable use of the rites is to achieve harmony."

子曰："吾十有五而志于学，三十而立，四十而不惑，五十而知天命，六十而耳顺，七十而从心所欲，不逾矩。"

Confucius said, "At fifteen I made up my mind to study; at thirty I was established; at forty I was no longer perplexed; at fifty I understood the will of Heaven; at sixty I listened to everything without feeling unhappy; at seventy I followed all my desires and none of them was against the norms."

子曰："其身正，不令而行；其身不正，虽令不从。"

Confucius said, "A man who is upright is obeyed even if he gives no orders; a man who is not upright is not obeyed even if he gives orders."

子曰："三人行，必有我师焉。择其善者而从之，其不善者而改之。"

Confucius said, "Whenever I walk with two other men, I can always find teachers in them. I can learn from their good qualities, and correct those faults in me which are like theirs."

子曰："己所不欲，勿施于人。在邦无怨，在家无怨。"

Confucius said, " Do not impose on others what you do not desire yourself. Bear no grudge against the state where you work; have no feeling of dissatisfaction when you stay at home. "

子曰："唯仁者能好人，能恶人。"

Confucius said, "Only the humane can love others and hate others."

子曰："志士仁人，无求生以害仁，有杀身以成仁。"

Confucius said, "A man with lofty ideals or humane man never gives up humanity to save his life, but may sacrifice his life to achieve humanity."

子曰："知者乐水，仁者乐山；知者动，仁者静；知者乐，仁者寿。"

Confucius said, "The wise enjoy water, the humane enjoy mountains. The wise are active, the humane are quiet. The wise are happy; the humane live long lives. "

子曰："父母在，不远游，游必有方。"

Confucius said, "While one's parents are alive, one should not travel to distant places. If it is necessary to travel, there should be a definite direction."

子曰："见贤思齐焉，见不贤而内自省也。"

Confucius said, "When one sees a virtuous man, one should think of exerting oneself to be like him; when one sees someone who is not virtuous, one should examine oneself. "

子曰："人无远虑，必有近忧。"

Confucius said, "He who does not think of the future is certain to have immediate worries."

子曰："躬自厚而薄责于人，责远怨矣。"

Confucius said, "One can keep hatred and grievance away by putting more blame on oneself and less on others for any fault."

子曰："过而不改,是谓过矣。"

Confucius said, "A fault that is not amended is a real fault."

子曰："君子喻于义,小人喻于利。"

Confucius said, "The gentleman knows what is right; the mean person keeps his mind only on gains."

子曰："君子坦荡荡,小人常戚戚。"

Confucius said, "The gentleman is open and at ease; the mean man is full of worries and anxieties."

子曰："无欲速,无见小利。欲速则不达,见小利则大事不成。"

Confucius said, "Do not want to do things quickly, and do not seek petty gains. You cannot reach your goal if you want to be quick, and you cannot accomplish great things if you seek petty gains."

子曰："有教无类。"

Confucius said, "There should be education for everyone without distinction."

子曰："性相近也,习相远也。"

Confucius said, "By nature men are similar to one another, but learning and practice make them different."

子曰："学而不思则罔,思而不学则殆。"

Confucius said, "He who learns without thinking will be bewildered; he who thinks without learning will be in danger."

子曰："温故而知新,可以为师矣。"

Confucius said, "He can be a teacher who finds what is new in reviewing what is old."

子曰："君子讷于言而敏于行。"

Confucius said, "The gentleman wishes to be slow in speech but quick in action."

子曰："君子耻其言而过其行。"

Confucius said, "The gentleman considers it a shame to talk more than he does."

子曰："君子不以言举人,不以人废言。"

Confucius said, "The gentleman does not recommend a man because of what he says, nor does he ignore what a man says because of his personality."

子曰："默而识之,学而不厌,诲人不倦。"

Confucius said, "To commit knowledge to memory quietly, to study tirelessly, and to enlighten others indefatigably."

子曰："见义不为,无勇也。"

Confucius said, "It is cowardice not to dare to defend righteousness when it is endangered."

孟子曰："以力服人者,非心服也,力不赡也;以德服人者,中心悦而诚服也。"

Mencius said, "When one by force subdues men, they do not submit to him in heart. They submit, because their strength is not adequate to resist. When one subdues men by virtue, in their hearts' core they are pleased, and sincerely submit."

孟子曰:"天时不如地利,地利不如人和。"

Mencius said, "Opportunities of time vouchsafed by Heaven are not equal to advantages of situation afforded by the Earth, and advantages of situation afforded by Earth are not equal to the union arising from the accord of Men."

孟子曰:"得道者多助,失道者寡助。"

Mencius said, "He who finds the proper course has many to assist him. He who loses the proper course has few to assist him."

孟子曰:"人之患,在好为人师。"

Mencius said, "The evil of men is that they like to be teachers of others."

孟子曰:"爱人者,人恒爱之;敬人者,人恒敬之。"

Mencius said, "He who loves others is constantly loved by them. He who respects others is constantly respected by them."

孟子曰:"鱼,我所欲也;熊掌,亦我所欲也。二者不可得兼,舍鱼而取熊掌者也。生,我所欲也,义,亦我所欲也,二者不可得兼,舍生而取义者也。"

Mencius said, "I like fish and I also like bear's paws. If I cannot have the two together, I will let the fish go, and take the bear's paws. So, I love life, and I also love righteousness. If I cannot keep the two together, I will let life go and choose righteousness."

孟子曰:"孔子登东山而小鲁,登泰山而小天下。"

Mencius said, "Confucius ascended the Eastern Hill, and *Lu* appeared to him small. He ascended the Mount Tai, and all beneath the heavens appeared to him small."

孟子曰:"民为贵,社稷次之,君为轻。"

Mencius said, "The people are the most important element in a nation; the spirits of the land and grain are the next; the sovereign is the lightest."

参考文献/Reference Books

[1] 鲍刚. 口译理论概述[M]. 北京：中国对外翻译出版公司，2005.
[2] 陈芳蓉. 英语口译听力[M]. 上海：上海交通大学出版社，2014.
[3] 陈科芳. 英语随同口译[M]. 上海：上海交通大学出版社，2014.
[4] 崔永禄，孙毅兵. 新编英汉口译教程[M]. 上海：上海外语教育出版社，2005.
[5] 陈菁. 视译[M]. 上海：上海外语教育出版社，2011.
[6] 李天舒. 最新简明英语口译教程[M]. 西安：世界图书出版公司西安公司，2001.
[7] [法]勒代雷. 释意学派口笔译理论[M]. 刘和平译．北京：中国对外翻译出版公司，2001.
[8] 李孚声. 英汉口译教程[M]. 北京：旅游教育出版社，2007.
[9] 雷天放，陈菁. 口译教程[M]. 上海：上海外语教育出版社，2006.
[10] [英]林超伦. 实战口译(学习用书)[M]. 北京：外语教学与研究出版社，2004.
[11] 卢信朝. 英语口译技能教程——听辨[M]. 北京：北京语言大学出版社，2012.
[12] 刘和平. 口译技巧——思维科学与口译推理教学法[M]. 北京：中国对外翻译出版公司，2011.
[13] 刘绍龙. 英语口译实务(三级)[M]. 北京：科学出版社，2008.
[14] 卢敏. 英语三级口译考试真题详解[M]. 北京：外文出版社，2005.
[15] 冯伟年. 汉英笔译[M]. 西安：西安交通大学出版社，2012.
[16] 冯伟年. 新编实用英汉翻译实例评析(第二版)[M]. 北京：清华大学出版社，2012.
[17] 戚文琴. 实用英语口译入门教程[M]. 北京：旅游教育出版社，2006.
[18] 梅德明. 中级口译教程[M]. 上海：上海外语教育出版社，2014.
[19] 梅德明. 高级口译教程[M]. 上海：上海外语教育出版社，2014.
[20] 梅德明. 通用口译教程[M]. 北京：北京大学出版社，2011.
[21] 梅德明. 通用交传——口译进阶教程[M]. 北京：北京大学出版社，2009.
[22] [法]塞莱斯科维奇. 口译训练指南[M]. 闫素伟等译. 北京：中国对外翻译出版公司，2011.
[23] 孙硕. 汉英口译技巧训练[M]. 北京：中国对外翻译出版公司，2015.
[24] 彭典贵. 实用英语基础口译教程[M]. 北京：清华大学出版社，2010.
[25] 王斌华，伍志伟等. 英汉口译——转换技能进阶[M]. 北京：外语教学与研究出版社，2012.
[26] 王丹. 交替传译[M]. 北京：外语教学与研究出版社，2013.
[27] 汪海涛，邱政政. 中高级口译口试备考精要[M]. 杭州：浙江教育出版社，2014.
[28] 王燕. 英语口译实务(二级)[M]. 北京：外文出版社，2007.
[29] 王炎强，冯超，何刚强. 视译基础[M]. 北京：外语教学与研究出版社，2013.
[30] 吴冰. 现代汉译英口译教程[M]. 北京：外语教学与研究出版社，2004.
[31] 吴云. 英语会展口译[M]. 上海：华东理工大学出版社，2008.
[32] 吴钟明. 英语口译笔记法实战指导[M]. 武汉：武汉大学出版社，2008.
[33] 詹成. 联络口译[M]. 北京：外语教学与研究出版社，2012.
[34] 詹成，王斌华，伍志伟. 汉英口译[M]. 北京：外语教学与研究出版社，2010.
[35] 周国强. 英语口译综合能力(三级)[M]. 北京：外文出版社，2004.
[36] 庄晨燕，邱寅晨. 口译学习与实践[M]. 北京：外语教学与研究出版社，2008.

[37] 仲伟合，刘绍龙. 英语口译实务(二级)[M]. 北京：科学出版社，2008.

[38] 北京周报[N]. 外文出版社，2014 (第 41 期)

[39] 北京周报[N]. 外文出版社，2014 (第 39 期)

[40] 北京周报[N]. 外文出版社，2015 (第 14 期)

[41] 北京周报[N]. 外文出版社，2015 (第 15 期)

[42] 北京周报[N]. 外文出版社，2015 (第 49 期)

[43] http://wenku.baidu.com/view/67d507a1284ac850ad024217.html

[44] http://www.kekenet.com/broadcast/201503/364213.shtml

[45] http://www.kekenet.com/broadcast/201409/327293.shtml

[46] http://en.dict.cn/news/view/13921

[47] http://www.qiewo.com/yingyuzuowen/kouyu/201009/233370.html

[48] http://talk.kekenet.com/show_1409

[49] http://www.kekenet.com/broadcast/201503/364280.shtml

[50] http://www.kekenet.com/broadcast/201409/330128.shtml